Art, Play, and Narrative Therapy

Art, Play, and Narrative Therapy shows mental health professionals how the blending of expressive arts, psychotherapy, and metaphorical communication can both support and enhance clinical practice. This book illuminates the ways in which metaphorical representations form who we are, how we interact, and how we understand our larger environment. Author Lisa Moschini explains how to couple clients' words, language, stories, and artwork with treatment interventions that aid empathic understanding, promote a collaborative alliance, and encourage conflict resolution. Chapters include numerous illustrations, exercises, and examples that give clinicians inspiration for both theoretical and practical interventions.

Lisa B. Moschini, LMFT, is the vice president and clinical director of Sanctuary Centers of Santa Barbara. She has been providing workshops, lectures, and training to therapists and educators since 1996. Her first book, *Drawing the Line: Art Therapy with the Difficult Client* (2004) has been translated into three languages.

Art, Play, and Narrative Therapy

Using Metaphor to Enrich Your Clinical Practice

Lisa B. Moschini

Routledge
Taylor & Francis Group
NEW YORK AND LONDON

First published 2019
by Routledge
711 Third Avenue, New York, NY 10017

and by Routledge
2 Park Square, Milton Park, Abingdon, Oxon, OX14 4RN

Routledge is an imprint of the Taylor & Francis Group, an informa business

Library of Congress Cataloging-in-Publication Data
Names: Moschini, Lisa B., author.
Title: Art, play, and narrative therapy : using metaphor to enrich your clinical practice / Lisa B. Moschini.
Description: New York, NY : Routledge, 2018.
Identifiers: LCCN 2018005387| ISBN 9780815371267 (hardcover : alk. paper) | ISBN 9780815371274 (pbk. : alk. paper) | ISBN 9781351170925 (e-book)
Subjects: | MESH: Art Therapy—methods | Play Therapy--methods | Narrative Therapy—methods
Classification: LCC RC489.A7 | NLM WM 450.5.A8 | DDC 616.89/1656—dc23
LC record available at https://lccn.loc.gov/2018005387

ISBN: 978-0-8153-7126-7 (hbk)
ISBN: 978-0-8153-7127-4 (pbk)
ISBN: 978-1-351-17092-5 (ebk)

Typeset in Minion
by Swales & Willis Ltd, Exeter, Devon, UK

Contents

Illustrations

Tables

Acknowledgments

I cannot express enough thanks to the following people for their assistance, thoughtful suggestions, and patience:

Lisa Brewer
Lauren Richardson
Liz Collins
Tanner Barge
Stephanie Soule-Maggio
Nina Guttapalle
Nikki Creel
Cyndie Westerhoff
Annette Longa
Barry Schoer

Lastly, I would like to express my very deepest appreciation to Anna Moore. You believed in this book from the moment we first spoke. From your valuable and constructive suggestions, to your ongoing support and guidance, your willingness to give generously helped make this book possible.

Introduction

Gentle Readers,

In an ever-evolving world, it is comforting to find one idea that interconnects, one concept that is not isolated or beyond understanding. A comprehension that far surpasses anything conveyed by verbal narrative, thus existing beyond our words. And to this I would say it is our figurative messages, a personal metaphor if you will, that encircle us; if we would just listen. From our cumulative life experiences, to our immediate thoughts, actions, and words, it is metaphor which can be found skulking in the corners or even laid bare through our repetitious patterns of behavior. Whether these patterns reveal themselves through language, creative endeavors, or activities, metaphor has the power to increase understanding.

In my work with the concept of a *symbolic abundance of ideas* (Moschini, 2004) the cumulative effects of an individual's personal expression often add up to much more than first recognized. It is with this in mind that the concept of metaphorical meaning has also grabbed hold of my imagination. Yet, how a metaphor is defined often goes against the grain. Webster's New World Dictionary (1988) defines metaphor as "a figure of speech containing an implied comparison" (p. 852), which I find to be rather antiseptic. On the other hand, comparable to the metaphorical representations that I will be discussing in this book is Kenneth Wright's (1976) description, "metaphor is a product of an ego that is going towards a problem and attempting to grasp it" (p. 98).

For it is within this struggle that every human can collectively empathize. Which one of us has not felt before we have thought? Which one of us can claim the rigid continence of Sisyphus when faced with fears that threaten to consume? In how many ways has an experience enriched your understanding?

Unlike other books on metaphorical psychotherapeutic techniques, *Art, Play, and Narrative Therapy: Using Metaphor to Enrich Your Clinical Practice* does not rely upon the therapist's hypothesis of a client's struggles but instructs the mental health professional on how to assimilate the client's natural metaphorical language into the therapeutic hour. Additionally, the identification of the client's repetitious words, language, stories, and artwork is coupled with treatment interventions that can aid empathic understanding, promote a collaborative alliance, and encourage conflict resolution.

So now we arrive at another series of questions. How does the mental health professional conceptualize a case? What theoretical orientation is utilized? How are treatment goals achieved? Which series of interventions are incorporated?

Each of these questions is of special significance because it is the mental health professional's chosen models of practice that define the applied interventions and ultimately determine the effectiveness of the treatment. Whether one seeks to make the unconscious conscious through the exploration of repressed conflicts (Psychodynamic therapy), extinguish maladaptive behavior patterns (Behavioral therapy), develop healthy communication patterns (Family Systems theory), promote the identification of irrational belief systems and automatic thoughts (Cognitive-Behavioral therapy), or acceptance and value through awareness of the here and now experience, each theoretical modality has a common and interlocking bond: all seek to expand insight and growth. Regardless of how objectives are met, or the terminology incorporated to define, theoretical assumptions serve as guides.

Thus, I have attempted to provide a focused exploration, regardless of the applied treatment approach, on how metaphorical representations form who we are, how we interact, and how we understand our larger environment. It is important to note that art, play, and narrative therapy are specific treatment modalities and, as such, require training and practice beyond the parameters of this book. Additionally, "because sandplay therapy probes the depths of being, the ego of the sand player must be sufficiently sturdy to withstand these rough undergoings. This can be a treacherous process" (Turner, 2005, p. 17). Accordingly, it is my firm belief that mental health professionals will incorporate the concepts presented herein in a prudent, thoughtful, and principled manner.

This book is divided into five chapters. In each chapter the case reviews, illustrations, and story narratives provide the reader with a mental picture of the presented individual's inner emotional life. As with all case histories within this book, the information concerning therapy and clinical matters is factual. However, the clients' personal information, including names (where applicable), dates, and places have been substituted to retain confidentiality.

The first chapter offers a brief overview of how a personal metaphor engages our emotions and often symbolizes the very essence of our character; how auditory, kinesthetic, and visual sensory preferences impact our experiences; and examples of how metaphorical meaning were incorporated into group, individual, and family therapy. Chapter 2 focuses on the transforming nature of development on personality. As such, it explores the role of morality, ethics, relationship development, and behavior concomitant with brain chemistry and growth. Chapter 3 incorporates an interdisciplinary approach where case examples are analyzed from a wide range of counseling methodologies. From Cognitive-Behavioral theory with its action-oriented emphasis on skills acquisition, Gestalt therapy highlighting the gaining of awareness, to psychodynamic therapy where healing is accomplished by making the unconscious conscious, to family theoretical models; all of these schools of thought can be woven into the fabric of metaphoric communication. Hence, successive case histories focus upon the interpretation of play, narrative, and artwork whereby coping mechanisms in the form of symbolic metaphors are explored. In Chapter 4 the verbal interplay of clinician and client brings into being a metaphorical communication found within the context of story characters, plot, spheres of action, and denouement. In each case review the client's metaphorical meaning is evaluated while the shared story offers new choices that facilitate the regulation of anxiety, fears, and humiliations. Chapter 5 explores the incorporation of sandtray therapy. As such, the sandtray miniatures are employed on a metaphorical level and represent personal symbols whereby a client's inner expression and experience can proceed unimpeded. Additionally, interpretive methods and skills are reviewed in an effort to augment the mental health professional's proficiency when assessing sandtray worlds. Lastly, Chapters 6 and 7 offer two guidebooks toward the blending of the arts and psychotherapy. As such, these guidebooks promote interaction, group cohesiveness, and most importantly illuminate the process while providing step-by-step directives designed for mental health professionals who wish to support the growing relational conflicts of their clients through the incorporation of art therapy. Though written with the group therapy client in mind, each guidebook can also be modified for treatment with individuals.

In the end, metaphor reaches toward self-understanding in a language that is individually ours. I hope you find the blending of personal metaphor with psychotherapy to be as enriching in your practice as I have in mine.

References

Moschini, L.B. (2004). *Drawing the line: Art therapy with the difficult client.* Hoboken, New Jersey: John Wiley & Sons.

Turner, B., (2005). *The handbook of sandplay therapy.* California: Temenos Press.

Webster's new world dictionary (3rd ed.). (1988). New York: Simon & Schuster, Inc.

Wright, K.J.T. (1976). Metaphor and symptom: A study of integration and its failure. *The International Review of Psychoanalysis*, 3: 97–109.

I
First and Foremost

1
A Personal Metaphor

> Once upon a time in a park there was a trash can. There was a ripped and dirty shoe inside. It was so ugly that no-one liked him. One day a poor man came to the park and he didn't have any shoes. The poor man looked into the trash can and he saw the shoe and said, "Your name is Eric. My name is Pepe. We'll have a lot of fun." Pepe put on the shoe and started walking. Pepe lived in the street with Eric. The next day Pepe was going to go walk. Pepe said, "I'm glad to have a shoe." Eric said, "I'm glad to have an owner." Soon Pepe got a job. He took Eric. He got a lot of money and he got some new shoes. He took Eric to this man so he could fix him. When Pepe went for Eric, he was a new shoe. He was nicer and they were happy together.

Every individual both receives and relays information in his/her unique metaphor. From the verbal communication of our statements to the metaphorical communication, which is witnessed in our actions, creatively incorporating an individual's metaphor into the therapeutic hour can provide the movement necessary for insight and growth. For personal metaphor lends meaning to our experiences, makes sense of both our external and internal worlds, offers respite from our fears while accentuating our conflicts, and provides a signpost for our hopes and desires.

Silvano Arieti (1976) in his exploration of creativity stated, "poets, playwrights . . . know very well that words often acquire great meaning not because of what they say, but because of what they don't say. What is not said, and at times is hidden, may then appear with powerful effect" (p. 89). Just as with the spoken or written word, metaphorical language explores the unconscious mechanisms that drive our interpersonal relationships, gives shape and form to our personal identities, and integrates the natural language patterns of the client.

As such, it has been my experience that when incorporating evocative therapy, an individual's metaphor can exist, in large part, through the manner in which they integrate the art media within their final creation. Consequently, these guiding metaphors are an unconscious product of the psyche and, "creatively using their metaphors strengthens the therapeutic relationship since it is a language tailored to 'fit' " (Riley, 1985, p. 119).

To that end, Edith Kramer (1971) outlined five distinct categorizations that illustrate how art media can be employed in the therapeutic hour. They are as follows:

1 Precursory activities: scribbling, smearing, exploration of physical properties of the material that does not lead to creation of symbolic configurations but is experienced as positive and egosyntonic.
2 Chaotic discharge: spilling, splashing, pounding, destructive behavior leading to loss of control.
3 Art in the service of defense: stereotyped repetition, copying, tracing, banal conventional production.
4 Pictographs: pictorial communications which replace or supplement words. (Such communications occur often in psychotherapy or in other intimate relationships. They usually remain unintelligible to the outsider.)
5 Formed expression, or art in the full sense of the word: the production of symbolic configuration that successfully serves both self-expression and communication.

(Kramer, 1971, p. 54)

Figures 1.1–1.8 have been provided to present visual illustrations of the five categories outlined above. In each of these samples, the reader can ascertain the unconscious use of metaphor inherent in the client's non-verbal and verbal communication.

Figure 1.1 Precursory Activity 1

Figure 1.1 was drawn by a 17-month-old. This scribble (typical for her age) is merely a kinesthetic activity as she learns to accommodate the crayon.

Conversely, the controlled scribble found in Figure 1.2 was completed not by a toddler but by a 16-year-old female. This young female spent the majority of her time monitoring and watching her peers. She had little trust in her own ability and exhibited frequent feelings of despair. Though verbally capable of expressing herself, this adolescent's lack of trust coupled with feelings of shame and doubt overwhelmed her to the point of immobility. Thus, her drawings were mainly completed in a style that consisted of random lines, colors, and shapes.

As with both of these drawings, the simple act of creating was necessary and important, albeit for varied reasons. The 17-month-old is assimilating and experimenting with objects within the environment, while the 16-year-old is discharging overwhelming feelings through a safe and controlled use of the media.

When Kramer discusses "chaotic discharge" she also interchanges the word chaotic with emotional, and nowhere are emotions higher than in a newly formed group of adolescents. Figure 1.3 typifies an art therapy group (in the early stages) where five adolescent males are working toward the completion of a clay town. In this example, the animal objects are being created and adorned with miscellaneous art materials. This depressed, 15-year-old male, had initially resisted coming to group, yet once there, he settled into the art activity with minimal difficulties. His work consisted of placing feathers on the background animals and listening to his peers as they talked about the projects and their day

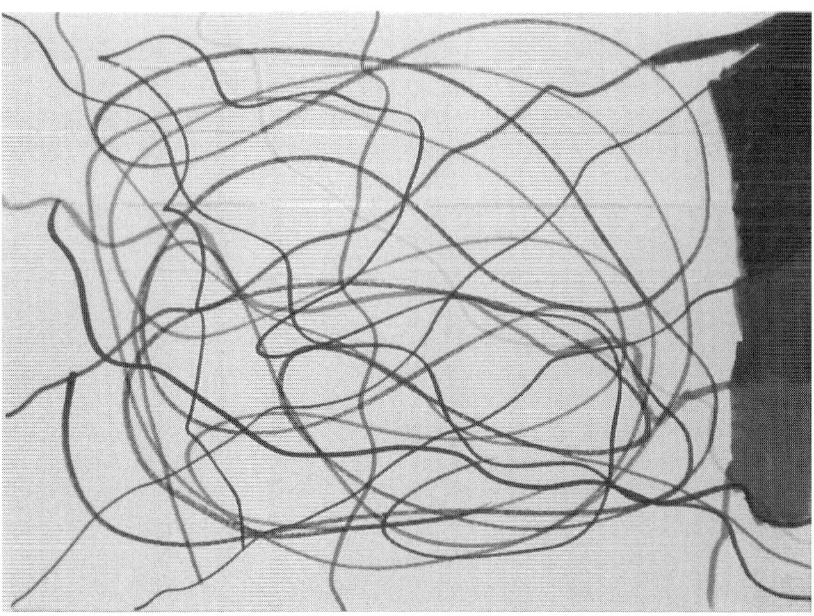

Figure 1.2 Precursory Activity 2

Figure 1.3 Chaotic Discharge

in general. Though he attempted to join in, his efforts were met with polite indifference. As the group wore on, and feelings of social incompetency increased, he pounded, trampled, crushed, and re-shaped his once 3-dimensional snake into the compressed form of Figure 1.3. In this way, a metaphor of devastation due to estrangement found venting through the art media.

In Figure 1.4 a pre-adolescent female resorts to defensive functioning to process the feelings of anxiety that threaten to devastate. Regardless of the directives offered, the media supplied, or the topics discussed, this client incorporates the repetition of devotion and fidelity within all of her art productions. Her history is such that this is not surprising. As a child, she was placed with a single foster family, and she and her siblings were not separated. However, her behavior was such that when the foster family wished to adopt the children, they adopted all but her. At this point, she lives in residential care seeking the devotion she craves through the physical intimacy of male peers and fantasy formations.

Conversely, the artwork of a high functioning, autistic female demonstrates the retreat into the safety of repetitious symbols (in Figure 1.5 this is expressed through stars, hearts, and butterflies). These representations (or stereotyped motor activities) serve to maintain sameness within her surroundings. As such, they provide a structured and ordered approach toward an environment that is frequently experienced as chaotic. Additionally, any interruptions of these patterns (whether they are expressed physically or pictorially) tend to result in withdrawal of the client or rage reactions.

Figure 1.4 Art in the Service of Defense 1

Kramer's fourth category, pictographs, is related to primitive styles of writing and drawing. A pictogram is a diagram or object whose use is to describe (in this definition graphically) an expression of anxiety. In the age of adolescence a

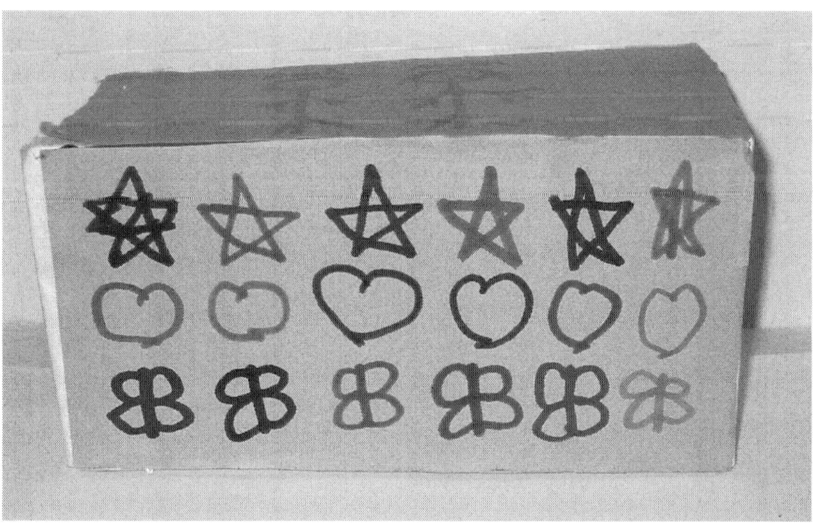

Figure 1.5 Art in the Service of Defense 2

child's space is of premium importance, as an aspect of their identity as well as an area for privacy, safety, security, and all manner (materialistically) of important things. They retreat to their "areas" as they learn to be themselves away from the need to share themselves with others.

In Figure 1.6, a group of adolescent boys was struggling with the "invasion" of their personal space. Many had been placed outside of their homes for the first time and the "sharing" as well as the loss of familiarity required expression. Thus, the directive, *"think about a room that is safe and comfortable. Draw your most private and comfortable space,"* was given.

On the left side of Figure 1.6, this male drew his idea, pictorially, of what such a room would look like. To a photocopy of a pre-drawn room (Dossick & Shea, 1988, p. 44) he added a bed, a television with PlayStation attached, and a cross (which was copied from a peer sitting next to him). In describing his "safe room" his verbal statements were as barren as the room itself. His need to lose himself within the fantasy of play (rather than to communicate his needs) was prominent. On the right side of Figure 1.6 was his depiction of a second directive, *"draw the security system that protects your most treasured possessions."* Here a red force field is drawn in front of his PlayStation while a secondary trap (a cage) falls from the roof to catch any interlopers.

The final rendering yields a plethora of information regarding this child's defensive structure as well as his emerging personality. Unable to verbally express his social distrust, dismay, and frustration, the illustration of entrapment articulated his internal feelings without the need for language.

Figure 1.7 requires little verbiage. Its visceral expression defines, in every sense of the word, a symbolic clay creation that both communicates a feeling state (in this case anger), as well as evocatively conveys the intensity of the emotion and ensuing destructive qualities if left unregulated. By itself, it provides a powerful representation of rage. In the form of a metaphor, it expresses internal processes that can be explored in a non-threatening manner and mediated through further evocative interventions. Consequently, feelings

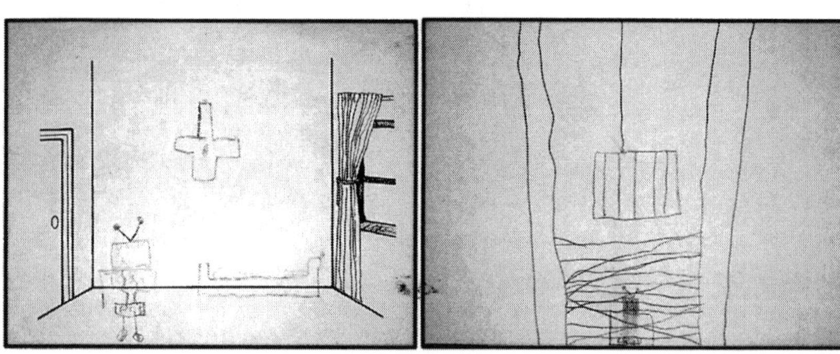

Figure 1.6 Pictographs

Figure 1.7 Formed Expression 1

exploration through the incorporation of media can make available an articulation of intensity and meaning that words merely disguise.

As a final example, a pre-adolescent male in a group setting completed Figure 1.8. The first part of the directive was to, *"choose one side of the box and draw what peace looks like."* While his peers worked quietly on representational drawings of the peace symbol or idyllic scenes found in nature, this young man grasped five colors within his fist and completed the left side of Figure 1.8.

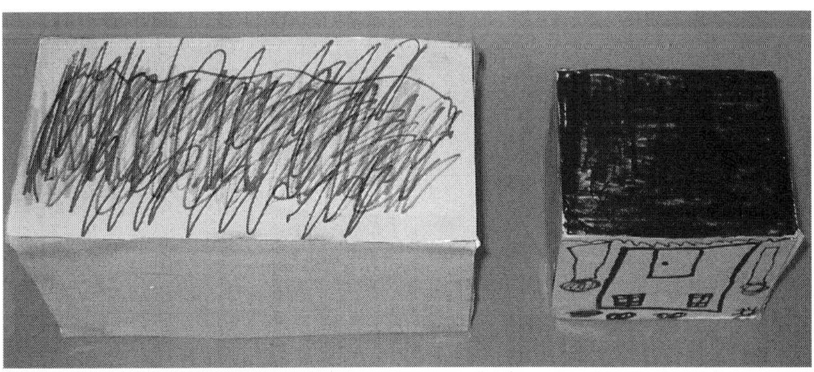

Figure 1.8 Formed Expression 2

As he looked at the final rendering, he requested a second box, as "this one isn't right." On his second box he wrote the word "peace" and then began a drawing of a person in the lower left. Again, he scrutinized his drawing and in a methodical fashion blacked out the entire side (right side of Figure 1.8).

The fervent feelings of anxiety, which he concealed verbally in his post-drawing discussion, did not escape the notice of his peers as the two boxes were displayed. Thus, this overanxious child has rendered peace primarily as an uproar of haphazard color, lines, and squiggles, while his second expression is that of emptiness. These two boxes compared represent a vacant and desolate landscape whereby peace is not experienced as harmonious or tranquil but instead as pandemonium (left side of Figure 1.8) and then isolative (right side of Figure 1.8). In the end, a metaphor that found expression through the art typifies this pre-adolescent's discomfort with strong feeling states and subsequent retreat into seclusion as he engulfs the projection of himself (recall he initially drew a figure underneath the black) which both protects and separates him from his peer grouping as peace is overshadowed by anxiety. As Kramer outlined, these last two examples are metaphorically both expressive as well as communicative.

It's Not the Heat, It's the Humidity

Consequently, the focus when exploring a personal metaphor can often be found within the symbolizing expressions of a client's non-verbal and verbal communication, a spontaneous representation that is frequently different from what it seems to be. Within the depiction of a ceaseless storm (Figure 1.9), one finds an adolescent male squaring off with an opponent as he compares the turbulent and formidable strength of the weather with an expression of rage simply explained as "when I get angry you can't stop me." To the symbolic significance of a psychotic male who was experiencing internal stimuli and in response drew an "alien" as a metaphorical manifestation of his own alienation (note the content of the word balloons) from the group members and the larger environment (Figure 1.10). These examples are but brief

Figure 1.9 An Enduring Storm

Figure 1.10 Alienation

representations of how metaphorical communication can provide a deeper level of understanding, aid in development, encourage insight, and grant access to unconscious fantasies and thoughts.

Thus, if we are to look at metaphors in this fashion all communication can be said to impart a measure of perception into the cumulative experiences that preoccupy our thoughts, feelings, and behaviors and has ultimately shaped how we interact. Lakoff and Johnson (1980) based their seminal book upon the belief that metaphors have a strong basis within everyday language and experiences and these events have formed the very fabric of our thought processes. One of many examples that Lakoff and Johnson provide revolves around the common belief that "the eyes are containers for the emotions" (p. 50). For we often speak of seeing fear in the eyes or flashes of anger, and love can be found within the eyes ("She is the apple of his eye"), as well as "seeing eye to eye" where agreement is achieved. In this way, facial characteristics suggest a metaphor of understanding of "the face for the person" (p. 37).

Figure 1.11 is an example of two masks created by an adult male (left) and an adolescent male (right). What do these masks reveal to you? Do they suggest admiration? Disdain? Do they silently speak of suspicions? Or perhaps loneliness?

Rather than being direct and confrontational, the metaphor of the mask (persona) facilitates a representation of the self that can both conceal and protect the fragility of awareness. Figure 1.12 symbolizes the psychotic decompensation of an adult male as he veils his hallucinations on a verbal level, but

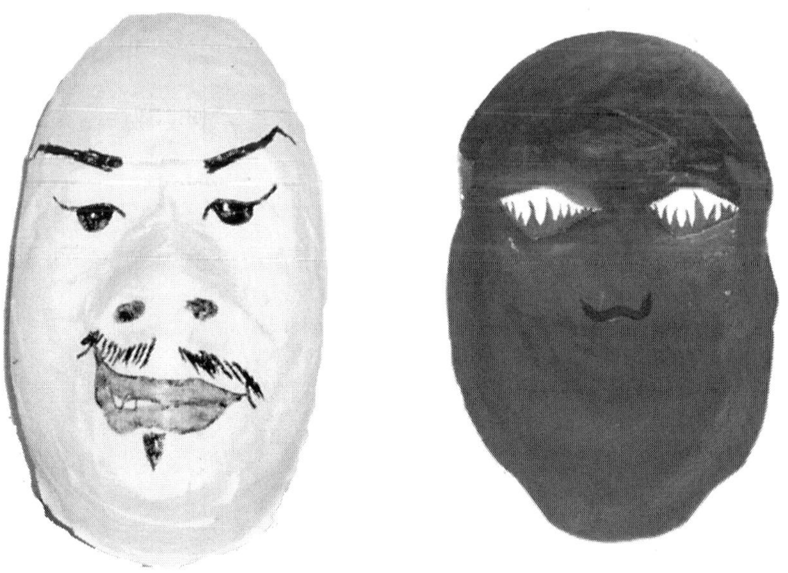

Figure 1.11 The Persona

expresses them without reserve evocatively. In a group therapy session, the members were instructed to *"paint your mask anyway you desire"* (left side of Figure 1.12). This male expressed his pride in his Mexican American heritage as he spoke of how the mask represents the self. In the subsequent session the group was instructed to, *"add anything to your mask that you think it needs"* (right side of Figure 1.12). During the post-drawing inquiry this male stated, "I dreamed about this mask. You know how some people's eyes are intense? They see things. I see things. All kinds of things . . . " As a result, within the language of metaphor this client was able to express and allow us to be a witness to the persona (the created mask), surmise the problem (visual and auditory hallucinations as expressed evocatively and through further verbalizations), and can reflect upon a resolution (medication management referral and continuing discussions with the client surrounding symptomology).

By the same token, Phillip Barker (1985) drawing from the work of Milton Erickson, applies the indirect communication of metaphorical language, stories, anecdotes, and tales within the context of therapy as the basis to change the systemic experiences of the whole. Hence, throughout the course of therapy the mental health professional integrates a therapeutic metaphor to address the clinical situation. An example from my practice revolves around an elderly male placed in long-term inpatient care. This gentleman would often render drawings of turtles either alone or in combination with other contrasting items (see Figure 1.13). In each group session, he offered no explanation, yet the turtle image emerged consistently.

The following week, this man spontaneously drew three items: a sad face, a tree, and his ever-present turtle (see Figure 1.14). Again, he chose to not share with the group. I had long before assessed this elderly man's growing

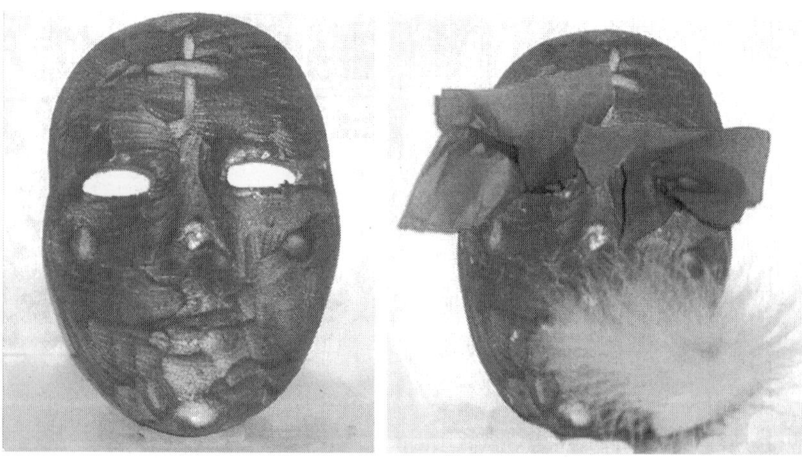

Figure 1.12 Eyes as Containers for Emotions

Figure 1.13 Turtle and Clown

despondency and self-absorption as he gradually retreated from interactions. It was at this point that I decided to tell an allegorical story in response to Figure 1.14. I began in this manner:

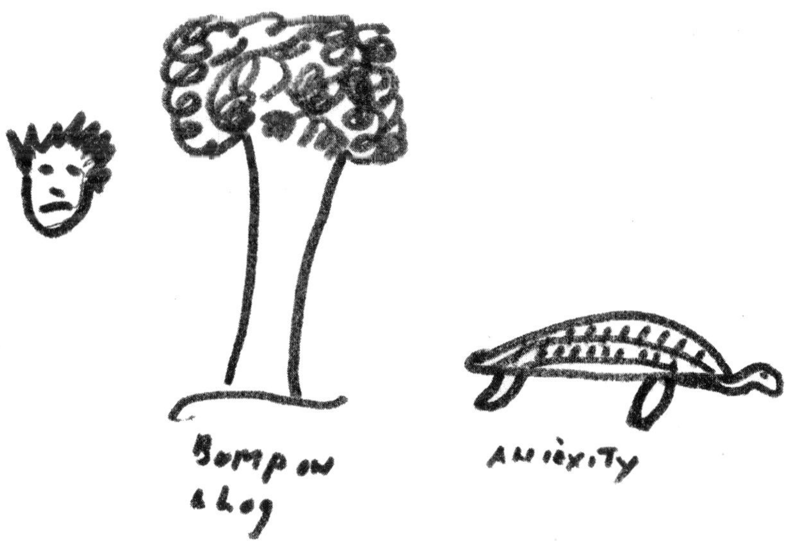

Figure 1.14 Anxiety

> That drawing reminds me of a Japanese Fairy Tale. It goes like this: One day a young boy named Urashima was walking along the beach. And in front of him were two bullies abusing a turtle. They were pushing it about, throwing it in the air, and not letting it swim back into the ocean. Urashima ran and helped the turtle who later returned to thank him for his kindness.
>
> The boy crawled onto the back of the turtle and they dove deep into the sea. Urashima was taken to a large castle where a maiden welcomed him. Everyone treated Urashima so well and for a long time he was very happy. However, one day he began to miss his family and he wanted desperately to return home. The turtle and the maiden reluctantly said their goodbyes and the maiden gave Urashima a sealed box. She told him never to open it.
>
> Once home he wondered what the maiden had put in the box, though he heard her voice telling him not to open it he did anyway. And in an instant, he became an old man.
>
> Even though Urashima thought he had been away for only a few days he had been gone for many, many, many years. It was only then that he realized that it was his old age that had been kept in that sealed box.

For a long time the group sat quietly and then the client wrote the words, "bump on a log" and "anxiety" under his drawings. After this he pronounced, "That's how I feel. Like my youth was stolen from me. Now I'm just a bump on a log. Worthless!" Thus, the turtle symbol that had preoccupied and beleaguered this client finally found voice through the verbal expression of despair. His life, much like Urashima's (McCarthy, 2000), felt diminished and pointless as he was not what he once was. His strengths and talents, rather than being applauded were bemoaned on a regressive level as he retreated from those around him. Yet it was the group and this man's eventual expression of sorrow that brought about the beginnings of a resolution, for the discussions that followed focused on his innate talents that though stagnated within the self due to despair, proved valuable to his peers.

Correspondingly, Mills and Crowley (1986) apply Erickson's metaphorical approach with that of Steven Heller's (1986) Neurolinguistic theory of communication. In this way, their work with children expanded to include a personal style of communication through the identification of "sensory preferences as manifested in language" (p. 106). It is their belief that each individual processes and internalizes new information and skills through these sense-based subjective representations. As such, the sensory system (made up of auditory, visual, and kinesthetic/tactile representations) provides a language which is both unique and universal.

Thus, if we pay attention, it is through our senses that personal modes of communication can be understood. Table 1.1 outlines the major learning styles which help explain how individuals experience their world and consequently provides a signpost to strategies which the therapist may employ.

Table 1.1 Sensory Preferences

Response Mode:	*React to:*	*Learn by:*
Visual	what they observe	Seeing
Auditory	what they are told	Listening
Kinesthetic	feelings in the body	Moving
Tactile	what they experience	Doing

Though Table 1.1 may look rather simplistic, it truly provides a plethora of information for the therapist regardless of the age of the client. If we look at each of the response modes and concomitant learning, the therapist can design personalized treatment planning merely by following the columns. As such, individuals with a visual sensory preference pay strict attention to details while possessing excellent creative skills (react to what they observe). Since they tend to learn by seeing they will frequently become impatient with purely verbal therapy; therefore, non-verbal models such as art and play therapy are particularly powerful. On the other hand, kinesthetic/tactile learners react to what they feel or experience. Their desire is to touch (clay is an excellent medium) and since they tend to learn best through trial and error art directives that link with one another in a repetitive fashion, it allows kinesthetic learners to process information thoughtfully. Additionally, role plays and movement-oriented interventions can provide effective learning opportunities. Lastly, those who have dominant auditory sensory preferences love to hold dialogues with or without reciprocity. Their communication can, at times, be overwhelming to those in their environment and due to this they may inadvertently alienate themselves. Since they react to what they are told, storytelling as an intervention for learning is remarkably influential.

To illustrate, a teenage female, whom I began working with, presented with a dominant representational system which surrounded auditory preferences while the visual, tactile, and kinesthetic sensory systems were blocked. In each of our meetings, I was besieged by a multiplicity of questions which kept this client tethered to content discussions and ultimately isolated her from those in her environment. However, that was not her intention, instead her rapid-fire questions served the purpose of helping her to learn (refer to Table 1.1) as she reacted to what was said. Additionally, it should be noted that when this girl spoke, with each inquiry, she employed a different intonation ranging from deep monotones to high timbres. It became evident that this client was absorbed with the different sounds that each of her manipulations created. Therefore, learning did not merely come by way of listening—she was also captivated, on an auditory level, with each of the sounds that her manipulations created. By way of example, in one session her questions were, "What do the doctors say? What do you say? Am I too tall? Is my face too big?

Am I smart? Why do I ask so many questions? Why do I use different voices?" In an effort to enhance her visual and kinesthetic systems, I incorporated Mills and Crowley's technique of "The Magic Puppet Theater" (p. 199) whereby the client designs his/her own paper puppets complete with scenery and action. Mills and Crowley state, "the puppets created by the child are themselves a metaphor of the child's environment and perceptions, and at the same time they function as a vehicle through which a metaphorical, therapeutic message can be delivered" (p. 203).

Figure 1.15, created over a period of several weeks, shows the finished puppet project. Using a variety of media (kinesthetic/tactile), this teenager first focused on the background scenery, choosing tissue paper that she shaped and crinkled into two brightly colored flowers. When this was complete, she then made stage curtains from corrugated cardboard and two puppets on popsicle sticks that she named Michael and Michelle (visual). Her initial story (auditory) was as follows:

> One day Michael and Michelle were in the park. Michael saw Michelle and wanted to talk to her. He went, "Ahem," but his face turned red and he couldn't talk. Michelle's face turned red too and she said, "I think I feel the same way as you do." From then on they were boyfriend and girlfriend and went on dates to the movies, restaurants, picnics, and the beach.

Figure 1.15 The Magic Puppet Theater

In this short yet symbolic story, you will note that auditory preferences prevail around the client's desire for affiliation and fidelity which she projected onto the main characters. Through an integration of the above-mentioned senses, learning was approached by including both visual and kinesthetic activities through the manipulation of the puppets. As such, ongoing art therapy sessions focused on placing the puppets in a multiplicity of relationship situations, together and with others, while her auditory preference was focused through the integration of storytelling, which therapeutically explored, practiced, and promoted improved social interactions in an indirect manner.

Applying the sensory preferences of Table 1.1 to the drawing task in Figure 1.16, the ensuing story, as told by an adolescent male, can be seen to point clearly toward a kinesthetic predilection. I have taken the liberty of italicizing the specific words in his story below:

The Boy Who Wasn't Accepted

> This boy is *fishing*. He is *playing* hooky from school and the building is a schoolhouse. The boy is a foster child. Everyone sees him as a troubled minor, but all he really wants to do is *relax* and take things as they come. He is real tired of being *hassled* by a lot of people. The reason he is *playing* hooky is because he *feels* he knows enough. He is always *running* from the truancy officers. He *plays* with his two friends. His other friends are mostly older adults that are considered menaces among their community. He is always *trying to help* his friends and trying to make the right choices. He wants to be considered a really good citizen but is considered an outcast.

If, as we have outlined, metaphor is a product of an ego that is going toward a problem and attempting to grasp it, this young man's issue clearly revolves around acceptance, or in this instance significant feelings of rejection. Even without understanding sensory preference predicates, the title alone says it all.

Mills and Crowley (1986) speak extensively of how "artistic metaphors" can communicate figuratively a client's personal language without the utterance of a single word. In this manner, the art task conveys the client's internal stressors, problems, and anxieties while offering external expression. By way of another example, a teenage male who had a significant history of navigating his environment through aggressive behaviors was seen in family therapy. The control that this adolescent wielded in the family system was a great source of stress for the adults; however, instead of voicing their discomfort they collectively acquiesced to his vengeful interactions. Over the course of many months, I had assessed this client's sensory predilection as kinesthetic/tactile and a family mural drawing (Landgarten, 1987; Moschini, 2004) was instituted to assist this family and clarify their experience on a visual level.

Figure 1.17 is the mural as completed by the client, his mother, grandmother, and grandfather. From the left of the drawing where a sun (son) defiantly sticks

Figure 1.16 The Boy Who Wasn't Accepted

out its tongue to the right side where the mother's drawing of the self has been accentuated in the breast area (dependency reactions), this client's renderings

Figure 1.17 Family

(the darkest colors of the overall mural) are found scattered throughout, over, and intrusively on top of his family's passive attempt at a unified image. The final rendering with its muddled boundaries and unhealthy bonds, symbolically articulated this family's struggles and conflicts.

In the end, what this family could not "see" when therapy relied upon traditional verbal therapy, they could not deny when the task was experienced on a kinesthetic level. The image was pointed out on a visual level, and each family member came together to voice his/her opinion (on an auditory level) in the post-drawing inquiry. Subsequently, the initial stage directive (family mural) provided metaphorical insight that highlighted the dependent interactions of the entire family as attendant victimization and passivity unwittingly endorsing egocentric relationship patterns.

Heart and Soul

In its totality, metaphorical expression engages our emotions and often symbolizes the very essence of our character. Whether this is articulated linguistically, conceptually, or through the non-verbal communication of an art production, the:

> Simple instances of making an object are all special cases of direct causation. They all involve prototypical direct manipulation. But they have one additional characteristic that sets them apart as instances of *making*: As a result of the manipulation, we view the object as a different *kind* of thing.
>
> (Lakoff & Johnson, 1980, pp. 72–73)

Take for example Figure 1.18 whereby a pre-teen placed out of her childhood home and into a large group home for the first time gathered a giraffe, cow, dollhouse, and fencing. After fencing in the "baby cow," she carefully placed the giraffe on the edge of the roofing. This benign scene, however, takes on a very "different form and function" (Lakoff & Johnson, 1980, p. 73) when the child has the mother giraffe tell the baby cow, "in order to get out of the cage you have to ride the largest, hardest, scariest, roller coaster in the world." With this superfluous comment, a mundane scene transformed into an expression that conveyed the anxiety and fears found within this child's persona.

Consequently, metaphorical communication provides an avenue to exploration and moves beyond the part of us that has learned to disguise and thus camouflage meaning. Within these conceptual images, the client can subtly be offered new alternatives, improved realizations, and the power of insight. In the case of Figure 1.18, I understood the metaphor of the client's fear of never breaking out of the "cage" of residential programming and focused on the promotion of a success identity by stating, "If you try hard enough, baby cow, you can do it, don't give up."

Figure 1.18 Don't Give Up

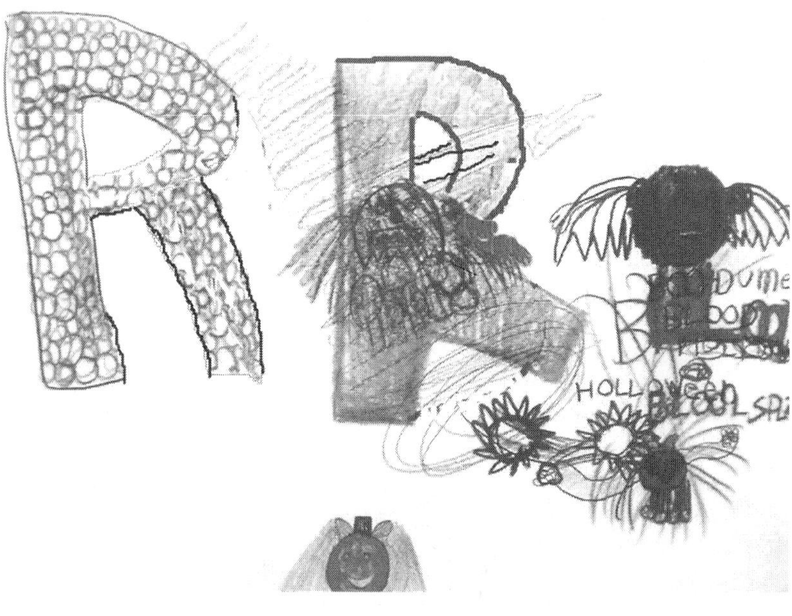

Figure 1.19 A Sense of Self

It is imperative that the mental health professional remain within the disguise of the metaphor. If the exploration becomes too manifest, it will impede the indirect message and as it moves too close to consciousness, play will inevitably cease, for as Battino (2002) has stated, "the art of the language of metaphor is that the listener makes the connection internally" (p. 55).

If, as outlined in Figure 1.18, metaphorical communication allows us to see beyond disguised meanings, then symbolism reigns supreme when it is applied to our initials, speaking to the very core of our being. Our initials represent our individuality, our self, and as such identity formation can be assessed when incorporating the directive, *"draw your initials as large as possible. Decorate them in any way you choose."*

Figure 1.19 illustrates an adolescent male's intensity of suffering, cloaked within a story of death and annihilation. Notice how the first initial (digitally changed) is unhindered by any decoration. While the second initial escalates until it begins to spiral out of control becoming progressively destructive as it devours everything within its path until it chaotically slips off the boundary of the page. This aggression, projected onto the drawing paper and created from the client's initials, paralleled this young man's interactions in the environment.

Untethered, without limits and boundaries and left to his own devices, he proves incapable of mediating within his surroundings, and thus resorts to hostility and violence.

By way of another example, aggressive mediations arise through the act of storytelling. This adolescent male, who preferred isolation to interaction, had a pattern of wordlessly suffering the indignations of both his peers and father and had a penchant to retaliate through aggressive actions when feelings of hopelessness swelled. He told the following story as it related to a collage image of a bird feeding her five babies:

> One day a mother hatched some baby chicks. These chicks were very cute. Someone saw somebody capture the babies and they knew it was wrong. But he didn't care. His name was Mr. Finch. Mr. Finch didn't like birds. So he killed them. He didn't like them because they crapped, they crapped all over his car and they crapped all over him. And that's the reason why he killed them. The mother bird was finding stuff to feed the babies. So when she got back to the nest she found out that her babies were dead and she was sad. So, Mr. Finch eventually found her and killed her. The moral of the story is just because something bothers you doesn't mean you have to kill it.

Here again this young man's story projects his suffering, incorporates the here and now dilemma of aggressive detachment, and imparts a hostile resolution focusing on revenge fantasies. Using the Mutual Storytelling Technique of Richard Gardner (1986) and incorporating sensory experiences, I placed special emphasis on the bird's nest as a place of safety surrounded by caring authority figures and a story ending that strengthened inner resources rather than the symbolizing issues of inadequacy and defeat.

> One day there were five baby chicks and they were left alone in their nest while their mother went out to get them some food. While she was gone the youngest bird noticed something strange, but didn't say anything to any of the other birds because he was scared they would tease him. Well, in that moment the tree started to shake and the next thing the babies knew, a big hand was taking them out of their nest. The birds were very frightened and began to shiver. All the way down they could hear mean Mr. Finch mumbling and grumbling about how the birds crapped on his car, made far too much noise, and he wasn't going to take it anymore. Slowly but surely, mean Mr. Finch decided he was going to kill each and every one of the babies. The birds were so fearful that they couldn't even speak until one of them, the biggest one of the bunch, started screeching and screeching, and it was ear splittingly loud. Well, soon the second bird started screeching, and then the third and fourth, and the smallest one tried, but just couldn't get out his words so instead he cowered in fear. Mr. Finch covered his ears and decided he was going to put an end to all the birds as quickly as possible. But, before you knew it, neighbors were coming into the yard and saying, "What's all this racket?" This made Mr. Finch pause and from far away the mother heard the crying and she flew down in order to get Mr. Finch. She swooped in and she pecked at him and screeched her anger. Mr. Finch was even madder and he went inside to get a gun. While he was rummaging around all the while and shouting for quiet, the mother picked up the largest bird and flew it back to the safety of its nest, she picked up the second and the third. All the while she was thinking, "I'm going to help my babies. I can do this." So she picked up the fourth and placed him in the nest, but now what do you think happened? That's right, mean old Mr. Finch came out and the mother was frantically looking for her youngest baby, when the fifth bird found his voice and began screeching and screeching and in bird-speak he was saying, "Hurry Mom, hurry, he's coming, he's coming to get me. I'm right here." The mother bird swooped in and quickly grabbed her youngest and placed him safely in the nest and away from mean old Mr. Finch. All the birds heaved a sigh of relief. From that day on, whenever there was a problem, the youngest bird never forgot to use his voice sooner rather than later.

As you can see I focused on the client's own wordless suffering that was projected upon the youngest and most fearful bird. Though this re-telling of the story was lengthier than what I would normally strive for, it was imperative that this adolescent male connected with a wordless world, as one that can either combat victimization or draw condemnation. In short, no matter the outcome, we are all responsible for and in control of our actions.

As outlined in Figure 1.16, the title of his story pointed toward both the client's problem and solution; in short, the therapeutic purpose. In the same way a moral can also provide a signpost to a client's personal and emotional struggles. In a series of story drawings, Figures 1.20 through 1.22, an adolescent girl's changing morals exposed initial relational difficulties and a subsequent budding personality formation which is inherently fundamental to growth. In each story, over a period of six weeks, the struggles in her daily life were both reflected and accentuated.

Her first story (Figure 1.20) revolved around Panda Bear's discarding of a golden ball which she thought was useless and inconsequential. The client's moral was, "He lost the ball." As will be outlined in Chapter 2, the ability to interpret context and incorporate higher-level meaning supports individuals as they move beyond concrete interpretations of their environment. Thus, it was important in subsequent sessions to assist this client toward a perspective which focused on feelings rather than merely the content of an interaction. As such, after each concrete story lesson, I offered one that assimilated friendship and intimacy. Therefore, in turn, my response to her moral was, "Sometimes we throw away that which is important to us." In this manner, the client and I discussed the story from a myriad of viewpoints with the goal of facilitating social understanding.

The next two times we met, her story morals continued to be concrete. In one session we repeated the fairy tale, "The Boy Who Cried Wolf." Her story lesson was, "The Kid Cried Wolf." While mine was, "If you trick people they won't be there when you really need them." Another story centered on Boo Boo who was often angry at Snoopy as he was impulsive in his attempts to receive attention. In the end Boo Boo went to the doctor to request a new dog. Her story lesson was, "You should never buy a dog that is annoying."

By the fourth and fifth week, helping this client ascertain the emotional component of the story lesson was beginning to show promise. The left side of Figure 1.21 encompasses a story surrounding bullying behavior which she titled, "The Creature and the Cricket." In this dual story a rabbit challenges a cricket to a race. When the cricket loses, he becomes enraged and my ending comment to the story was, "Maybe it wasn't fair of me to challenge you. Next time I'll pick on someone that I can actually race." When asked for the moral she replied, "Never challenge somebody who is weaker than you. It's just not fair." Conversely, the right side of Figure 1.21 focused on "Friendship" and forming bonds with others rather than being non-inclusive. Her moral was, "Treat friends nicely because you never know when you will need them."

As a last example, Figure 1.22 explores models of leadership and is titled, "The Growing Tree." In this story, the client outlines the return of Panda Bear but this time, "now instead of being a child she was 17." Slowly, all friends but

Figure 1.20 Papa Bear and Panda Bear

one decide to touch a magical leaf from the growing tree and they too become 17. However, one is too frightened and refuses. The moral as given by the client was, "Never feel pressured to do something you're not ready to do."

The metaphor inherent in her story drawings concentrated on her growing identity while the verbal and written expression of thoughts, feelings, and ideas promoted identification, allowed conflict resolution, and encouraged relational stability; for an individual needs to know that they can be loved and in turn love.

Figure 1.21 The Creature and the Cricket and Friendship

Along the lines of the Mutual Storytelling Technique, clay provides both a metaphor for feelings expression and symbolically represents a container for our projections. As such, the act of creating in clay grants access to a multiplicity of sensory preferences from the kinesthetic/tactile, whereby the client shapes, forms, and feels the clay, to the visual whereby the end product is newly fashioned. Figure 1.23 illustrates a latency-aged female's response to the directive, "*make an expression of your grief using the clay.*"

While this kinesthetically oriented child pounded her clay, she stated, "It's a robot, but it isn't." Further speech became regressive as she added a row of buttons, and large vigilant eyes. When her "robot" creation was discussed, no mention was made directly referencing her grief and loss issues. However, Figure 1.23 with its unconsciously omitted mouth symbolically delineated the need for an emotionless expression. As the session continued, the client stated, "Robots are strong," while she demonstrated their methodical and determined walk in the room. She also said, "Robots only follow commands. They have fake stuff in it. No hearts." If we take this interpretative metaphor one step further, the absence of a heart, the process of thoughtless acquiescence, coupled with mechanical expressions, protects the client from any future pain, grief, or loss.

In this singular clay creation, the experience and subsequent metaphorical expression is such that the desire for mechanical functioning serves as a wish. As Arlow (1969) has stated, "metaphor constitutes an outcropping into conscious expression of a fragment of an unconscious fantasy" (p. 7).

Figure 1.22 The Growing Tree

Across the Board

The act of integrating a personal metaphor into therapeutic practice is one that requires the establishment of objectives coupled with the implementation of techniques and methods to further the chosen goals, for it is the mental health clinician's theoretical modality which proves fundamental within the practice

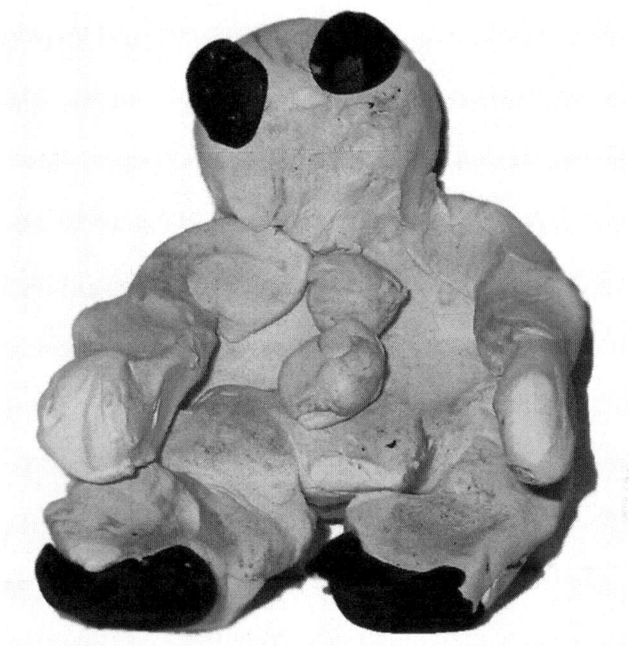

Figure 1.23 It's a Robot, but It Isn't

of psychotherapy. Just as our world, our appreciation of the world, and our interactions within the world are shaped by a myriad of events, the use of a single theory severely limits the potentials of both the client and the therapist. As such, effective treatment interventions tailor the goals and objectives to the needs and resources of the individual client.

In recent years the Cognitive-Behavioral model of intervention has gained favor among Marriage and Family Therapists and psychologists (Norcross, Hedges, & Castle, 2002; Northey, 2004); due in large part to favorable research, its action-oriented emphasis on skills acquisition, and here and now problem-solving, clients gain insight into self-defeating cognitions. Moreover, the client's schema or cognitive beliefs can provide the helping professional with the figurative language of the personal metaphor.

The following is a brief case history of a kinesthetically tactile young adult female who was abandoned by her mother as a toddler and admonished by her father throughout her childhood. In addition, she exhibited significant sibling rivalry issues coupled with diffident interactions in the here and now. Her verbalizations were replete with comments such as "I was never protected" and "They (*parents, sibling*) don't love me, they don't care about me, so no-one else will either." These remarks coupled with low frustration tolerance and aggressive emotional outbursts underscored her interpersonal relationships with peers and authority figures. During individual sessions, she frequently exhibited dependency reactions combined with a passive aggressive style of communication.

Conceptualizing this case from a Cognitive-Behavioral standpoint, this adolescent's irrational belief system ("If it wasn't for my sister, things would be perfect" and "I have to fight for everything") resulted in dysfunctional conclusions and ongoing negative patterns of thoughts with underlying feelings of fear. Her tendency to incorporate the schema of emotional reasoning, when discussing here and now events, only furthered her maladaptive thinking style.

Due to this adolescent's resistance to verbal exploration, an examination of her basic values was arrived at through the elaboration of an imaginary narrative.

The directive for Figure 1.24 was adapted by me from Shorr's (1972, p. 35) examination of conflict and imagination. In this book the use of *bi-polarization* can be defined as employing a client's opposing tendencies toward the modification of cognitions.

The Conflict Collage directive is an excellent intervention for kinesthetically predisposed clients. Additionally, it has many levels and to be most effective, should be undertaken in the order outlined. Provide your client with a collage box filled with animals only. One box should contain predatory animals and the second box animals of prey. Make certain to offer a wide variety and, for the purposes of this exercise, have the animals be single pictures rather than using images that have more than one animal in any given image. Provide the

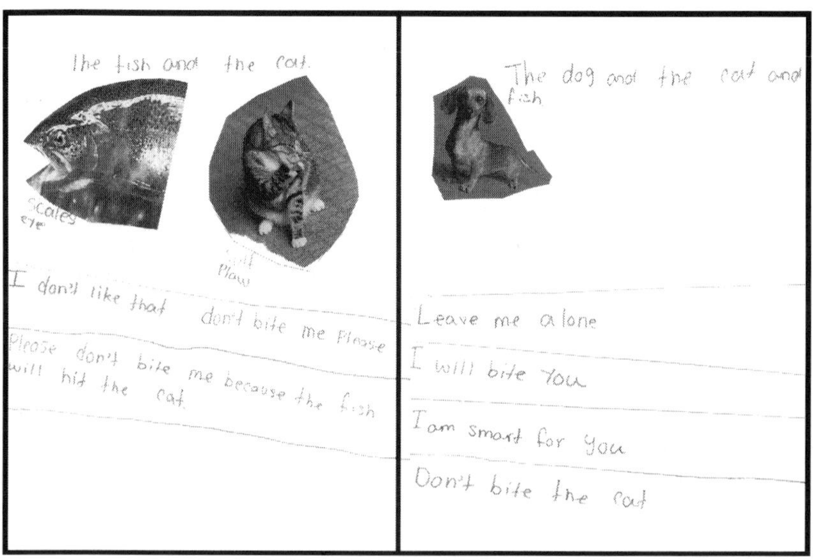

Figure 1.24 The Conflict Collage

client with one basket and ask the client to, *"choose one animal and glue it to the paper."* After removing the first basket (so the client will not choose a second image from that basket), provide the second basket and ask them to, *"choose one animal and glue it to the paper."* Once this is completed, remove the second basket and instruct them as follows: *"Underneath each animal write down words that describe them."* Now have the client, *"choose one of the animals and write what they are saying to the other animal."* Then, *"write the second animal's reply."* Lastly, *"choose one of the animals and write what they are thinking."* Now, *"write what the second animal is thinking."* After this, a story narrative is introduced and the client is instructed to, *"tell a story about the animals into the tape recorder."*

The client's first story related to the left side of Figure 1.24.

> Once upon a time there were two animals: a cat and a fish. The cat had soft paws and claws. One day the cat saw the fish and the fish had scales and large eyes. Its scales were shedding and with its large eye it looked around and saw everything. One day the cat walked up to the pond and saw the fish. "Hello Mr. Fish, I'm a cat." The fish said, "I don't like that. Don't bite me please. Please don't bite me because I will hit you." Soon they were fighting and the fish was scratching and the cat was looking. The cat was surprised at how mean the fish was and so the cat got mad and the fish got mad and the more the fish got mad the more the cat got mad. So one day the fish swam away so the cat didn't have to get him or catch him.

After this story, no interpretation was provided. Instead, remaining in the metaphor, a discussion ensued surrounding the irrationality of the conflict and viable problem-solving that the fish or the cat could have utilized if they had thought rather than felt.

In the next session, after speaking briefly of a recent peer conflict, the client wanted to hear her story again and insisted on adding a third animal to her first story. The dog, on the right side of Figure 1.24, was chosen.

> Once upon a time there were three animals: a dog, a cat, and a fish. One day in the forest the three animals ran into each other. They needed exercise. So all three of them went swimming. While they were swimming the dog said, "leave me alone," to the fish. And the fish didn't care. The cat said to the dog, "I will bite you." And the dog said, "I'm too smart for you." The cat laughed and the fish said, "Don't bite the cat." The dog didn't know what to do so he decided to hang out with other animals. The dog found a group of dogs and they played games, they played chase and run. The dog was happier hanging out with these friends.

Though the second story encompassed problem-solving on the part of the dog, the chain of inferences and self-defeating messages (personal metaphor) persists whereby attempts at cooperation, friendship, and affiliation are met with failure and ensuing aggression. Thus, subsequent insight was garnered through challenging the antecedent cause of her fear (rejection as delineated in her *Conflict Collages*), identification of her automatic thoughts ("I will never be good enough"), and action-oriented responses (cognitive homework assignments). By the fourth session, the indirect use of collage was supplanted with here and now verbal interpretations, challenges on her faulty thinking, and the incorporation of productive assumptions around her exaggerated fears of rejection. On the whole, the assimilation of evocative art into a Cognitive-Behavioral approach offered a safe method to identify this client's fears and the resultant anxiety through an imaginative art directive without heightening her already fragile sense of self.

As Shorr (1972) states, "the principal *functions* of imagination is that it is used to resolve the conflicts between the outer reality and the inner fantasy and can be thought of as the *modus vivendi* which harmonizes these opposing forces" (p. 11).

Not unlike individual sessions, therapeutic styles within a group setting are as broad as the clinician's proclivity to embrace a modality of treatment. Whether healing is acquired through a humanistic, directive, or abreactive approach, "changes in our conceptual system do change what is real for us and affect how we perceive the world and act upon those perceptions" (Lakoff & Johnson, 1980, pp. 145–146). As such, techniques incorporated into group psychotherapy may contrast but the phases of group development remain venerable. Whether one is adhering to Yalom's (1985, pp. 300–310) formative stages of a group or the five stages of the group life cycle as outlined by Dies (1996, pp. 35–51), these structured concepts, when viewed metaphorically, offer corrective interpersonal experiences toward mutuality, greater responsibility, and ultimately differentiation.

Figure 1.25 offers an example of an assertiveness skills group with four adolescent males. Each of these clients exhibited primitive coping mechanisms coupled with significant impairment related to shared interactions. As a group, these members had met each week for over six months. They were quite adept at identifying and rectifying here and now issues with the guidance of an authority figure. However, their ability to navigate interpersonal relationships without adult intervention was lacking. The directives for Figure 1.25 emphasized the group's need to increase member-to-member communication with a concentrated focus on problem-solving and resolution.

The group was instructed to *"each choose one collage image and when this was completed, to decide which of the four choices they would use in the collage."* At this point a rousing debate ensued around whose image would be chosen. Throughout, group members argued, compromised, and alternately looked for help from the therapist. When the group was informed that the decisions were entirely up to them, they decided upon a warrior image (upper left). The young man whose picture was chosen (whom I will call Alan) proudly glued his collage onto the butcher paper.

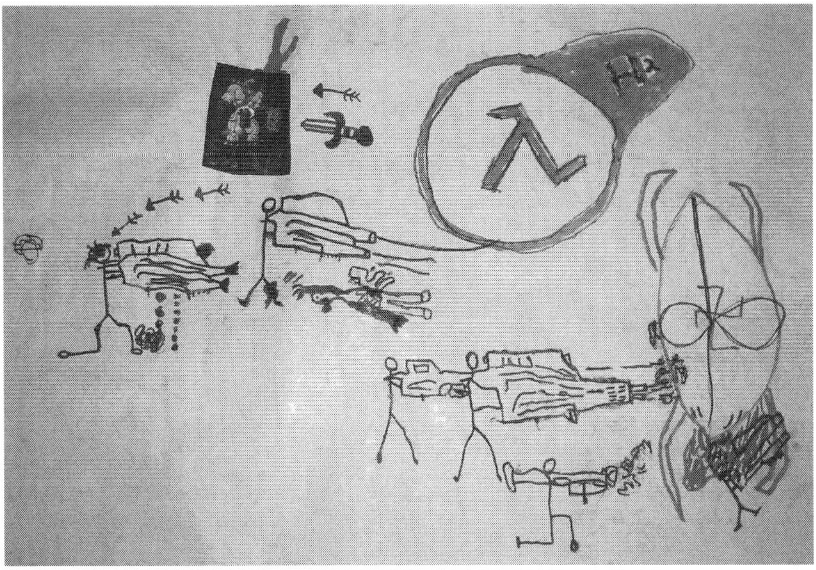

Figure 1.25 Group Mural

The second part of the directive was for *"each group member to take turns drawing anything around the collage image. Decide who will go first, second, third, and fourth, and begin when you are ready."* Quickly a group order was decided upon and the first two boys launched arrows at Alan's warriors (upper left) while Alan increased the number of warriors and the last boy drew blood spurting from the collage warrior and exclaimed, "He's dead." As the drawing continued it became clear that Alan was to be the target. His guns were tampered with and made ineffective, shields were created to ward off his attacks, dying men crept silently into his camp and ambushed his warriors, blood ran from open wounds, and a poisonous beetle (right side of image) were some of the drawing items which epitomized the violence and ruin. With each attack Alan could be heard laughing and saying, "That's not right, man," while anxiously awaiting his turn to repel the assaults. The carnage continued until slowly each member ceased to draw. As each of the group members returned to their seats they immediately began discussing the mural drawings around what they had added, attempted to add, improved upon, and decimated within the art project. No mention was made of the interpersonal relationships or process until this writer confronted the issue.

As we review the process of group therapy and the many models of group psychotherapy, Dies (1992) divided group therapists into three distinctive categories based around their leadership style. They were outlined as: (1) psychodynamic, (2) action-oriented, and (3) interpersonal. For purposes of this discussion, I will remain within these categories for the conceptualizing of Figure 1.25.

As such, from the psychodynamic approach I would give attention to the manifest metaphorical content (warfare) by linking it with the unconscious process of overpowering aggressive opposition. Through the exploration of feelings, the affect-laden conflicts within the art project (group process) would be focused upon to help the members gain insight into their unconscious motivations. An example of an action-oriented approach would include Cognitive-Behavioral therapy, which in this case would center on the dysfunctional beliefs and automatic thoughts of the members (expressed through metaphor) as a way to gather information on thinking styles. Additionally, the post-drawing discussion would work to challenge the maladjusted behaviors through an exploration of individual and collective strengths, the affective experience that accompanied the client in the drawing task, and solutions from the group as a whole. The last approach, as outlined by Dies (1992), is the interpersonal approach whereby socializing skills, self-awareness, group cohesiveness, and the development of empathy play a primary role. Exploring Figure 1.25 from this methodology, the peer relationships and the resultant exchange of the mural task would be of primary concern. Thus, each member's patterns of interaction, their feelings expression, and the rationale for subsequent relations would be opened up to the group in an effort to decrease social isolation through member-to-member interaction and provide a corrective appraisal of here and now behavior which can first be practiced within the safety of the group atmosphere.

Yalom (1985) has stated that group therapy goals, methodology, and interventions vary according to the theoretical orientation of the leader. Though very true, it is important to note that regardless of the model of psychotherapy (dynamic, interpersonal, or action-oriented), a common element comes to light: the expression and exploration of feelings. As such, each model places emphasis on the "experience" whether it is focused on catharsis, identification of automatic negative thoughts, or discovering new coping skills through interpersonal communication, an experiential process is paramount.

Correspondingly, the incorporation of figurative communication and metaphor within the therapeutic hour illuminates a client's natural "language" whereby the symbolic identification of problems is experienced on both a verbal and non-verbal level.

When assessing metaphorical communication in a family session, my preference is to utilize the family mural drawing as referred to earlier in this chapter. This simple art therapy directive not only illustrates the interactional patterns of the entire family but also can be used as a metaphor in future communications. Figure 1.26, with its large overpowering form items, smattering of tiny details, and the anxious representation of an underwater chase between a mother and her young adult daughter, characterizes this family of three perfectly. In all, this mural could be interpreted on a multiplicity of levels, from its formal or structural aspects to the insight-oriented comments by the family in the post-drawing inquiry where they stated that the ocean in the mural reflected that there is "always stuff going on underneath."

However, if we explore Figure 1.26 from a family systems perspective, the father complacently interacted in an emotionally distant manner (adding only the "trimmings" to the drawing) all the while desperately wanting to connect to both wife and daughter. On the other hand, the mother dominated through overpowering decision making (grass, vines, last shark) in an effort to compete and surpass her daughter's accomplishments. Alternately, the daughter, attempting to launch from her family, opposed her mother's overbearing pronouncements through a series of larger (cat) and more imposing interactions (submarine). All told, it could be said that each person in this system was projecting their unmet needs through dysfunctional communication and behaviors.

Based upon Figure 1.26, the goal of the subsequent directive was to provide this family with an experience of separating in a healthy way (the young adult female to have more independence and the parents to join as a couple). Integrating metaphorical expression, two distinct boxes were initially drawn (Figure 1.27) in the hopes that the parents would join in one box while the adult client would focus independently on her own needs in the second. Additionally, the bold pre-drawn boxes would provide a clear boundary for the family members to respond with congruent communication patterns rather than defensive and indistinct roles.

Figure 1.26 Quiet Time

Figure 1.27 Congruent Communication

As the family was presented with two pre-drawn boxes the daughter chose the box on the right side while the father, though vacillating, chose the left. As the wife went to the mural paper she immediately chose her husband's box and the provider complimented each member for their selections as it pointed toward healthy potentials. The drawing task continued in turns; the parents were given permission to speak with one another and negotiate, while the daughter had to remain silent, focusing entirely within her own "box." This directive was initiated to assist the family in identifying healthy methods of interaction while strengthening relationships.

Over the course of the next few months, family therapy focused on the familial strengths, rather than faults. Hence, when anxiety arose, as it was bound to do, each member was verbally referred back to the relationship metaphor of Figure 1.27 and informed that they needed to "remain in their own box," or that one or the other was "stepping out of their box." This allowed each individual to clarify the roles that must govern them if they were to develop stronger and healthier selves.

Thus, whether the mental health professional incorporates Cognitive-Behavioral interventions (identification, exploration, and modification of shared schemas), psychodynamic interventions (clarification, confrontation, and interpretation of inner conflicts), or humanistically oriented family therapy interventions (point out, refocus, and encourage healthy communication patterns) "therapeutic metaphors . . . can tap a variety of experiences, beliefs, and ideas that have been dormant in the listener's mind" (Barker, 1985, p. 13).

In the end, the identification and exploration of a personal metaphor provides an enriched experience for the client, and ultimately this individualized expression can be incorporated into the therapeutic hour to promote insight, growth, and experience.

> Much of psychotherapy consists in identifying previously unconscious metaphors and discovering how we unwittingly live by them. As one's sense of the self changes with therapeutic work and experimental action in the "real world," these metaphors will gradually be reshaped.
>
> (Siegelman, 1992, p. 67)

And So to Bed

Throughout this chapter, though varied expressions of metaphor have been presented, identical messages have repeated: metaphorical communication touches our instinctive self and connects internally to provide understanding to the conflicts that drive, regulate, join, and interconnect our beliefs and understanding of the world around us.

Whether metaphor is found within our daily language, as Lakoff and Johnson (1980) have postulated, is communicated figuratively through "artistic metaphors" (Mills and Crowley, 1986) or it is adapted to change the systemic experiences of the whole (Barker, 1985), it is not an isolated expression.

Ultimately, the union of a client's personal metaphor with an established treatment methodology allows the clinician to enter the symbolic world of the client in a language that is altogether theirs because it lifts away the veil of reflexive defenses and in due course provides understanding for the characteristics that make up the person.

References

Arieti, S. (1976). *Creativity: The magic synthesis*. New York: Basic Books, Inc.

Arlow, J.A. (1969). Unconscious fantasy and disturbances of conscious. *The Psychoanalytic Quarterly, 38* (1), 1–27.

Barker, P. (1985). *Using metaphors in psychotherapy*. New York: Brunner/Mazel.

Battino, R. (2002). *Metaphoria: Metaphor and guided metaphor for psychotherapy and healing*. Wales: Crown House Publishing.

Dies, R.R. (1992). Models of group psychotherapy: Sifting through the confusion. *International Journal of Group Psychotherapy, 42* (1), 1–17.

Dies, R.R. (1996). The unfolding of adolescent groups: A five-phase model of development. In P. Kymissis & D.A. Halperin (Eds.), *Group therapy with children and adolescents* (pp. 35–53). Washington, DC: American Psychiatric Press.

Dossick, J., & Shea, E. (1988). *Creative therapy 52 exercises for groups*. Sarasota, Florida: Professional Resource Exchange, Inc.

Gardner, R.A. (1986). *Therapeutic communication with children: The mutual storytelling technique*. Northvale, New Jersey: Jason Aronson Inc.

Heller, S., & Steele, T. (1986). *There's no such thing as hypnosis*. Phoenix: Falcon Press.

Kramer, E. (1971). *Art as therapy with children*. New York: Schocken Books.

Lakoff, G., & Johnson, M. (1980). *Metaphors we live by*. Chicago: University of Chicago Press.

Landgarten, H. (1987). *Family art therapy: A clinical guide and casebook*. New York: Brunner/Routledge.

McCarthy, R.F. (Ed.). (2000). *Urashima and the kingdom beneath the sea (Kodansha bilingual children's classics)*. Japan: Kodansha International.

Mills, J.C., & Crowley, R.J. (1986). *Therapeutic metaphors for children and the child within*. New York: Brunner/Mazel.

Moschini, L.B. (2004). *Drawing the line: Art therapy with the difficult client*. Hoboken, New Jersey: John Wiley & Sons.

Norcross, J.C., Hedges, M., & Castle, P.H. (2002). Psychologists conducting psychotherapy in 2001: A study of the division 29 membership. *Psychotherapy: Theory, Research, Practice, Training, 39* (1), 97–102.

Northey, W.F. (2004). Reflecting on the profession: Who are marriage and family therapists? *Family Therapist Magazine: The Association for Marriage and Family Therapy*, November/December, 10–17.

Riley, S. (1985). Draw me a paradox? . . . Family art psychotherapy utilizing a systemic approach to change. *Art Therapy Journal of the American Art Therapy Association*, (2), 116–123.

Shorr, J.E. (1972). *Psycho-imagination therapy*. New York: Intercontinental Medical Book Corporation.

Siegelman, E.Y. (1992). *Metaphor and meaning in psychotherapy*. New York: Guilford Press.

Yalom, I. (1985). *The theory and practice of group psychotherapy* (3rd ed.). New York: Basic Books.

2
Psychological Maturity

> Once upon a time, there was a girl who was very mean to another guy. And that girl was named Lisa. Lisa was very mean to a guy named Jerry. Jerry was just about fed up and so he told her off. Not only was she the meanest person alive, she also made him tell a story he didn't want to tell in the first place. And he was hyper so he really did like the group and everybody in it. And that was the end.

One of the most enduring principles of developmental theory lies in the belief that ability progresses in stages. This epigenetic perspective also encompasses an individual's ability to adapt to changing relationships within any stage of the life cycle. In the story outlined above, the interaction between this adolescent male and me is a prime example of a metaphor created out of a relationship. Thus, the story metaphor could be viewed as a symbolic representation of his oppositional and aggressive relationships with select family members whereby this client has associated our present relationship with the parental demands of the past. This substitution, accentuated through the indirect method of storytelling, illustrates the intensity of a therapeutic metaphor as it corresponds to transference for "they both refer to the carrying over of meaning from one set of situations to another" (Arlow, 1969).

The antagonistic defiance found within this client's story parallels his desire for autonomy ("so he told her off") but is met almost immediately with guilt and doubt as threats to his basic sense of security is heightened ("and he was hyper so he really did like the group and everybody in it"). The hostility generated in the story reflects the internal struggles of a growing independent identity from that of "parental" injunctions. In the therapeutic setting, the identification of these internal struggles combined with mature interactions and self-understanding is often equated with psychological growth.

As a result, the emotional experience of early relationships places an indelible mark upon human development and within the therapeutic setting, it becomes all important as the transference is unconsciously acted out. This story, replete with unresolved conflicts, exaggerated responses, and relationship resistance symbolizes the quest for an independent identity. The processing of this personal metaphor could be accomplished subtly, though less disguised based upon the realistic characters, to encourage autonomous behavior and greater awareness without direct confrontation. An example would be as follows:

> Once upon a time, there was a girl named Lisa and a guy named Jerry. Every time that Lisa and Jerry met, it seemed that Lisa was asking Jerry to do something. Sometimes she wanted him to sit up straight, settle down, or listen. Jerry was fed up with Lisa's requests. He didn't want to sit up, or settle down, or listen. Sometimes he just wanted to slouch, run around with his friends, and yell as loud as he could. Jerry felt that no matter what he did he got into trouble, so he decided to just give up. But when he gave up Lisa, his family, and his friends started to think he didn't care, and that was wrong, Jerry cared very much. He didn't know what to do. So, one day, instead of doing nothing, Jerry decided to do things about the stuff that bothered him. He wasn't able to change everything, but he noticed that the more he did for himself the less angry he felt. The end.

On the other hand, the story metaphor could be explored candidly through any established treatment modality goals and/or theory. In this vein, the resistance, transference reaction, and hostility in the story could be verbally identified as a way for Jerry to express his anxiety around external demands, all the while seeking a unique identity. Whether direct or indirect means are utilized, the "discussion of one's immediate thoughts and feelings helps the patient sort out his identity by having to express it; the patient is offered the ego-enhancing opportunity to clarify for self and others who he is" (Bauer, 1993, p. 18).

In this example, the psychosocial crisis according to Erikson (1963) would be equated with the developmental phase of identity versus repudiation or role confusion. Hence, the client's contradictory statements provide the necessary solution, as metaphorically, his symptoms serve as the very indicator of his needs. This phenomenon is not only found within this one case example, but can be tracked throughout the entire transforming nature of development. In effect, psychological growth can be likened to the necessary social development of our relationships, for these relationships shape our personality, character structures, and ultimately meet the demands of maturational intimacy.

As such, the experience of need is an underlying structure that if overlooked, can result in adaptive failures. Whether these failures are regarded psychosocially as Erikson's identity crisis (Erikson, 1956), psychosexually as outlined by Freud, or through the lens of Kohut's self-psychology as in a developmental arrest, it is the ever-widening relationships that support the growing individual as he or she navigates through his or her expanded world. Thus, the relational qualities between therapist and client become increasingly important as the symbolic behavior and its subsequent underlying meaning is identified, processed, and corrected.

Fill the Bill

In my work, the developmental challenges of psychological maturity have often been counterbalanced by an under-utilized method of intervention called pair therapy. The psychosocial approach of pair therapy accentuates the relationship development between a set of peers and centers on the promotion of emotional and shared responsibility within the here and now. The intimate nature of this two-person group, coupled with the mental health professional's supportive, empathic understanding, facilitates the integration of adaptive skills and in its ideal, the recommencement of developmental growth. In short:

> This approach actively encourages both children to engage with one another in real-life issues such as the inevitability of peer conflict, the discovery of mutual support, the experience of managing feelings of jealousy and competition, and the magnetic and infectious joy of cooperation and shared experiences.
>
> (Selman, Watts, and Schultz, 1997, p. 11)

The structure of pair therapy is such that the two children chosen exhibit opposite personality traits, what Yeates, Schultz, and Selman (1991) refer to as *self-transforming* and *other-transforming* interpersonal orientations. "By pairing opposites in this way, the counselor can praise both children's competencies (e.g., restraint or assertiveness) and encourage each child to practice the positive aspects of the other's negotiation style" (Karcher, 2002, p. 124).

It is also important to note that this intervention requires that the pair decide upon an activity (at the beginning of each group) which they are to engage in together. After the initial session, subsequent group sessions provide time to reflect on the prior activity with an emphasis on psychosocial maturity.

In Figure 2.1 two latency-aged girls attended pair therapy sessions as the first (whom I will call Beth) exerted an inordinate amount of control and intimidation (other-transforming) over Laura, who preferred a passive style of interaction (self-transforming). These two girls, though exhibiting intense relational conflict, were inseparable. On this day, however, they each entered the group individually. Beth was rambunctious and verbally expansive as she bounded through the door, while Laura insisted that her assigned staff member escort her into the room arm-in-arm. As one can guess Beth with Laura reflexively acquiescing, decided the activity for the day which was to be felt boards.

While Laura focused on a familial picnic scene, Beth struggled with the activity as she enviously watched Laura's adeptness at the task. In no time, Beth began to insist that Laura help her find the pieces she was seeking. However, each time Laura would do so, Beth would dismiss the felt piece and request another. After a multitude of such exchanges, Laura silently avoided interacting with Beth.

Beth's felt board **Laura's felt board**

Figure 2.1 Pair Therapy First Session

Toward the end of the therapeutic hour, time is set aside for the two clients, directed by the mental health professional, to review the session as negotiation skills, the here and now experiences of behavioral choices, and mutuality over egocentricity are explored. On a purely representational level, the completed felt boards revealed an individual psyche that embodied each client's underlying character structure. As such, Beth's completed felt board outlined her egocentric needs as two attending horses flank the princess (note how the hat is masking the princess's face), while Laura's clearly spoke to the demands of the basic family, with care and devotion as the emerging theme. By the same token, the communicative aspects coupled with the non-verbal components of the session's play provided a metaphor for their relationships, interactions, needs, and desires both in and outside of the group. Laura painfully in need of acceptance and protection, suffered the discomfort and indignation as she sought to "belong," much as an infant seeks to belong to a central caregiver. In contrast, Beth masked her intimacy needs beneath a seething jealous rage while her conflicting verbal commands spoke of the self-doubt that often accompanies the beginnings of assertive, autonomous behavior.

Looking at these two contrasting, yet comparable factors (symbolic and representational communication), the entire task was processed as a metaphor for their larger relationship. Though Laura did not possess the skills to verbalize her frustration, the relational interactions remained the central focus as I pointed out and clarified issues where intimacy and autonomy diverged.

For the next three weeks, Beth continued to dominate while Laura conceded on every count. Whether they engaged in games (where Beth blatantly cheated when faced with her inadequacies) or art tasks where Laura excelled, the process of Beth controlling the relationship persisted. However, in subsequent sessions Laura's passive acceptance of emotional deprivation had begun to wane. During the process illumination, after each chosen activity, Laura slowly began to voice her desire to choose an activity and that she felt "frightened" when Beth would get angry. Though Beth's response was minimal in the seventh session, Laura insisted that the girls draw (Figure 2.2).

This was the first time that Beth had acquiesced to Laura's wishes. While the pair drew individually, Beth clandestinely watched Laura's rendering take shape. Out of the corner of her eye, she closely monitored each form item and tentatively attempted to copy it on her own paper. With each effort, she failed. As her frustration grew, so did her aggressive behavior. She began to push at the table, mumble under her breath, and complain about the inferior art supplies. It was at this juncture that Beth was encouraged to request help from Laura on a verbal level, while processing her feelings of frustration that what she truly endeavored was gratification. Cautiously, Beth asked for Laura's help in adding a tree and sun to her drawing. The result, Figure 2.2, was a milestone in the relationship, as the unilateral play of the prior months turned cooperative.

For the next several months, the pair continued to focus on their growing relationship as the process of negotiation and reflection enhanced their developmental deficits. In this way, Laura's passive acquiescence to external demands was diminished by a growing ability to express her feelings of both need and discontent.

One such example of expression was a dual story told by the pair. It is important to note that the therapist does not participate in the telling of a dual story. In their narrative, Laura tests the strength of the pair's connection through the metaphor of Gypsy and Snoopy's relationship.

> Once upon a time, there was a wolf named Gypsy, who lived in a forest. Gypsy got lonely one day and went to the village. And she met Snoopy. Snoopy and her went walking down the forest. When they walked they heard something move and Gypsy went to see what it was. Then Snoopy went to go see to. They got tired and Gypsy said, "Let's go hide together." "Okay, let's go." As they played in the forest Snoopy thought that Gypsy was tricking her. She said, "I know that you're not tricking me?!" "No, I'm not." And Snoopy believed Gypsy. Gypsy just wanted a friend. And they both said okay.

Figure 2.2 Laura and Beth Work Cooperatively

This dual story illustrates how Beth's profound antagonistic social skills were beginning to show mediation through her growing sense of industry. In this way, the safe environment of the pair therapy sessions allowed Beth to freely acknowledge her inadequacies as feelings of inferiority were replaced with expressions of need, coupled with less dependency on the environment. As shared storytelling became the preferred activity, Beth initiated the following tale:

> Once upon a time there were two tigers. One was named Jewel and the other Jade. They lived in a jungle. And they fought with each other. After fighting then we apologized to each other. And then we became friends. Then they said, "Do you want to go for a walk?" Then they went for a walk and talked to each other about all sorts of things. Then we played hide and seek after we went for the walk. Then we will hide and nobody will find us. After we hid where no-one can find us we found a house. We went into the house and looked around. And then we found something special. That special thing was two rings. They were gold and metal and had a diamond in it. The rings were beautiful. They each wore the friendship ring and their friendship went real good. And they lived happily ever after. The moral is friends always stick together at all times.

The path that these two females walked, from relational conflict to social skills development is not an isolated incident if, one believes as Erikson does, that psychosocial change is rooted in both relational crisis and resolution, then interpersonal orientation of pair therapy can prove invaluable. For within the symbolic play, a metaphor of socialization emerges. Moreover, the manner of reflection in pair therapy avoids direct confrontation in preference to metaphorical learning experiences.

A spontaneously shared story from two adolescent males personifies this integration of a social metaphor.

Bear vs. Killer Dog

> Once upon a time there was two animals, a dog and a bear. They both were not getting along at all so one day they both caught something at the lake. When they caught something at the lake they both caught something big. Well, the bear caught something small and the dog caught something big. The bear was bigger than the dog, so the dog was smaller. So, they had a big conflict and they got into an argument. So, what happened was they started being aggressive and started fighting. Basically, no-one was getting anywhere. The ending is basically they worked it out by saying, "I'll get this half and you get that half and everything will be good." It ends up they accepted that and they both shared and went on with their life and had a good life.

Child's Play

In the quest for relational intimacy and understanding it is often those divested of such love and nurturance who exhibit the most conflict-laden symptoms. These conflicts, between the person and the environment, often take the form of fantasies whereby the deprivation is mastered through omnipotent favor, fame, and fortune, or combated in its opposite, as a separation of self and others. In either case the traumata of early experiences is often set forth repetitiously in play to master the situation. As such, this symbolic play material can help an individual to cope with loss, fears, and connected feelings of inadequacy.

These developmental impairments, often witnessed as anxiety or aggression, frequently find relief in the action-oriented and compensatory fantasies of metaphoric communication. The following Figure (2.3) illustrates the power of masked conflict and abounds with planes, boats, and armored cars each outfitted with "protective" armaments.

A group of adolescent and pre-adolescent males had been meeting regularly for over eight months. The focus of the group was on assertive communication skills and each member was presently in the fourth stage of the group life cycle according to Robert Dies (1996). As such, the clients were taking a greater responsibility for the group process while generalizing this self-awareness and

Figure 2.3 I Wish . . .

understanding into the larger community. The art directive was for each member to, *"draw a wish for the entire group."* This client (Figure 2.3) wrote, "I wish this group would have its own island," with further elaboration he stated, "the house in the middle has love and money."

As you look at the final image, what had been intended as a safe refuge has instead been rendered as a depiction of aggressive fear. Needless to say, the group response was not overwhelmingly positive. Members, in turn, stated their displeasure at the amount of "violence" that surrounded the island. While the artist defended his fantasy, I viewed the image as a symbolic distortion and processed the drawing through the lens of Sarnoff's (1987) work on stress and humiliation:

> What are the tactics available to the child to master overwhelming stresses? First, the child can do to another what has been done to him. Second, the child can talk about the experience directly. Third, the child can develop a fantasy to master the circumstances of the situation that stresses him.
>
> (Sarnoff, 1987, p. 42)

In this image, the aggression, so disproportionate to the client's verbalized meaning, with its excessive protection from unseen external forces, had me wondering what had occurred in the here and now. A simple question surrounding the client's recent experience in school brought forth a wealth of meaning. The client spoke of numerous humiliating experiences over a four-week period that had ultimately culminated in a final embarrassment. Thus, this client's conflict-laden wishes were disguised as intense and prominent metaphors, both verbally and artistically.

In some instances, fantasy can also distract from the necessary affiliation and intimacy of an evolving relationship. Therefore, once an individual has moved beyond the stage of latency, fantasy is forsaken as "reality" gains prominence. However, the establishment of self-esteem through ongoing fantasy can inhibit the formation of intimacy and isolate in its intensity. Freud (1989) states, "the motive forces of phantasies are unsatisfied wishes, and every single phantasy is the fulfillment of a wish, a correction of unsatisfying reality" (p. 439).

Figure 2.4 is the symbolic equivalent of a deprivation that has been expressed through repetitious, superhero, fantasy drawings.

This young man constantly reverted to superhero formations in an effort to resolve the emotional problems of parental abandonment and subsequent deprivation. The image on the right was described as a person who was "cut in half," bleeding, and stomping on multiple victims as he concurrently "powers up" and yells that they have failed in their attempt to "kill" him. This thinly veiled revenge fantasy, a metaphor for the parent-child relationship, permeated his interactions and subsequently interfered with his developmental maturation. Though his symbols revolved around omnipotent compensation, this adolescent male communicated through dependent exchanges as he internally hoped and waited for rescue.

Figure 2.4 Now I Will Kill You

The growing child, while navigating the larger environment is regularly faced with changes, both psychologically and physiologically, as new experiences supplant the familiar. As these experiences intensify, it is within the created fantasy that conflict and tension seek release. This masked form of communication is often apparent within the metaphorical expression of uncontained destructive rage. The regressive tendency found within Figure 2.4 offers an example of how "feelings toward the primary objects or their substitutes are safely displaced onto symbols" (Sarnoff, 1987, p. 24).

Moreover, as conflict and tensions within the environment gradually intrude upon daily reflections, a discharge of the drive is imperative. In some cases, the welling up of overwhelming feelings, with a sudden and forceful release in-and-of-itself, provides satisfaction. Figure 2.5 is an example drawn by an adolescent male who exhibited chronic anger management issues. The directive was to, *"draw a time when you were angry."*

In Figure 2.5, the client has drawn a series of word balloons, building one upon the other, as an argument escalates out of control. This drawing requires no words be placed within the cartoon bubbles for the viewer to comprehend the energy contained within the expression. What motivated this client was a reduction of his anxiety. What goaded caregivers was the determined pleasure found within this client's aggressive release which occurred regularly in the program setting. Regardless of the substitute problem-solving offered, any compromise for fighting was found to be fleeting and unsatisfactory.

Whether one is psychodynamically delving into the discharge of drives with their tendency toward unconscious repetition or identifying the automatic recurring negative thoughts of Cognitive-Behavioral theory, the metaphorical meaning within our communication binds the emotional experience. For the

Figure 2.5 Discharge of Drives

dynamic representation of thoughts, sensations, and reaction, imparts a powerful message and places the expression into a context for further exploration.

Correspondingly, the developmental processes with their transformative aspects are experiential, vibrant, and direct, an integrative sequence that allows for the vicissitudes of life with all of its attendant order and chaos. This growth process does not end in young adulthood, needs and drives extend throughout the life cycle and up until the moment of death. These needs and desires are illustrated in Figure 2.6 where an elderly, institutionalized male was asked to render, *"On one side of your paper, draw you doing something outside the hospital and on the other, you doing something inside of the hospital."*

The left side of Figure 2.6 shows the client sitting isolated at a riverbed feeding his beloved birds. The right side of Figure 2.6 was described by this client, from bottom to top, as him smoking while thinking about life, a cat and dog intermingled, a friend who was happy, a hoped-for group of friends in the community, an adult board-and-care, and his cat. This side reveals a child-like Symbolist drawing much in the style of Gustav Klimt's painting entitled, "Death and Life." In Figure 2.6, as in Klimt's painting, "the ornamental flatness of the drapery, the organic, undulating contours, and the arbitrary placement of figures, such that they seem to float and hover as they would in dream" (De la Croix & Tansey, 1980, p. 809), embody the replacement of intimacy over isolation. "When people are prevented from satisfying their drives, the natural

Figure 2.6 Inside and out

reaction will be anger and frustration. When there is no hope of having drives satisfied at any time, the consequence of striving without achieving goals can be alienation" (Brun, 1993, p. 7).

Thus, both sides of Figure 2.6 typify this adult's continued need to be needed. Whether he is feeding birds or rendering his present and future relationships, these drawings provided a signpost that gave direction to the therapeutic hour. A flight of fancy and imagination, which would have been difficult to express in purely verbal terms, was experienced symbolically by both client and mental health professional.

Betwixt and Between

The developmental psychology of Jean Piaget (1973) has outlined four stages of adaptive cognitive development marked by the intellectual growth of the child. As such, his analysis ignores the social influences of Erikson's theory and instead accentuates the conscious mental operations in children's intellectual experience. Though Piaget's research and exploration lay within the realm of human intellect rather than the unconscious processes (Maier, 1978), Piaget "shared with Freud that the important aspects of the mind lie beneath the surface" (Gardner, H., 1982, p. 18). During a speech presented in 1920, he responded to Freud's premise regarding the basis of intuitive thought within the unconscious:

> The conscious and the unconscious are everywhere entangled, often inextricably; if these two aspects of the life of the mind have been treated as in violent contrast with each other, and thus also psychoanalysis and the psychology of intelligence, this was a simplification of reality.
>
> (Piaget, 1977a, p. 56)

As such, Piaget relied upon symbols, and symbolic processes, as a form of assimilation, which is defined as "the act of incorporating objects or aspects of objects into learned activities" (Lefrancois, 1995, pp. 329–330). Accordingly, his approach to symbolic activity would focus upon the cognitive sphere and associated intellectual achievements while a psychoanalytic approach would view the projected symbols as an expression of the self's needs, conflicts, and desires.

A teenager who was directed to, *"draw your feelings in the here and now"* completed Figure 2.7.

Piaget (1970) would interpret Figure 2.7 based on the child's mental growth in relation to perception and spatial representation. Hence, this child's drawing characteristics would be evaluated based upon schemas, knowledge of the environment, dimensional organization of objects, and the depiction of space. This Constructivist point of view identifies knowledge as an assemblage of personal experiences, based on sensory perceptions, which are then structured to form larger concepts as the growing child adapts to his/her environment.

Figure 2.7 A Deserted Island

Conversely, a psychoanalytic approach would view the same drawing (Figure 2.7) as reflective of the fundamental personality of the creator. In this manner, the client's verbal statements, the structural (placement, quality, perspective, and size), and formal aspects (detailing, accessories, and symbol interpretation) combine to produce a qualitative and quantitative approach to image interpretation (Buck, 1973; Caligor, 1957; Machover, 1949).

Arieti (1976) has stated:

> Creativity as a cognitive function is to be distinguished from intelligence; it is not a unitary or uniform function but is to be accounted for in terms of a large number of factors, or primary mental abilities. The intellect can be divided into memory and thinking. In creativity it is thinking that counts. In its turn, thinking can be divided into cognition, production, and evaluation.
>
> (Arieti, 1976, p. 17)

Hence, awareness and understanding of the larger world is not purely composed from logical observation but through symbolization, fantasy, and imagination.

As we explored in Chapter 1, metaphorical representation is found within our daily language (the conceptual metaphor) and our sensory system (with personal preferences predominating). Additionally, the incorporation of evocative interventions with its thrust toward imagination and verbalization integrates the left and right hemispheres of the brain as the logical and verbal left side is united with the symbolic and emotional right hemisphere. Together these two systems "govern our abilities to create, in language and in art, and to discover new connections in the world" (Ornstein, 1991, p. 135).

However, "there is now an impressive amount of evidence that, as a consequence of brain damage to the right hemisphere, individuals lose the ability . . . to honor the conventions of the fictive realm" (Gardner, H., 1982, p. 182). As such, Gardner has found that clients with right hemisphere damage often exhibit problems when attempting to ascertain the moral of a story. He states, "either they simply repeat an element of the story or they seize upon a concrete feature of the story and convert that into the moral" (p. 314).

A situational example of this difficulty can be found in the following tale. This teenager was referred to individual therapy due to excessively aggressive peer interactions. As part of my assessment routine, I instituted a dual story. By the second sentence, this client's impairments were quickly identified as her ability to augment the story's characterizations, theme, and/or plot (i.e., imaginative pursuits) was hampered. As such, I have italicized her contributions to the narrative.

> *Once upon a time*, there was a *boy named John*, and he *lost a ring*. John loved the ring because *it was special to him*. John's ring was special because *he got it from one of his friends*. John got *on his horse, named Spirit*, and

> was *riding on the farm looking for it.* It turns out that *the dog stole the ring* and *then buried it in the dirt.* And the boy *didn't know that he buried it in the dirt.* John was *on Spirit* and he *started chasing the dog.* While John was chasing the dog *he led John to the ring* and *John found the ring.*
>
> So, the lesson or moral is: *John shouldn't have lost the ring.*

Throughout this story, the client exhibited significant cognitive-communication problems typified by poor reasoning and difficulty with organization. Her responses were concrete in nature and were interspersed with long periods of silence as she struggled with the sequential events in the narrative.

Equally, damage to the frontal lobe can produce impairments which extend to motor functioning, memory, language production, impulse control, and social and sexual behavior. Ultimately, the frontal lobe controls our emotional responses and metaphorically gives shelter to our basic personality (Kolb & Milner, 1981). A young male, whom I will call Donny, had suffered a head trauma with significant right frontal lobe damage. After the accident, he began to evidence signs of behavioral problems, motor and vocal tics, with compulsive tendencies. As he got older his reality testing worsened, his impulse control declined, and euphoria increased as he experienced what Blumer and Benson (1975) refer to as "pseudopsychopathic" behavior. Subsequently, his sexual acting out increased and his aggressive tendencies became inexhaustible.

Donny was seen with other adolescent males who had been diagnosed within the Autistic Spectrum in weekly group sessions. These clients exhibited a range of impairments in their social and interpersonal skills, verbal fluency, cognitive functioning, and problem-solving abilities.

Figure 2.8 is Donny's completed clay dinosaur and environment. Due to his head trauma, Donny's motor skills (especially fine motor skills) were notably disturbed. His dinosaur, a tangle of twisted and balled clay, took an inordinate

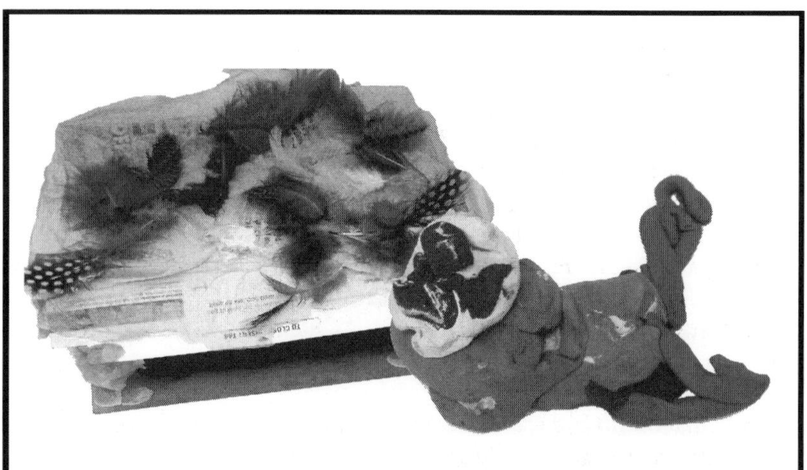

Figure 2.8 Donny's Dinosaur and Roach Motel

amount of time and concentration. However, this did not stop him from making a shark (not shown) with an attempt at a third animal before limits were imposed. As the group shared their initial creations, only Donny had created exclusively predatory animals.

As he set to work on his environment, he was adamant that the box in Figure 2.8 would be the home for his dinosaur. He called this enclosure, "The Roach Motel." At this point, he had used each of the materials supplied, attempted to make two more clay creations, and begin another cardboard environment. If not for verbal limits by the group members and staff, his inclination toward "free" expression (and perseveration) would have been boundless. This situation was primarily neurologic rather than emotional as his brain injury created a dichotomy of impulsiveness and apathy. With diminished regulation of judgment there was no dampening of primitive drives. Thus, his primitive brain (archipallium) where aggression and self-preservation govern, took over and his actions were often unfettered. For the remainder of the project only markers were presented. Through this intervention, I hoped to make Donny's participation within the group project success-oriented rather than one of mere limit setting.

In all, it has been noted that brain-damaged clients experience grave difficulties in the comprehension of metaphors and idioms (Myers & West, 1978; Foldi, Cicone, & Gardner, 1983; Weylman, Brownell & Gardner, 1989; Stowe, Zempleni & Hoeks, 2003). This reliance upon concrete interpretations places organically damaged individuals at a disadvantage as nonrepresentational perception facilitates understanding. Faced with a wealth of personal and often symbolic experiences, the assimilation of concepts, the understanding of events, and the integration of these real-world experiences propels learning. Thus, abstract thinking often relates to higher levels of cognitive development.

Unlike younger children, the ability to interpret non-literal language is acquired by the age of 12 (Johnson & Pascual-Leone, 1989). Piaget views this as the transition to formal thought (*formal operational thinking*) whereby, "youths become capable of thinking propositionally, of conceptualizing, and of using hypotheses" (Lidz, 1976, p. 92). As such, young children, lacking metaphoric comprehension and higher reasoning skills, provide literal interpretations (Ackerman, 1982; Gardner, H., 1982; Johnson & Pascual-Leone, 1989) when presented with idiomatic expressions.

Ackerman (1982) has stated, "that young children are sensitive to the use of non-literal utterances in some situations, but cannot explain these utterances" (p. 449). Consequently, communicating contextual information can assist the younger child (up to latency age) in the comprehension of idiomatic interpretations.

Figure 2.9 illustrates the drawings of a regressed pre-teen (upper and lower left side) and a developmentally aged appropriate eleven-year-old (upper and lower right side). The idiomatic expression, "left out in the cold" was initially given without any context being provided. As you can see, each child related a

Figure 2.9 Left out in the Cold

literal meaning with the upper left depicting a door being closed while a figure waits outside and the upper right image of a woman standing in the snow at a bus stop. After a brief discussion of the initial drawings, I provided the group members with a framework by focusing on the psychological and emotional context of the idiom. At this point, the female on the right began to discuss "feeling left out in the cold" when a friend did not invite her along to the movies. Additionally, the regressed female on the left processed "feeling left out in the cold" when her mother did not arrive for a scheduled visit. The bottom drawings in Figure 2.9 were created after the discussion and show a party occurring with two figures wishing they had been invited (left side bottom) and a memory of sibling rivalry where the client was consequenced and unable to attend a concert with her family (right side bottom).

With a shift from literal communication to figurative expression, the client is afforded an opportunity to share on an abstract level the vicissitudes of his/her thoughts, actions, and emotions.

As a final example, Figure 2.10 represents the frustration that can accompany uncertainty, confusion, and embarrassment.

This developmentally delayed pre-teen decided to illustrate the idiom "treading on thin ice." She began with a squared block of ice and then added the mixture of diagonal swirls which she stated was a "hack saw." As she spoke,

Figure 2.10 Treading on Thin Ice

this literal interpretation began to perplex her and she quickly took back her comment while attempting to cross out the hack saw image. With each stroke her frustration intensified until she left the table in a flurry of motion and loud shouting. In the beginning, she was inconsolable as she stormed around the room complaining that she did not know what the idiom meant. In due course, her extrinsic anxiety dissipated and uncertainty was replaced with contextual information.

Figure 2.11 was her second drawing and shows two people interacting (this therapist and a self-portrait of the client) whereby the therapist has a darkened dialogue bubble to represent her limits and boundaries, while the lighter dialogue bubble is the client's depiction of her yelling in anger. She then stated, "I tread on thin ice when I raise my voice and scream at people."

In all, comprehension of idiomatic and metaphorical language is dependent upon numerous factors and this comprehension is a driving force behind systematic and logical solutions within any given problem. In addition, the ability to reason abstractly forms the basis of critical thinking as well as universal ethical principles.

If we return to Figure 2.8 and the case of Donny, his frontal lobe damage impacted not just the control of impulses, but also hampered his ability to follow a moral code of conduct. Shermer (2004) has stated:

Figure 2.11 A Context Is Provided

> To the extent that morality is linked to impulse control and the delay of gratification, if there is a moral module in the brain, it is either in the frontal cortex or directly linked to it and is heavily mediated by brain chemistry and experience.
>
> (Shermer, 2004, p. 228)

Overall, Donny's numerous interpersonal difficulties were not merely aggravated by his neurologic impairments but were also due in large measure to the social isolation he suffered within the everyday environment. In the end, people learn through experience. Thus, "moral development, then, is not a process of imprinting rules and virtues but a process involving transformation of cognitive structures. It is dependent on cognitive development and the stimulation of the social environment" (Duska & Whelan, 1975, p. 7).

Read Between the Lines

Not unlike the benefits of pair therapy, the development of a moral code of conduct provides the necessary framework for mutuality, reciprocity, and the sharing inherent in cooperative play.

Lawrence Kohlberg's, "theory of moral development was dependent on the thinking of Swiss psychologist Jean Piaget and the American philosopher

John Dewey. These men had emphasized that human beings develop philosophically and psychologically in a progressive fashion" (Barger, 2000). As such, Kohlberg outlined six stages with three marked levels of maturation.

The *Pre-Conventional* level is defined by the concept of "good" and "bad." To this end, it is an egocentric mindset with concrete understandings and deference. The second or *Conventional* level appreciates the importance of intimacy and mutuality whereby the social group and identity formation is given credence. The final category is often called the *Post-Conventional* or *Principled* level. At this stage, "there is a clear effort to define moral values and principles which have validity and application apart from the authority of the groups or persons holding these principles and apart from the individual's own identification with these groups" (Duska & Whelan, 1975, pp. 46–47).

When working in the therapeutic hour, understanding the intricacies of each stage moves beyond mere academics as the knowledge garnered can provide the helping professional with processing information. It is important to note that Kohlberg believed that individuals could only come to terms with one stage beyond their present level of reasoning, hence his belief that the propagation of cognitive conflicts or "disequilibrium" produces insight (Duska & Whelan, 1975). Additionally, "according to Kohlberg, what defines a person's moral reasoning is not the specific moral choice, but the reasoning used to justify that choice" (Hursh, 2005, p. 3). Subsequently, the process illumination stage of any therapeutic session can yield information connected to growth possibilities.

One example of how Kohlberg's work was applied in the group setting was with a newly formed group of adolescent girls who, after having completed the drawing task, were in the midst of the feedback discussion. One particular female was angered at two of her group members and whenever they spoke, asked a question, or chanced to look at her she responded with increasingly disrespectful comments. As we processed her obvious disdain, each group member pronounced, in one form or another, that her manner of interacting was "wrong." Though the peer comments were helpful in setting a moral code of conduct (rules, cooperation, mutuality) it did not yield the reasoning behind the understanding.

To elicit the moral justification I asked each group member this question, "When people are mean to some and nice to others it is wrong because . . . ?" Of the six adolescent girls in the group, one aligned with the first level, *Pre-Conventional* stage of thinking and replied, "Because you'll get punished." While a second fell into the *Pre-Conventional* stage two level of thinking, "because then someone will get you back." The last three group members provided reasoning from the *Conventional* stage three thinking and stated, "Because it hurts feelings," "because it makes them upset and feel left out," and, "I wouldn't do it because I want to be nice to people." The offending group member's reasoning for being rude and disrespectful was found in the *Pre-Conventional* stage of thinking as she loudly exclaimed, "They were mean to me!"

Alone, these responses provide an understanding of how one group member's comments can affect the larger whole. However, when taken in concert with Kohlberg's theory of moral development, each group member's response provides the mental health professional with an identifiable stage of awareness, cognitive maturity irrespective of chronological age, and the interactional process of the group and of the individuals which make up that group.

As such, the promotion of empathy and reciprocal interactions will require a variety of interventions as "cognitive conflict is only experienced when the considerations being introduced emanate from one stage above the individual's usual stage of reasoning about moral conflicts" (Duska & Whelan, 1975, p. 104).

In this case, the group members were in various stages of cognitive understanding, thus the process illumination was tailored to fit the growing needs of the individual. Consequently, questioning focused on one stage above their present level of reasoning. The client at *Pre-Conventional* stage one was asked, "When you are with other people, what type of friends make you happy? How do they act toward you? How do you act toward them?" This level of questioning focused the stage one client on the pleasure principle and moved her from a rigid position of egocentricity. Conversely, the stage two clients processed other people's needs and feelings (moving from egocentricity to group identity skills) by answering questions related to the "Golden Rule." Equally, the *Conventional* level, stage three, peers were prompted by questions focusing on not merely the group, but society and social rules as a whole.

Additionally, an assessment of moral development can be ascertained through the incorporation of specific directives. These can be designed with an eye toward group and individual needs. One such directive is what I call *Storytelling in the Round*, which combines a group story with drawing tasks. This directive illustrates the projected self through both verbal and visual symbolic expressions. Given complete freedom to relate a story and then to choose one part of the story to draw, the group members are faced with multiple decisions. First, the storyteller begins a story that is wholly his/her own and at their discretion, another group member then picks up the story. The tale is thusly narrated until all members have had an opportunity to add to the initial story. Once the story is complete each member of the group chooses a portion of the tale and this is depicted on his/her paper.

A group of early adolescent males related the following shared group story:

> One day a bunch of soldiers called the Red Ribbon Army went up against Gilbro. Gilbro fought hard but he got shot and the Red Ribbon Army flew out the window. Gilbro's friend, he was called Piccolo, was angry and went to find the people who shot his friend. Soon, all kinds of people were chasing the army. When Piccolo returned he found Gilbro dead so he took him to his cave and tried to heal him. The soldiers returned and people came to

help but the soldiers shot everyone and threw bombs. Gilbro healed and he fought one of the army guys who had blown up his house. After this the police came and calmed everything down. Gilbro was sad because he was put in jail with the soldier for fighting. But Gilbro only stayed for the night and when the cops let him go he teased the soldier and they fought again. Gilbro was put back in jail and was electrocuted in the chair after spending almost all of his life there.

Figure 2.12 offers the completed drawings of two of the group members. The upper drawing depicts the electrocution of Gilbro. The client related that "Gilbro didn't listen and so he deserved to die." *Conventional* adults would look upon an electrocution for teasing as excessive; however, in the mind of the *Pre-Conventional* thinker, Gilbro flaunted his mockery rather than showing respect for those in authority. Thus, the severity of the punishment was justified.

On the other hand, the lower drawing of Figure 2.12 represents the police's arrival and subsequent arrest of Gilbro and the soldiers. This client stated, "Gilbro had to go to jail. He was destroying things and that's wrong. He had

Figure 2.12 Storytelling in the Round

to be arrested." In this response we see an orientation toward punishment; however, in this client's reasoning it was not due to unequivocal obedience toward authority figures, but instead that social control and order is necessary as the *Conventional* thinker believes in upholding the law and accepting the inevitable external consequences.

Beyond these client's drawings and the subsequent moral reasoning, the composite elements of the narrative generated an interchange of ideas, symbolic fantasy, and understanding, as communication and cooperation walked hand in hand. The story theme with warring factions, attacks, and miraculous acts of healing allowed each member to satisfy base needs through fantasy formation while practicing pro-social relationship skills. Additionally, just as the artwork provided a kinesthetic release, the story allowed verbal and visual expression in the form of metaphor (acts of aggression displaced) and reasoning (the client's moral interpretation). This abstraction, coupled with the incorporation of multiple sensory preferences, allowed each client to succeed; it replaced egocentric concerns with that of the larger whole, and ultimately through imaginative play expressed their concerns, fears, and worries without adult interruption or censure.

By way of a second example, a young adult female, unable to tolerate feelings, experienced life through the lens of Kohlberg's *Pre-Conventional* level of development. As such, her focus was on singular comforts centered on self-interest and rewards, chronic impulsivity, and egocentrism. All total, these values led her to feelings of sadness, frustration, and ultimately of loneliness. Though by witnessing her interactions with others one would never guess the pervasiveness of these negative emotions as her propensity was to hide behind false salutations of joy and excitement. This method of interacting both protected her true feelings and allowed her to hold painful thoughts and feelings at bay.

If we believe that moral reasoning evolves in progressive stages, then this young adult would benefit by moving into the *Conventional* level of moral development through the cultivation of internal values, mutual relationships, and shared feelings. Concomitantly, the assessment and incorporation of her primary sensory preferences would aid in choosing a corresponding media which would augment her strengths and drive her weaknesses. In this vein, kinesthetically tactile response modes described her method of processing information. Overall, she learned through experience, and experienced feelings physically as opposed to emotionally. As a result, the medium of papier maché was ultimately employed.

Figure 2.13 is the first picture from a series of drawings where this client is asked to choose feeling words—in this case, "jealousy"—and render the emotion using shape, form, and color with water-based markers. The use of water-based markers is purposeful, as this is ultimately used for the strips of paper when composing her papier maché shapes.

Figure 2.13 Jealousy

As discussed in Chapter 1, linking directives, one with another, allows kinesthetic learners to process information thoughtfully. Thus, succeeding directives were designed to offer a variety of balloons, in an assortment of shapes, which both metaphorically and literally provided the necessary support for her papier maché sculpture as well as her fragile sense of self. Figure 2.14 illustrates how the drawing, once combined with the flour and water (to form the paste), allowed the colors to run and bleed, adding a further layer of symbolism, whereby her emotions have now become part of the three-dimensional shape, giving tangible form and function, representing how nothing is separate or isolative.

In all, when working with an individual and exploring moral growth, the use of art therapy can provide a sense of safety and protection for the painful thoughts that impede the human experience. If we return once again to Chapter 1, the *Conflict Collage* with its emphasis on imaginative pursuits provides the client with a forum to express needs, desires, wishes, and conflicts while processing the experience in masked form. In the assessment of maturational development, this directive can prove fruitful as a means of evaluation. If you will recall, the directive is comprised of two animals chosen from a collage box, and the resultant imaginary conversation highlights thoughts, feelings, and actions. The strength of this intervention lies within

Figure 2.14 Papier Maché Sculpture

the ego-distancing technique of collage, which provides a safe refuge for our humiliating experiences and the projected verbal conflict that references and symbolizes our experience.

When augmenting this directive with moral and ethical reasoning, a broad stroke of awareness related to the client can be ascertained. If we return to Figure 1.24, this female struggled with feelings of failure and aggressive responses as her attempts at friendship and affiliation were met with disregard. Even though direct questions related to moral reasoning were not instituted with this client, the inherent themes of her two stories imparted a working metaphor. In each story the third stage of Kohlberg's moral development could be perceived. As such, the animals initially sought approval with a willingness to "obey the rules" of acknowledgment and welcome. However, the interaction quickly turned aggressive as the stereotypical desire to be nice was superseded by stage two egocentric thought.

In all, the post-narrative discussion surrounding the stories of Figure 1.24 allowed this client to expand her understanding of "good" and "bad" while exploring the process not as a participant, but as an observer. Additionally, the incorporation of Cognitive-Behavioral interventions provided a thrust away from egocentricity (the first two stages in Kohlberg's model) toward that of mutuality, understanding, and cooperation as the heart of interpersonal relationships.

The concepts of "right" and "wrong," "good" and "bad," have far-reaching implications especially as identity issues and autonomous pursuits take preference, for it is this maturational path and emergent self-awareness that provide the maturing person with a basis for relationship formation. Whether psychological maturity is defined as psychosocial competence (Erikson), cognitive advances (Piaget), social order and morality (Kohlberg), or psychosexual stages (Freud), each theory relies upon the growing child's sequential advances and his or her ability to adapt to changing circumstances. From egocentricity and single-minded pleasurable interests, to the tolerant consideration of others, this internal process is often arduous and conflictual.

> Contrary to an impression one might gain from Freud's concept of the origins of the "superego," superego directives do not emerge like Pallas Athena, full-grown and fully armed, out of the father's head at the closing of the oedipal period. Ethical development, very much like intellectual growth, depends upon gaining experience and relating to different people in various settings, which gradually diminishes children's egocentricity, and, as Kohlberg has shown, depends very greatly upon cognitive development.
>
> (Lidz, 1976, p. 295)

Equally, Piaget's focus on the development of cognition and conceptual thought revolved around that of logical patterns and interaction. As such, it was the experience of life that propelled learning (Maier, 1978) as the process of imaginative play "becomes more and more adequately adapted to reality" (Piaget, 1977b, p. 517).

Figure 2.15 is an example of Piaget's study on the dialogue of children. In this illustration, two pre-adolescent boys involved in a group sand play therapy session engaged in *progressive collaboration*. Piaget (1973) has defined this stage of conversation as an "association in the sense that everyone listens to and understands the speaker, but there is no collaboration because each child speaks only of himself, of his own action, or of his own thoughts" (p. 73).

The play of these two boys began with the first, and most timid, (whom I will call Larry) asking the second child (whom I will call Jack) a series of questions: "What man should I put in? Are we playing army? Where are the army men at?" His questions soon turned to mumbles and diffidence as Jack worked feverishly to hoard weapons and miniature people. As Larry settled on building an enclosure (left side of Figure 2.15) he eventually chose a woman, much to Jack's chagrin who stated, "Let's leave the women out of this. They want to fight."

Larry, realizing he had not collected any weaponry begins to search, but Jack has already cornered the market and states triumphantly, "I can't leave them (*weapons*) for you to find and want them really bad." Thus, the right side of Figure 2.15 illustrates the final battle and metaphorical destructive longings as Jack sought control over Larry verbally and through the action of play.

Figure 2.15 Progressive Collaboration

As time wore on, Jack continued to engage in group sandtray therapy. These ongoing experiences, with a myriad of partners and peers, produced the learning experience, which would afford Jack an emerging sense of mutuality. In these and subsequent sessions, Jack had decreased his egocentric speech as he adapted to a social environment that required both knowledge and interaction.

Figure 2.16 demonstrates a sandtray that was to be a nodal point in Jack's development. In this tray, the aggressive destruction of soldiers turned to the projected fears of the unknown and unforeseen, as "ghosts" and people are swept away in the aftermath of natural disasters (left side of Figure 2.16). Yet, instead of mere devastation and chaos, Jack and two other peers completed the tray by placing one of the victims in a makeshift operating room (right side of Figure 2.16) as imaginative play and reality intermingled. Piaget refers to this as *socialized speech* where:

> The child really exchanges his thoughts with others, either by telling his hearer something that will interest him and influence his actions, or by an actual interchange of ideas by argument or even by collaboration in pursuit of a common aim.
>
> (Piaget, 1973, p. 33)

Working egocentrically, Jack's sandtrays suggested omnipotent power as his symbols metaphorically represented his overwhelming need for protection and security. However, over time, as experience and action guided Jack's exchanges, his communication became increasingly cooperative and within his figurative play a metaphor of integration was undertaken as he safely practiced that which is fundamental to psychological growth.

As a final example, Figure 2.17 symbolizes an adolescent male's search for meaning in a constrictive world. With a kinesthetic sensory preference his tendency was to traverse emotional relationships through a series

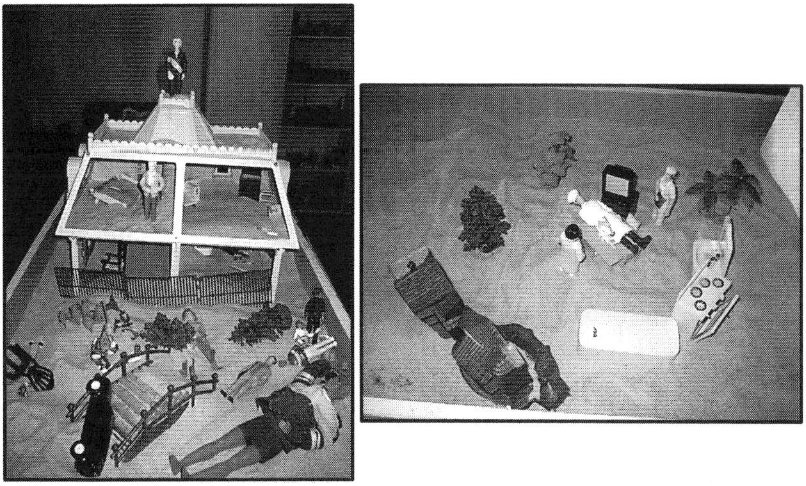

Figure 2.16 The Rescue Attempt

of rebellious and impulsive actions. However, his behaviors do not stand merely as anti-social responses to a tumultuous life but represent his personal metaphor toward mastery.

Figure 2.17 Hip Hop Sad

As such, if we view Figure 2.17 metaphorically, his drawing epitomizes much more than the anxious lines, bold color, and geometric shapes of the formal image. Instead, the picture is replete with figurative meaning as all elements of the task are taken into account: from his manner of drawing (both thoughtful and frenetic) to the disguised "sad" in the title (which only one peer noticed, as the focus was on "Hip Hop") and finally to his intentionally regressive voice as he described the completed drawing.

The extreme emotion contained within Figure 2.17 stands alone as an overpowering symbol, yet it is the constructivist's perspective, which permits all the sense impressions to be incorporated. It is an implied comparison of the projected self's internal struggles. As Mary Watkins (2000) has so aptly stated:

> The art therapist . . . is someone alert not just to the literal image which is drawn, but to images in the patients' gestures, tones of voice, ways of interacting, presenting complaints and history. Through this alertness she helps the patient interact with the image being expressed in order to see more metaphorically his or her daily struggles, fears, and preoccupations. Her questions and suggestions are aimed at extending the presentation of the image as it is, and in helping to establish a way of reflecting on images such that they begin to move the imaginer from the figured page to an awareness of multiple moments when an image is being lived. The art therapist should attend to the structure of an image, so that its myriad details are seen not as random expressions, distortions, or disguises, but as necessary to the precise meaning of the whole image.
>
> (Watkins, 2000, pp. 198–199)

And So to Bed

In summary, maturation, cognition, psychosocial proficiency, and psychological growth transpire due to the cumulative effects of our experiences. Consequently, each theorist has outlined progressive shifts from the self-absorption of our early years to the necessary structures of interaction that require shared exchanges. No matter how these periods of growth are assessed, a metaphor of learning and understanding can be ascertained. From Freud's psychosexual stages to Erikson's psychosocial polarities, the linguistic underpinnings are prominent. When Freud speaks of his psychosexual stages, he is speaking both metaphorically and literally. The orality of the infant whereby the mouth is the focus for pleasure, can be viewed in a concrete sense, but it can also be regarded in the metaphorical sense as the need to take in information ("A thirst for knowledge") or its converse as in "biting sarcasm" (Hall, 1954). These characterological traits, should they persist into adulthood due to early frustration or anxiety, are metaphors for the growing personality and can be said to pave the way for future interactions.

Erikson included polarities to clarify the inner conflicts of the growing individual. In this way, throughout each psychosocial crisis a series of *psychosocial modalities* have to be integrated. And it is these modalities that retain the metaphorical component so important to the growing infant's development. Thus, as the infant meets his or her third year of life (the stage of *initiative vs. guilt*), Erikson (1985) has stated, this "stage adds to the inventory of basic social modalities in both sexes that of 'making' in the sense of 'being on the make.' The word suggests head-on attack, enjoyment of competition, insistence on goal, pleasure of conquest" (p. 90).

Additionally, Erikson attached a series of qualities to each of the stages and called these *basic* virtues. In many ways these correspond to Kohlberg's stages of morality, as pro-social moral reasoning is not an isolated learning experience but one that depends upon social interaction, emotional development, and new patterns of relating.

By the same token, Piaget's theory of cognition relies heavily upon the metaphor of emerging awareness as the child experiments within and explores his or her ever-widening world. For Piaget, experience, which begins as sensory, becomes egocentric only to see the child gain a greater objectivity as symbolic activity is replaced with the universal principles found in Kohlberg's Level III social perspectives. In the end, reason predominates as knowledge, morality, and continued interaction with the environment structure the development of the mind.

Anderson (1995) has stated:

> The stages of life during immaturity represent not only different levels of advancement in how the mind thinks concretely in childhood, abstractly in adolescence, and relativistically in youth—but also the kind of input the mind accesses to create its understanding of the world: five senses or all six senses.
>
> (Anderson, 1995, p. 42)

As such, the mind and all of its complexity must be taken into account as physiological changes, bodily traumata, and genetic predispositions can impact the social and interactional process. The individual who has experienced right hemispheric damage often has extreme difficulty in understanding a metaphorical world. Thus, literal interpretations often take precedence as cognitive impairments affect comprehension (Shields, 2005).

If the mental health professional is to successfully intervene (regardless of theoretical modality) it is imperative that the client's inner strength and resources, which may simply be lying dormant, be encouraged, supported, and processed.

References

Ackerman, B.P. (1982). On comprehending idioms: Do children get the picture? *Journal of Experimental Child Psychology, 33* (3), 439–454.

Anderson, A. (1995). *The stages of life.* New York: The Atlantic Monthly Press.

Arieti, S. (1976). *Creativity: The magic synthesis.* New York: Basic Book, Inc.

Arlow, J.A. (1969). Unconscious fantasy and disturbances of conscious. *The Psychoanalytic Quarterly, 38* (1), 1–27.

Barger, R.N. (2000). *A summary of Lawrence Kohlberg's stages of moral development.* Retrieved May 20, 2004, from www.nd.edu/~rbarger/kohlberg.html.

Bauer, G.P. (1993). *The analysis of the transference in the here and now.* Northvale, New Jersey: Jason Aronson.

Blumer, D., & Benson, D. (1975). Personality changes with frontal and temporal lobe lesions. In D. Benson and D. Blumer (Eds.), *Psychiatric aspects of neurologic disease.* New York: Grune & Stratton.

Brun, B. (1993). Symbols of the soul. In B. Brun, E.W. Pedersen, & M. Runberg (Eds.), *Symbols of the soul: Therapy and guidance through fairy tales* (pp. 5–17). London: Jessica Kingsley.

Buck, J.N. (1973). *The house tree-person technique,* (rev. ed.). Los Angeles: Western Psychological Services.

Caligor, L. (1957). *A new approach to figure drawing.* Springfield, Illinois: Charles C Thomas Publishers.

De la Croix, H. & Tansey, R.G. (1980). *Garder's art through the ages* (7th ed.). New York: Harcourt Brace Jovanovich.

Dies, R.R. (1996). *The unfolding of adolescent groups: A five-phase model of development.* In P. Kymissis & D.A. Halperin (Eds.), *Group therapy with children and adolescents* (pp. 35–53). Washington, DC: American Psychiatric Press.

Duska, R., & Whelan, M. (1975). *Moral development: A guide to Piaget and Kohlberg.* New York: Paulist Press.

Erikson, E.H. (1956). The problem of ego identity. *Journal of the American Psychoanalytic Association, 4* (1), 56–121.

Erikson, E.H. (Ed.). (1963). *Youth: Change and challenge.* New York: Basic Books.

Erikson, E.H. (1985). *Childhood and Society* (35th ed.). New York: W.W. Norton and Company.

Foldi, N.S., Cicone, M., & Gardner, H. (1983). Pragmatic aspects of communication in brain damaged patients. In S.J. Segalowitz, (Ed.), *Language functions and brain organization.* New York: Academic Press.

Freud, S. (1989). Creative writers and day-dreaming. In P. Gay (Ed.), *The Freud reader* (pp. 438–443). New York: W.W. Norton & Company.

Gardner, H. (1982). *Art, mind, and brain: A cognitive approach to creativity.* New York: Basic Books.

Hall, C.S. (1954). *A primer of Freudian psychology.* New York: The World Publishing Company.

Hursh, T. (2005). *Moral reasoning.* Retrieved May 23, 2005, from http://moodle.ed.uiuc.edu/wiked/index.php/Moral_Reasoning

Johnson, J., & Pascual-Leone, J. (1989). Developmental levels of processing in metaphor interpretation. *Journal of Experimental Child Psychology, 48* (1), 1–31.

Karcher, M.J. (2002). The principles and practice of pair counseling: A dyadic developmental play therapy for aggressive, withdrawn, and socially immature youth. *International Journal of Play Therapy, 11* (2), 121–147.

Kolb, B., & Milner, B. (1981). Performance of complex arm and facial movements after focal brain lesions. *Neuropsychologia, 19* (4), 505–514.

Lefrancois, G. (1995). *Theories of human learning* (3rd ed.). Pacific Grove, CA: Brookes/Cole.

Lidz, T. (1976). *The person* (rev. ed.). New York: Basic Books.

Machover, K. (1949). *Personality projection in the drawing of the human figure*. Springfield, IL: C.C. Thomas.
Maier, H.W. (1978). *Three theories of child development* (3rd ed.). New York: Harper & Row.
Myers, P.S., & West, J.F. (1978). The speech pathologist's role with right hemisphere damaged patients. In R.H. Brookshire (Ed.), *Clinical aphasiology: Proceedings of the conference*. Minneapolis: BRK Publishers.
Ornstein, R. (1991). *The evolution of consciousness of Darwin, Freud, and cranial fire: The origins of the way we think*. New York: Prentice Hall Press.
Piaget, J. (1970). *Structuralism*. New York: Basic Books.
Piaget, J. (1973). *The language and thought of the child* (M. Gabain, Trans.). New York: World Publishing.
Piaget, J. (1977a). Psychoanalysis in its relations with child psychology. In H.E. Gruber & J.J. Voneche (Eds.), *The essential Piaget* (pp. 53–59). New York: Basic Books.
Piaget, J. (1977b). Response to Brian Sutton-Smith. In H.E. Gruber & J.J. Voneche (Eds.), *The essential Piaget* (pp. 515–517). New York: Basic Books.
Sarnoff, C.A. (1987). *Psychotherapeutic strategies in the latency years*. Northvale, New Jersey: Jason Aronson Inc.
Selman, R.L., Watts, C.L., & Schultz, L.H. (Eds.) (1997). *Fostering friendship: Pair therapy for treatment and prevention*. Hawthorn, NY: Aldine deGruyter.
Shields, J. (2005). Semantic-pragmatic disorder: A right hemisphere syndrome? [Electronic version]. *British Journal of Disorders of Communication*, 26, 383–392 (1991).
Shermer, M. (2004). *The science of good and evil: Why people cheat, gossip, care, share, and follow the golden rule*. New York: Henry Holt and Company.
Stowe, L.A., Zempleni, Z., & Hoeks, J. (2003, August). *Processing idioms in the left and right hemispheres*. Retrieved June 16, 2005, from www.amlap.psy.gla.ac.uk/programme/node3.html
Watkins, M. (2000). Six approaches to the image in art therapy. In B. Sells (Ed.), *Working with images: The theoretical base of archetypal psychology* (pp. 186–207). Connecticut: Spring Publications.
Weylman, S.T., Brownell, H.H., Roman, M., & Gardner, H. (1989). Appreciation of indirect requests by left- and right-brain-damaged patients: The effects of verbal context and conventionality of wording. *Brain and Language*, *36* (1), 580–591.
Yeates, K.O., Schultz, L.H., & Selman, R.L. (1991). The development of interpersonal negotiation strategies in thought and action: A social-cognitive link to behavioral adjustment and social status. *Merrill-Palmer Quarterly*, *37* (3), 369–405.

II
The Eternal Verities

3
Clinical Applications

> Once upon a time, a long time ago, there were two people, an old lady and an old man. They used to live together, they used to have fun, they used to have good times together. One day she decided to take an airplane and go see her grandkids. Her grandkids were jumping up and down they were so excited. But something happened and the grandmother died. The kids were sad and lonely and their mom said it was okay. It would be okay. They went to the funeral and they had ice cream and stuff. Their grandfather came and lived with them. They were feeling bad about themselves and lonely. Whenever they felt lonely they went to their grandpa and asked him to tell them a story about grandma. And he told good stories that made them laugh, giggle, and have fun. At bedtime they prayed every night for their grandma.

When exploring treatment and treatment approaches, the mental health professional should not be blinded by the strength of the image alone, nor should the behavioral and verbal interactions stand as an indicator of deficits, developmental delays, and intrapsychic conflicts. Instead, the two should be viewed as harmonious; a unity of verbal, historical, and non-verbal cues by which the clinician may integrate a sense of meaning beyond the overt communication.

In this vein, it is both the dynamic encounter and the overall context that should drive the theoretical assumptions. The story outlined above, at first glance, appears to highlight the emotional conflict surrounding loss issues. Yet, if one were to understand the context that precipitated this tale of grief, a different picture would emerge. During a group therapy session, a member (whom I will call Paul) was struggling with the recent loss of his grandmother. His anxiety was palatable and though peers were attentive and offered words of advice and guidance, his emotional turmoil was evident through a combination of disorganized, abusive, and resistant behaviors. As days passed, Paul's anxiety did not abate. Eventually, one by one, members of the group ceased offering condolences as their apprehension increased in direct proportion to Paul's. In the end, this metaphorical story as given by another peer, offered hope and encouragement that remembrance and memories which endure can serve as reminders of love lost.

Ultimately, in this group context, the treatment was not solely focused on the individual who had suffered the loss but upon all within the group as their struggles with empathy and problem-solving required exploration. And found within this young man's basic story was the distancing of displacement coupled with the natural resources of the environment toward the binding of anxiety.

In the end, regardless of therapeutic orientation, it is the emotional experience that most influences the therapeutic outcome. In the scenario outlined above, the profound loss that Paul suffered was not assuaged through the promotion of empathy, active listening, understanding, and acceptance. His estrangement arose from feelings of uncertainty and meaninglessness in a world where individual control is imaginary at best. Accordingly, advice, sympathy, and support did not address the myriad of social, emotional, and behavioral difficulties that had inundated this adolescent to the very core of his identity. Yet, the story metaphor, with its emphasis on experience over cognition provided not only a displacement for the painful feelings but highlighted the natural resources of both the client and the environment.

As Howard Gardner (1982) has stated:

> It proves impossible to think of symbolizing activity apart from human imagination and creativity: man lives in a symbolic universe. And in the process of symbolic activity, human beings inevitably engage in meaning-making, in imaginative problem-solving, and in equally creative problem production.
> (Gardner 1982, p. 44)

Consequently, the symbolizing of our feelings, thoughts, and actions form a common element in our interactive processes. For the progression from concrete to abstract thought can determine how an individual will counter all of life's experiences.

Often cognitive-communication problems interfere with the basic need to belong. In the case of loss and grief issues the emotional vulnerability can cause a retreat into the self, an anxious isolation that can separate feelings and thoughts. In the presence of developmental delays it is the individual's self-concept that is challenged as experience frequently opposes perceptions.

By way of example, an adolescent girl (Figure 3.1) presented with impulsive interactions consisting of aggressive verbal outbursts, difficulty concentrating on tasks, and poor memory. In all, her communication problems together with her significant cognitive delays impacted her peer relationships as her lability of mood had peers either distancing themselves or catering to her needs in the hopes that she would not lash out upon them. This client's presenting problems though numerous were not uncommon. As such, a myriad of treatment approaches could be incorporated with great success: Behavioral therapy with its focus on symptom removal, Humanistic therapy and the facilitation of self-awareness and trust, Analytic therapy highlighting the role of the ego and intrapsychic conflict, and/or Cognitive-Behavioral therapy whereby irrational thoughts and behaviors are replaced with balanced, life-affirming values and beliefs.

Yet in deciding upon a specific perspective, it is important to note that within any treatment approach, it is the similarities of the goals that are striking. The attention placed upon the development of insight and understanding in Analytical therapy parallels the self-exploration of blocks to growth (Humanistic therapy), the study of current behavioral choices which has led to maladaptive behavior (Behavioral therapy), and the examination of thoughts and exaggerated fears (Cognitive-Behavioral therapy) as all strive to capture an action-oriented methodology to the role of cognition, feelings, and behaviors. In each therapeutic modality, the techniques utilized embody an active contribution from both client and therapist. From the philosophy of learning to clarification, interpretation, and confrontation it is the emotional experience that shapes the success of any intervention or treatment approach.

To return to the example, Figure 3.1 illustrates a group art therapy directive where each individual begins a drawing and at pre-determined times the image is passed around the group so that each member has an opportunity to add to another member's drawing. This group pass-around technique provides both the group leader and group members with metaphorical information related to interpersonal difficulties, conflicts in the environment, and the natural resources utilized when faced with anxiety-producing situations.

The left side of Figure 3.1 represents this client's first attempt at the directive. Her contribution can be found in the anxious scribbling and haphazard coloring on the door. As her concentrated attempts at drawing stars turned into unconstrained scrawling marks, her kinesthetic sensory preference resulted in giggles and snickers, which were not diminished by the protestations of her peers. In the post-drawing discussion, group members focused on her callous disregard of the group effort (behaviors). As the process illumination continued, the group

Figure 3.1 If at First You Don't Succeed

moved from mere complaints to an exploration of feelings with an emphasis on problem-solving. The client, at first defending her position, was finally able to accept the confrontations and spoke of her frustration as her attempts to create a "nice drawing like the other girls" was thwarted by her lack of drawing ability. At this juncture, rather than proceed with discussion, I instituted a second drawing experience (right side of Figure 3.1) with emphasis placed on what the client had heard in the feedback (auditory sensory preference) over her preferred model of interaction (kinesthetic).

The right side of Figure 3.1 illustrates the applied techniques of what the client heard ("That's what you do to us. You take over."), what she had stated (inferiority produces anxiety), and a final kinetic experience of controlled interactions with the second intervention encouraging improved boundaries (her additions are found, *contained*, within the coloring of the windows only).

Taken as a whole, the incorporation of metaphorical interventions and analysis becomes useful in the therapeutic hour as a way to connect the major treatment approaches in a dynamic manner, explore patterns of relating, modify sensory preferences, and improve negotiation, problem-solving, and conflict resolution skills. In this manner, the projections of the client are found within the drawing task (rather than being externalized), hence the therapist-client relationship can proceed without hindrance as empathic communication encourages the processing of reality-based resolutions, past traumata, and the generalization of therapeutic interventions into the larger community.

More Here Than Meets the Eye

Shirley Riley (2004) has stated:

> Making an art form involves movement, tactility, vision, memory, and imagery; therefore, all of the brain functions . . . are brought into play. Emotional intelligence is stimulated as the image retrieves memories and associations and engages the cognitive capacities and self-regulators. A drama is played out with all the senses adding texture to the dialogue. The therapeutic conversation can be wordless, or it can be through verbal metaphors that later become concrete expressions.
>
> (Riley, 2004, pp. 189–190)

In the therapeutic hour the effectiveness of experience over logical understanding cannot be overstated. The act of creation, far from being simplistic in nature, has the power to structure reality, alter emotions, and reconcile internal and external conflicts.

Concurrently, the integration of theory and treatment planning provides the mental health professional with guiding principles and strategies to incorporate into the therapeutic hour. Within these procedures are the techniques, which guide the course of treatment as individualized interventions process thoughts, feelings, and behavior. From Psychodynamic theory with its expression of intrapsychic concerns to a Cognitive-Behavioral model whereby helping the client understand and change irrational thoughts in order to replace maladaptive behaviors with adaptive ones, or the incorporation of Gestalt principles of self-regulation, sensory, and emotional awareness, each theoretical model stresses the importance of a supportive relationship whereby therapeutic rapport is paramount.

Table 3.1 outlines some of the major individual theoretical modalities and juxtaposes the role of the therapist with the role of the non-verbal directive.

In each of the preceding models outlined in Table 3.1, relational qualities are stressed, whether this is between therapist and client or client and peer grouping, while the goals of separation-individuation predominate. Hence, the natural resources of the client must be taken into account as the client's desire for change, concomitant with past and current successes, becomes the focal point.

As such, when incorporating the expressive arts into any therapeutic modality, the therapist is charged with "listening" to both the covert and overt communication of the client, recognizing the messages and themes inherent in the communication, and finally selecting the appropriate time to interpret and process the repetitious patterns of behavior. Generally, the process of interpretation relies heavily upon the theoretical modality of the mental health professional; however, the timing of an interpretation flows from the session and cannot be measured in a formulaic manner. Instead, the therapist must rely upon his or her knowledge, as related to the ego strength and readiness of the client, to accept and internalize any such analysis. In instances where an interpretation is presented prematurely, the client's natural tendency will be to dismiss its importance. "A general principle of interpretation is that it should always start from the surface and go only as deep as the patient is able to go while experiencing the situation emotionally" (Patterson, 1980, p. 323).

Figure 3.2 represents the drawing of an adolescent male as he reconciled the contradictory feelings of acceptance and rejection. On the day of this session, he had recently moved into a new dorm consisting of 12 high functioning male peers. Though excited, the reality of the move had left him feeling sullen, confused, and anxious. Noticing his withdrawal, I requested that he draw *"an interest that brings pleasure."*

As quickly as the directive was given, this young man created Figure 3.2 and spoke of how hummingbirds, "work together, look out for one another, and are playful." At this juncture I could have interpreted "a free hummingbird" on a surface level by relating this to a wish for him and his new dorm mates, on a deeper level by linking this with the transference wish for his family, or remain in metaphor and enhance the feeling experience. In this case, I sensed that a shift from a figurative discussion into either the here-and-now or

Table 3.1 Theories Compared

Psychoanalytic	
Role of Therapist	Join, observe, reflect, interpret the meaning of present behavior as it correlates to past experiences, act as benign superego
Role of Art	Bring repressed material to consciousness, supply unconscious information for interpretation, a vehicle of transference
Client-centered	
Role of Therapist	Caring, non-judgmental, believe in capacity for growth and self-direction, observe and listen reflectively
Role of Art	Means to reflect and clarify feelings, facilitate self-knowledge and broaden expression
Cognitive-behavioral	
Role of Therapist	Praise success, build collaborative and trusting relationship, stress client ability to control own fate
Role of Art	Means for modeling/teaching skills, identify and change behaviors in an indirect manner, practice adaptive thoughts and behaviors, development of control, structured and goal-directed activities
Gestalt	
Role of Therapist	Active, assist client to experience feelings, thoughts, sensations, assist in sharing his/her wisdom, pay attention to non-verbal body messages/cues
Role of Art	Means to integrate conflictual feelings, establish/restore sensory and motor functions, develop self-support, awaken awareness and expression of emotions, acceptance of self
Transactional Analysis	
Role of Therapist	Re-parent, collaborative, interactive
Role of Art	Means to increase awareness and intimacy, allow for new decisions to be practiced, emphasize choice
Existential	
Role of Therapist	Authenticity, therapist becomes a microcosm of other healthy relationships
Role of Art	Means for shaping direction, growth, and awareness, exploration of feelings, helps client create their own meaning in life

Figure 3.2 A Free Hummingbird

the then-and-there would have engendered a retreat into the self or increased defensiveness. Consequently, I consciously made an effort to incorporate all the sensory preferences and replied, "I wonder if you felt the same way I did when I heard you say that? It made me feel a longing to be that safe and secure." After much thought he answered, "I love hummingbirds because they are nice to us; I care about them."

In this scenario it was not important that I understand which relationship association this young man was revealing. What was significant was the metaphorical wish for closeness and protection. Thus, I viewed Figure 3.2 as the culmination of his conflicted childhood needs and the ongoing desire for a family (or family-like connection), which is met with the fear that others will reject his advances, while the self (longing for intimacy and security) responds with passive adoration as he fantasizes the ideal. This experience, played out by the client in multiple settings, lent itself to my choice of intervention.

As such, this feeling-oriented interpretation was significantly less threatening to the client's already fragile sense of self. In this situation the client made the connection and we proceeded to discuss the here and now issues that overwhelmed him. However, the benefit of remaining in metaphor is that conflict-laden material can be processed both literally and symbolically, which allows the client to ascribe his/her own tacit meaning, in his/her own time, employing his/her natural resources to the understanding and insight.

Any Port in a Storm

Case Illustration 1

This case, though not considered a treatment success, embodies the power and experience of the projective metaphor as applied to the family constellation and the therapeutic relationship. It involves the client introduced at the beginning of this chapter whom I named Paul. Paul was a 13-year-old, loquacious male who presented as affable and confident; however, these traits belied his deep-seated insecurities and anxieties. Conceptualizing this case from a Bowenian perspective, the family constellation was characterized by marital discord, conflictual emotional fusion between mother and son, and subsequent emotional cut-off. Paul's one connection in life was his grandmother who during the course of treatment passed away. This singular relationship provided Paul with compassionate patience, which was counter to the disquiet that permeated his immediate family. Unfortunately, Paul's identity was intertwined with the family's view that he was "a failure," as this unstable system sought relief by projecting their negative energy on Paul.

In the early stages of therapy, I explored Paul's level of identity formation through a metaphorical exploration of the self. Figure 3.3 represents the directive, *"on one side draw how others see you and on the other side draw how you understand yourself."*

These two renderings, completed on the outside of white lunch bags, initially appear innocuous. However, upon closer inspection they can be said to incorporate metaphorical elements related to the dysfunctional roles Paul has adopted. On the left, his "goofy and silly" persona conveys both the impertinence and fragility of one who is not taken seriously. While his self-reflection (right side of Figure 3.3) exposes the defiance and consequent feelings of rejection that only a "mischievous" identity could produce. As the process was discussed, Paul was typically verbose, yet his statements continued to yield little information, as they were inclined to be superfluous. However, he did make one comment repetitiously, "trust deceives;" unfortunately, he refused to elaborate.

For the next month, Paul's work in some way incorporated his new credo, from images that exclaimed, "Trust could be deceived," and, "Those who believe are deceived," to a new-found fascination centering on Egyptian mythology with emphasis on the Gods' penchant for betrayal and ambiguity. As each day passed, Paul continued to erect walls of defenses and consequently his symbolism became increasingly pronounced. Before long, his drawings took on the appearance of pictograms (Figure 3.4), a personal expression that would not be shared with others. Paul's two comments about Figure 3.4 were, "It's a fairy tale, but I'm not telling which one," and the title, "Don't get conned into what other people say."

I viewed this secret language as Paul's search for the self, to have power over another as only he possesses the answer, to understand the world with certainty rather than be puzzled by its vicissitudes. Sarnoff (1987) states, "The child who cannot articulate his demands in words and so change the external

Figure 3.3 And Don't Forget It!!!

world, develops symbols and fantasies to create a comforting inner world" (p. 43). Additionally, if we return to my interpretation of Figure 3.4, the creation of his own cryptic language provided him with information that no-one else possessed. How could someone with such ability not be taken seriously? How could someone with such knowledge not be accepted?

It was in this way that I began to explore with Paul the importance of chronicling his beliefs, opinions, and values. Using narrative, I hoped Paul could safely communicate the divergent thoughts, feelings, and behaviors in his life rather than employ secrets or emotional distance for self-preservation. Moreover, stories reflect our personal identity, and narrative is a tool, which enhances understanding. From the roles we adopt in select stages of life to the private experiences that shape our interactions, storytelling can address conflict-laden issues with an eye toward mastery.

In Paul's first narrative, a riddle of deceit and duplicity emerges, as trust is forsaken.

> The black-hearted people are as dangerous as a bear, but not as sly as a fox for they are very cunning but easily deceived. So don't believe in what you see or hear for it may be a lie rather than the truth.

Figure 3.4 Don't Get Conned into What Other People Say

As with most stories, imaginary encounters can isomorphically be related to both problem and solution. In this case, as Paul grapples with the challenges of basic developmental growth, the path to an autonomous identity will require the power of a bear and the cunning of the fox. Yet, internally Paul has adopted a personal credo of guarded mistrust. Does he have the ingenuity to surmount the challenges?

Toward this end, subsequent stories as told by Paul reflected on the theme of the hero's journey. The basic metaphor found within this themed story is the rite of passage with all its attendant danger, triumphs, subjugation, and personal hazards (Battino, 2002). This quest for meaning often occurs in stages and is centered on the initial departure, a struggle, a chance meeting with one who is wiser, transformation, and a return often in the form of a triumphant homecoming. The verse narrative *Gilgamesh* (Mason, 1970) is an excellent example of the transformation from egocentric tyrant to self-discovery and integration so fundamental in the hero's journey.

The following excerpt is from Paul's second story, which he chose to end abruptly. This entire narrative took roughly four weeks to conclude:

> Once upon a time in the land of Kalidor, lived a king and a queen who ruled the lands with all their might to keep it running steadily. There was a knight named Josh who always got the short end of the stick at jobs.

> Finally, he got a knight's job after his best friend had died in battle . . . . One day a fairy named Sarah passed by. This fairy was told to help people whoever she passed by. She noticed Josh who was having a lot of trouble trying to get the long end of the stick of his job, but the king would never let him do anything else but guard the perimeter of the castle. The fairy had passed by and had noticed Josh getting very angry and starting to fake sword fight with the shadows on the walls . . . . Josh had come back with no money whatsoever while everybody else had got five pieces of gold from the king . . . . This was the fairy's chance to try to find a way to talk to Josh. For about a half an hour she had pondered a way of figuring out how to talk to the knight without startling him, since that was her job. She said she will not hurt him and told him her name, "I'm Sarah the fairy and I'm here to help you with your problems." "I'm Josh. The knight of Kalidor. But my only job is to guard the castle perimeter. I really want to go out and battle and fight for what my friend tried to fight for. But the king will never let me." She and Josh tried to figure out a way to get the king to let him join battle . . . . The king, after being asked plenty of times, decided to finally agree. "Yes, but it is a dangerous battle that we are fighting and I do not want to see you die." Now the knight found out that he was not trying to be mean to him but was only trying to help him not risk his life . . . . That morning he and Sarah the fairy quickly saddled up the horse and rode all the way to camp. It took a few hours to get to camp because it was a long road. He thought he had gotten lost but no, Sarah the fairy knew the way . . . . That morning he'd woken up and everybody was already out there. He noticed that he had accidentally slept in past time and quickly ate breakfast, of course in a sloppy manner as he always did, and quickly ran out to get ready for training. The knights were taunting him about the way he was eating and the way he was dressed. He forgot to grab his sword, so everybody else was prepared for training and he wasn't. He ran to his tent and grabbed his sword and his armor. Training had almost started; he was lucky to make it on time.

The telling of this story betrays in projective metaphor the worries, hopes, desires, and problems that haunt Paul both symbolically and literally. Unable to assume the level of respect and control he craved, Paul ultimately becomes a victim of circumstances, relying on courage but exhibiting no confidence. In reviewing the story opening Paul expresses the frustration of partiality which is reminiscent of emotional reactivity ("There was a knight named Josh who always got the short end of the stick at jobs . . . the king would never let him do anything else but guard the perimeter of the castle"). As we reach the middle of the story his relationship with the fairy parallels that of the care-giving therapeutic connection ("I'm Sarah the fairy and I'm here to help you with your problems") yet the knight remains dependent and incompetent. It is here that Paul is unable to provide a closing, figuratively implying that a successful transformation is beyond the "failure's" reach, as feelings have overwhelmed thinking and reason.

It is important to remember that we live the stories we tell; though they are modified by our experiences:

> The individual sees all his problems from a perspective which is his own creation. Thus, he also sees the environment which trains him with his own self-created perspective and accordingly changes its effect upon him for better or worse.
>
> (Adler, 1956, p. 212).

As such, the Bowenian case conceptualization, which I provided earlier, is merely one that could adequately describe Paul's experiences and symptomology. I could just as easily illustrate Paul's family from a Structural viewpoint by focusing on the parents' difficulty in coping with Paul's changing developmental needs as they instead adapted through a series of unhealthy alliances and detouring coalitions. Equally, an experiential perspective could be employed whereby this family's roles and rules were guided by dysfunctional communication styles each designed to diminish the importance of true feelings and maintain balance.

It is my belief that regardless of how a case is conceptualized, the interventions need to be tailored to the client's individual strengths, abilities, interests, and sensory preferences. Thus, the techniques for insight and growth should be based on the personality and developmental needs of the client irrespective of age. As such, my focus for Paul was on his struggle for an individual identity separate from the family's myths and controlling dominance. Working on an individual basis, it was my belief that an existential therapeutic approach would provide Paul greater self-awareness, personal responsibility, and increased choices as our relationship could form a basis for other healthy interactions. Additionally, his feelings of helplessness coupled with the engrained fixation on his incompetency, required more than a non-judgmental approach or the monitoring of cognitions. Paul would require a methodology steeped in visceral understandings and an interactive journey much like that which Sarah afforded Josh.

Paul's next story voluntarily retained the main characters of Josh and Sarah in both name and temperament. The condensed story opens in this way:

> This is a town unlike any other. It is surrounded by a forest. There is a mystery to this town known as Hangan's Hollow. It has no electricity so people have to rely on fire for warmth and light. It has a shortage of food so they rely on the forest for food. Though many are afraid of the forest. You may be wondering why live in a place like this?
>
> Our story begins with a family that was tired of the city life and decided to live in the wonderful valley . . . . Their Mom being a very busy person

> always tried to get into the action but their Dad was always a little short on cash for he always had less than a decent paying job . . . . Their family was always so busy that Josh was left alone to do as freely as he wanted . . . .
>
> The next day Josh's mom showed him the schoolhouse. Josh never liked anything that happened in school because he thought that it was cutting into his time to hang in the forest. When school ended he hadn't made a lot of friends except for one, a girl named Sarah. She was from the city but had been there a couple of years with her family.

Again, Paul unconsciously relates a hero's journey with a separation from the familiar into the "mysterious" unknown. Yet, in this narrative, Paul includes observations of the familial dysfunction associated with emotional cut-off ("Josh was left alone to do as freely as he wanted") while the father adopts the tragic role of one who disappoints. This story opening, as with most rites of passage, parallels the search for personal meaning and life goals beyond the here and now.

Paul's quest continues to unfold as Josh and Sarah find a common desire to explore the darkened forest.

> Sarah said she hardly ever wandered through the woods for everybody was scared. As they were talking, they decided to talk more about the forest. As Josh and Sarah were wandering closer toward the forest some town's folk were following them wondering why they wanted to go to the forest. As they saw this, one of the villager's spoke up, "Why go to the forest? People say these parts are haunted. But many do not exactly know why. I suggest never going into the forest. That's why all of us are scared; we believe there is a curse upon it. Please, leave, never go to the forest." But Josh and Sarah disobeyed and quickly ran into the forest. As they were going they noticed the further they went in the thicker the woods got. For the woods were darker and a lot more scarier for Josh because he did not remember to bring his flashlight.

The villager's attempts to warn Josh and Sarah are met with indifference as Paul's characters brave their fears and impulsively embark, unprepared for the challenges that lay ahead. Here again, Paul's penchant for mischievous behavior is transferred onto the main character of Josh, and it is this impish decision that thrusts him into the darkened forest and the ensuing existential anxiety (for things which are beyond individual control). Tresidder (2000) states, "being lost in the forest, or finding one's way through, is a powerful metaphor for the terrors of inexperience and the achievement of knowledge – of the adult world or of the self" (p. 74).

As Paul's story continues, Sarah and Josh stumble upon an "Indian Wiseman" living alone in the woods. He tells a tale of separation from his family, "When I had to move out from my people things didn't seem as they used to . . . everything has been false. Nothing has seemed to go right." This simple comment, remarkably similar to Paul's familial circumstances and repetitious comments of "trust deceives," speaks to the core vulnerabilities of disconnection and abandonment.

At this stage of the hero's journey, a decision is usually made to either confront the fears that threaten to overwhelm or in the case of Paul's prior story, forsake the journey.

> That night Josh went to bed and pondered what the Indian Wiseman had told him. And wondered what could be haunting him. He knew that he would never be allowed in the forest, but knew that he must go back knowing that his journey starts in the forest. Knowing that no matter what had happened back then he must still go in there and help the Wiseman get back to his people and know that they are safe and the villagers would figure out that it was just a figment of their imagination. But for all that he needed to go back into the forest. He planned out that he would have to get supplies in his backpack especially his flashlight and go back to the Indian Wiseman's hut. All this he pondered in his mind wondering how he was going to do it and when.

It is at this point that Paul begins to actually formulate a plan, rather than respond impulsively. His new-found resolve, however, is short lived. In the next session, Paul relates:

> When Josh got back from school, he decided to quickly grab his backpack and start off but he noticed that his mom was standing in the doorway. She knew that he wanted to go back in the woods and said that he must stay in the house and not even leave the house for any reason; not even to see his friend Sarah. This made him feel angry . . . . The next morning the stuff in his backpack was taken out and was not in his room. When he went downstairs, his mom asked him why he had that stuff in his backpack. He knew he had been caught officially. There was no way of getting his stuff back besides his mom was holding his set of keys.

The dependent regression witnessed in this paragraph corresponds perfectly with Paul's struggle for individuality, choice, and freedom. With each step, Paul's mother would thwart his independence through a series of well-timed consequences and interventions, all designed to restrict autonomous choices. It is interesting to note that once Paul's character Josh takes measures to "plan" for his quest, his family who was always "so busy that Josh was left alone to do as freely as he wanted," impedes his search for personal meaning.

Luckily, Sarah, Josh's benign superego, "handed Josh the set of keys that his mom was holding earlier . . . . I waited until your mom had left the room and I found the box and brought it back here. I noticed that there would not be a box there when your mom returned so I put an old one like it, but more beautiful in its place with a lock." Josh, in his turn, "was thankful for what Sarah had done and gave her a hug."

The exchange of a regular box for one that was more beautiful metaphorically embodies the harmonious beauty of transformation. A power that Sarah intuitively recognizes and Josh can barely imagine. As Paul moves his story from conflict to climax, Josh's character begins to personify courage, competence, and self-determination.

> Josh had quickly figured out that the boat was tied not just to their rope but someone else had tied it to a tree. Josh quickly grabbed his pocketknife and cut it. He got into the boat and rode it toward Sarah . . . . "
>
> "Why can't we go back now?" Sarah said.
>
> Josh said, "No Sarah, we must stay. We must try to talk to these people and see what is going on."
>
> "Why do we have to do this?"
>
> "I don't know but we have to do it," Josh said.

Needless to say, I felt that a breakthrough had occurred with the shift from Josh's lack of self-reliance and action to one of confidence and inner strength. As the story continues, Sarah and Josh witness a stranger being tied to a pole while they watch; they too become captives.

> "Who are you? Why have you come?
>
> "We are just peaceful people from the next village over. We were just going to—searching around the woods." Josh was getting scared not knowing what the man may do, his voice deep and dark sounding.
>
> The man added that he was to be executed the next day. Josh didn't want anyone to die or to see death happen. "I've got a pocketknife in my back pocket. Maybe we could cut ourselves loose and leave."
>
> "There are guards out in front little boy."
>
> "I can cut a hole out of the material and we can go out the back way."
>
> The man started to get interested in the way Josh thought. "You think like a wise man. I bet you are going to be a great man when you get older."

When exploring the narrative for metaphor, it is important to notice the repeating patterns, because what *is* important *will* repeat. In Paul's first story a riddle of deceit emerged. In his second story, the metaphor focused on incompetence. In this story, the theme of capture and escape evolves as Josh leaves his old life, breaks his mother's firm grasp through the help of Sarah, and eventually through action and forethought, cuts the ties that bind through the shrewd use of his pocketknife. In this way, Paul faces his fears and worries, comforts those around him through his prudence and intellect, and moves closer to solving the "riddle" of his own life.

Unfortunately, this would be the last story that Paul would relate. In the next session faced with a story that personified Josh as the hero rather than a failure he sat passively and then spontaneously exclaimed, "I can't finish this story! I'm not a writer. I can never be a writer." The anxiety that plagued Josh had derailed the actualization process.

No amount of empathy or discussion moved Paul from his failure stance, so engrained was the myth and experience of failure that a biased understanding had become an objective truth. He adamantly refused to return to the story narrative. It was at this juncture that after a brief illness Paul's grandmother had passed away which increased his distance and rejection of anything that brought him praise and accomplishment. Metaphorically speaking, Paul began to "abandon" interests and accomplishments just as he had been "abandoned" by the death of his grandmother. He replaced his past interests with a religious fanaticism in an effort to solve the riddles of death and loss. Regrettably, this focus on investigative pursuits removed him from the experience, ensconced him once again in the role of victim, and allowed him to avoid social and emotional contact. Paul had regressed into a state of existential anxiety.

From each of his story narratives, I ascertained that prior to Paul having Josh plan for his journey, the main sensory mode was auditory. Here his plot focused on what he had heard about the forest or what he was instructed to do. However, by the end of the story Paul's sensory predilection shifted from that of auditory to kinesthetic/tactile. In this vein, the action and experience came to life as Josh began to touch, feel, and surmount obstacles. In an effort to promote continued kinesthetic "successes-oriented" preferences, and aid Paul's identification of feelings, I instituted a body/mind outline.

This directive begins by measuring a sheet of butcher paper to reach the full length of the client. After taping the butcher paper to a wall, I have the client lean against the paper in any way he or she chooses, as I trace his/her body outline. For some clients the tracing of their outline can feel exceedingly intrusive. In these instances, I supply the client with one of the two pre-drawn outlines (see Figures 3.5 and 3.6).

In Paul's case, I traced his outline, Figure 3.7, and then had him choose a series of three feeling words. He decided upon angry, sadness, and jealousy.

During the session, Paul was instructed to "draw each of your chosen words on the tracing in the spot where you feel it the most." His first feeling word was angry. As he drew the blackened heart with an arrow through it, he spoke of feeling "vicious" and lashing out at others. He then added the tears and the single-lined mouth to denote sadness. Before exploring this emotion he quickly drew jealousy just above the eyes and spontaneously related how when he feels jealous of others, he "teases" and "hurts their feelings." Once more, Paul's reflections point toward auditory preferences with an externalized feeling expression. In this way, Paul protected himself by erecting external defenses that denied him genuine acceptance and understanding.

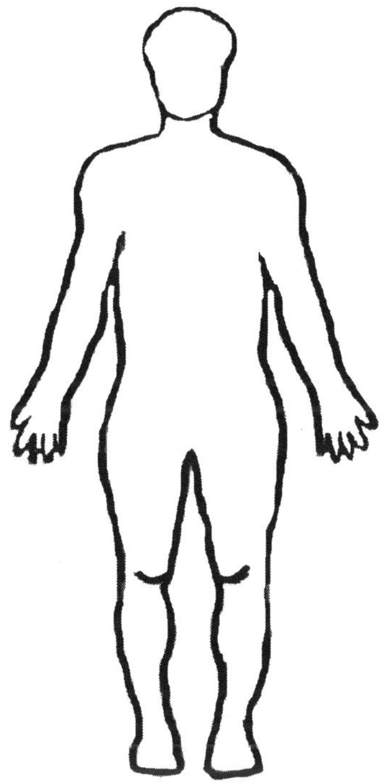

Figure 3.5 Body Outline – Adult

Figure 3.6 Body Outline – Child

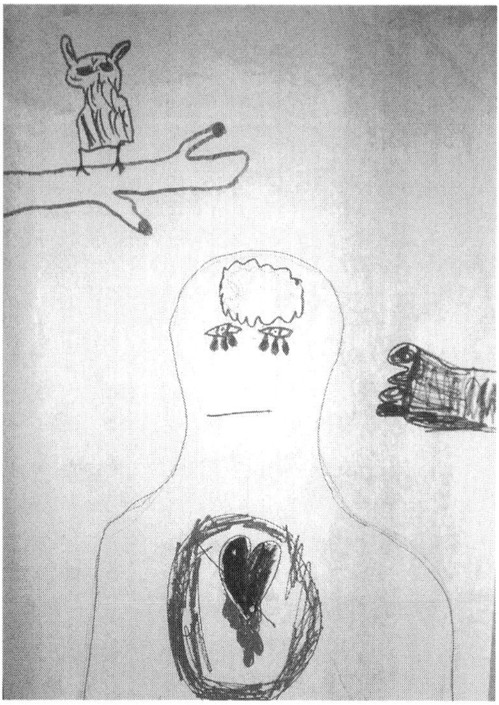

Figure 3.7 Body/Mind Tracing

Knowing Paul's penchant for mystery, I then directed him to "draw a secret feeling and add it to the body tracing where you feel it the most." He thoughtfully added the owl and tree branch found in the upper left of Figure 3.7. After I attempted to guess, unsuccessfully, at what the emotion could be Paul related that his secret feeling was "frightened." He explained how the owl symbolized his "fear of the dark." The owl, often identified with night and death (Cirlot, 1983) as well as experience and wisdom (Biedermann, 1994), is an apt representation for the fears, anxieties, and concerns that tied Paul to his family or origin and intruded upon his search for personal meaning.

Up to this point I had not commented upon or confronted the repeating patterns found in Paul's art and stories, and as we approached the upcoming sessions I decided it was important to challenge his experience through a personal search for meaning. As such, I expanded upon the body/mind tracing by requesting that Paul, "Draw your experience of lonesomeness on the outline." If you refer to Figure 3.7, you will notice a heavily shaded circle around the heart and a darkened hand extending toward the figure on the right side of the drawing. These illustrations resulted in conversations related to Paul's relationship with the death of his grandmother (the darkened hand reaching toward the figure of Paul), his feelings of isolation (the circle of hurt around his heart), and reassurances which normalized his feelings.

From Paul's narrative themes of estrangement with resulting tragedy, to his highly symbolic illustrations, Paul's manner of interacting in the world was one of a mere spectator awaiting his truth. In successive sessions, I related to Paul how his statements and beliefs affected me with an emphasis on his distancing pursuits that both protected his fragile sense of self but also kept him tethered to feelings of loneliness. In one of our final meetings, I requested he draw, "*what's in your mind?*"

While exploring the tangled lines of Figure 3.8, Paul's finger lightly traced the sections as his jumbled thoughts recalled issues related to control, courage, friends turning against you, and a smattering of stars, which stood for goodness. The drawing reminded me of a maniacal labyrinth. As such, I asked, "Is there a way out?" As I waited for Paul to answer, silence filled the room. I slowly slid a pack of colored pencils and paper toward Paul. Eventually he stated an emphatic, "yes." Figure 3.9 represents his freedom.

In Figure 3.9, Paul began the process of defining himself without the interference of his family's expectations. He spoke of escaping into a tranquil world where "people see exactly what is there. They don't force us to believe." The "stars of goodness" lay on solid ground rather than buried within the

Figure 3.8 What's in Your Mind?

Figure 3.9 Life, Life, and Life Again

vast expanse. Over many sessions, I centered the post-drawing discussion on the metaphor of a sailing ship where the rigid rules of reality were replaced by the guiding principles of transition. Paul's voyage, much like his hero's journey, required navigation through the treacherous obstacles, which alight the path and hopefully bring forth a call to action rather than indecision. Additionally, the ocean, both responsive and antagonistic, offered a working metaphor that paralleled his family relationships. These opposing forces, founded on Paul's experiences, had shaped a personal identity of inadequacy and overriding malaise.

As therapy continued, it became apparent that the transitional scene of Figure 3.9 was not something that Paul could reach out and touch; a personal identity where choices beget responsibility and challenges exist both externally and internally was a future construct beyond his imagining; a metaphor that existed temporarily in the therapeutic hour. As Adler (1956) outlined, "The greater the feeling of inferiority that has been experienced, the more powerful is the urge to conquest and the more violent the emotional agitation" (p. 116). In this manner, regrettably, Paul's behavior escalated to such a degree that he was removed from treatment.

A Whole New Ball of Wax

Case Illustration 2

This case involves a now early adult whom I will call Harris. Harris' childhood was marked with chaos, fear, and feelings of abandonment, consequently by the time he was an adolescent he found solace in substance use (methamphetamine and cannabis) which would eventually result in a psychotic break consisting of visual and auditory hallucinations, hyperactivity, and confusion. By late adolescence he was diagnosed with methamphetamine induced psychotic disorder without use, and for the next 15 years he would use both methamphetamine and cannabis as a way to control his psychotic symptomology.

As such, due to the chronicity of his symptoms, Harris had been in and out of inpatient treatment programs for nearly a decade. This case history explores Harris' treatment via one art therapy directive, coupled with Gestalt theory, which was applied over a multi-year period with a one year long interlude between treatment sessions. However, the direction that this singular directive took could not have been more divergent.

After an interlude where Harris was stabilized on antipsychotic medication, and assurances, through urine drug screens that he was both sober and abstinent from street drugs, Gestalt therapy was eventually chosen as the preferred treatment modality. Due to longstanding neglect concomitant with a preference to isolate, whether that was through drug use or insulating himself from personal interactions, feelings, sensations and thoughts were not in his vocabulary. Thus, introducing Gestalt therapy with its preference for moment-to-moment experiences, unfinished business, and its focus on integrating conflictual feelings Harris could hopefully begin to gain awareness of the struggle within.

Before we begin with the case illustration it is important to review a technique that I often use when incorporating Gestalt theory. This is a multi-step directive and may require a "practice run" to become familiarized with the procedure. Returning to Figures 3.5 and 3.6 you will notice two pre-drawn body outlines. For the purpose of this directive you can utilize these Figures or any body outline that you may prefer. It is helpful, however, that one appears childlike while the other is a more mature presentation. This offers the clinician an opportunity to view the internal representation that the client identifies with developmentally.

To begin, offer the client a choice of one of the two, distinct outlines making certain that you have made three copies of both so that once the client chooses you have enough copies for each of the Gestalt emotional states: 1) feelings, 2) thoughts, and 3) sensations. After the client chooses one of the outlines, provide them with that blank body outline and on the front write the word "feelings." Ask the client to arrive at five "feeling" words. Have them create a "key" by choosing one word and a corresponding color, and writing that word, in that color, on the front of the first body outline. Have the client choose a different color for each of the remaining words they have selected, and also write them on the body outline. At times a client will choose all positive or all negative words. Make certain that there is a balance between these emotional states, normally this will be three positive words and two negative or vice versa. On the second blank body outline write the word "thoughts" and have the client repeat the same key, writing the same "feeling" words in the assigned colors on this page. Have the client repeat this same procedure one last time, with the title, "sensations." Oftentimes it is prudent to ask the client to define each of the words they have chosen before moving on to the next step in the directive.

Beginning with any of the body outlines remove two from the table so that the client can only see the ones they are working on at the moment. For the outline titled, "sensations" ask verbatim: *"Draw where you experience (refer to one emotion from the key created by the client) sensations in your body. Please draw it on the outline."* Complete the entire key of feeling words in this manner. For the outline titled, "thoughts" ask the client: *"Where in the body do you experience (refer to one emotion from the key created by client) thoughts? Please draw it on the outline."* Once the entire key is completed move on to the body outline titled, "feelings" and ask: *"Draw on the outline where you feel (refer to emotion from the key created by client)."* Do this for each of the feeling words.

At this juncture the post-drawing inquiry can begin. I often ask the following question for the completed body outlines: *"Take a look at (choose one of the outlines) and tell me what's going on?"* It must be noted that at times I will not preform the post- drawing inquiry for each body outline. At this point it is important that the therapist use their instincts, knowledge of the client, and the visceral feeling that the therapist senses from the drawings to inform their decision. It is, however, essential that the provider allows the client to process their drawings in any way they desire; remaining in the present moment, whether they talk specifically or generally, openly or disingenuously. Thus, it is not the therapist's place to interpret for the client but instead the mental health professional should concentrate their attention on what the client is communicating. In this manner, the clinician is free to take note of expressed unmet needs as unfinished situations are allowed to come to the forefront.

Now let us return to Harris' case illustration and Figure 3.10 which is an example of his feeling body outline. The other two outlines are not being presented as they were very similar to his "feeling" drawing. Generally speaking either the sensation or feeling body outline has the most information to yield when we are discussing linking directives. It has been my experience that many clients rely upon words, or more specifically thoughts, rather than experiencing fully all of their feelings thus I utilize the "thought" body outline less than the other two. Note that in Figure 3.10 Harris chose the developmentally childlike representation which aligns closely with his lack of acceptance as an adult, couched in a childlike awareness he need not look toward self-support but could instead rely upon others unendingly.

Figure 3.10 Feeling Body Outline

The feelings chosen in Figure 3.10 were peace, exhilaration, contentment, sadness, and disgust. But it was the darkest color chosen, disgust, which catches the therapist's eye, and overtakes each of the other colors. As you can see, it springs from the top of the drawing until it touches the figure's feet in diminishing lines of anxiety. In this way, it not only surpasses but blots out the colors of peace and contentment until all that is experienced is loathing.

The next few sessions were spent discussing, and having him draw depictions for the words and accompanying feelings of peace and contentment; innocent choices that would keep Harris safe. Eventually, however, he would get to deeper expressive feelings with disgust being the principal emotion given his completed body outline. When that time came Harris was asked to "*Draw disgust.*"

Figure 3.11 depicts his completed drawing. When asked about this drawing Harris replied that he is behind the door, but he is not protected. He added that disgust brings on feelings of guilt and shame and he hesitates to walk through the door because to do so would mean he would have to face his fears.

It was at this juncture that a linking directive was introduced based on the door that Harris was so afraid to confront. Linking directives allow the mental health professional to work off the client's verbal statements while allowing the client to fully experience the moment toward the gaining of awareness.

Figure 3.11 The Door of Disgust

The best directives tend to originate from the client's personal experience and often arises naturally out of their comments, whether that be verbal or in a drawing title, or areas in their renderings that show particular emphasis, or simply through the clinician's instincts, in all cases the direction is best ascertained based upon the here and now relationship.

In this instance a copy of Harris' door of disgust was copied and three sides of the door were cut open while a second piece of paper was glued behind the first. When Harris came into the next session he was presented with the cut out door and was asked to *"draw what is behind the door."*

Figure 3.12 was the completed rendering replete with what Harris described as a "person in anguish" whom he went on to state was his future self. This peering figure appears to suffer defenselessly as he accepts the brightly colored flames which border a grimacing mouth. Further elaboration had Harris stating that the figure was searching for something that he hasn't "seen in a long time" and his advice would be to tell the figure to "step up." Harris then made a casual comment that the figure was reaching out of the enclosure for help but he could not draw in perspective.

The symbol of this projected, future self paralleled Harris' acceptance of vulnerability and detachment as an ordinary occurrence in his life. Based upon his

Figure 3.12 Harris' Anguish

statements this figure did not merely need to "step up" but more importantly to step out of the enclosures which blocked forward progress. For this follow up directive clay was chosen both for its tactile qualities that could similarly bypass some of Harris' stated obstacles, mainly his inability to draw what he saw within his mind's eye, and would afford him the developmental opportunity to work on competence and industry.

In his first clay representation (Figure 3.13) the directive was to "*make the man out of clay.*" It was purposefully worded in that manner to relay the idea that the figure was a man, not a child, and as such to reinforce the process of adulthood. As one can see, an upper body with a single hand reaches outward for help; a point that Harris was clear to communicate. While he created the sculpture, he mentioned that he wanted people to know that he is still trapped but he is "okay" and most importantly that "he has found peace with the bad feelings of guilt, shame, fear, and disgust." He titled Figure 3.13 "Fear of the Unknown." Though his verbalizations appeared confident the message did not match the method. It seemed impossible that peace, one of his original feelings in the body outline, had been achieved in such short order. A metaphorical indication of this was the creation of a torso with no ability to be ambulatory and oversized heavy hands desirous of assistance.

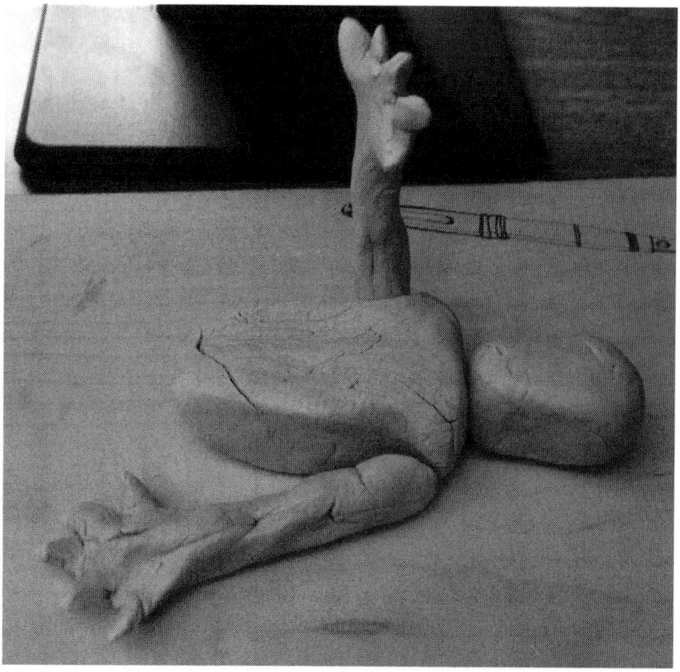

Figure 3.13 Fear of the Unknown

Overall, I believed Harris needed to stand before he could successfully face his overwhelming and often immobilizing feelings. Thus, it seemed important that his symbolic, future self, stand as a gesture of confidence for the expected trials of life that lay ahead. For the next month Harris struggled with the metaphorical and literal process of self-support. He was initially hesitant to add the finer points to his figure and admitted to his difficulty in attending to "details." Over a period of four weeks he created a face and legs while stating that he has been "muscling his way through things." However, it was the process of having his figure stand that took the most time, yet he persevered and Figure 3.14 was completed.

Shortly after finishing Figure 3.14 Harris left inpatient programming and moved to supported housing. Shortly after this transition he relapsed on methamphetamine, left housing, and did not re-emerge for another year. At the time that he returned to inpatient programming he had been sober for over five months but feelings of inferiority, isolation, and incompetence persisted. With a concerted focus on vocational training he enrolled in school and eventually found part-time employment. As his self-reliance grew this interlude was replaced with a return to art therapy and Harris was reunited with the "door of disgust" (see Figure 3.11). Harris was presented a copy of the door and asked to *"draw what is behind the door."*

Figure 3.14 Standing on His Own Two Feet

When he saw the year-old drawing Harris stated he recognized the picture but did not remember anything else. After sitting for an extended period of time he drew intently without comment. Once he put down the marker he said, "This is what's coming up in my future." His pictographs represent: a diploma, a job, his family, meeting a partner, and owning his own home. He titled his drawing, "Things Pending" and spent many moments closing and opening the door.

Replete with unfinished business, as well as developing awareness, Harris spoke of the closed door as if "there isn't anything on the other side" yet when he opened the door he expressed feeling "surprised . . . . It's a path. There's an order . . . . They'll find a way into my life . . . . I've been behind in life, what I was attaining in life escaped me . . . . I've gotta go out and do the work. There are steps to take . . . . It's been a long time since I had a life like that where all the pieces fit; where they make up a complete life."

Of all that Harris expressed I felt that one of his most perceptive statements was when he referred to his symbols as a path. The best linking directives rely upon the client's remarks and "the therapist's job is to invite clients into an active partnership where they can learn about themselves by adopting an experiential attitude toward life in which they try out new behaviours and notice what happens" (Gestalt Therapy: Overview and Key Concepts, 2007).

Figure 3.15 Things Pending

In this case, to assist with focusing awareness on present situations and navigate beyond avoidance it was reasoned that play therapy could best address his present needs.

However, before this could be undertaken copies of the pictographs were made as they would be utilized on the path, which he would soon be creating, as board pieces. This would also serve to figuratively remove the "door of disgust," as it was time for Harris to walk toward growth and wholeness.

In Figure 3.16, Harris was asked to *"draw your path."* Note how many of the twists, turns, and tight switchbacks run past the boundaries of the page. This pointed to Harris' propensity to overlook the margins of his world and react impulsively with little concern for the larger picture. Symbolically, Harris' path would not be straightforward. As the session unfolded Harris was given the photocopies of his pictographs and asked to *"place them on your path anywhere you choose."* Harris named his path, "Captain of Your Own Ship," while commenting that this was a "voyage" and how he must "stay on course." As he reflected on his game board he closed with, "I've never had all this. This is what I've always wanted."

For the next few sessions Harris was challenged to explore his fragmented and one- dimensional road. Initially he appeared puzzled but eventually

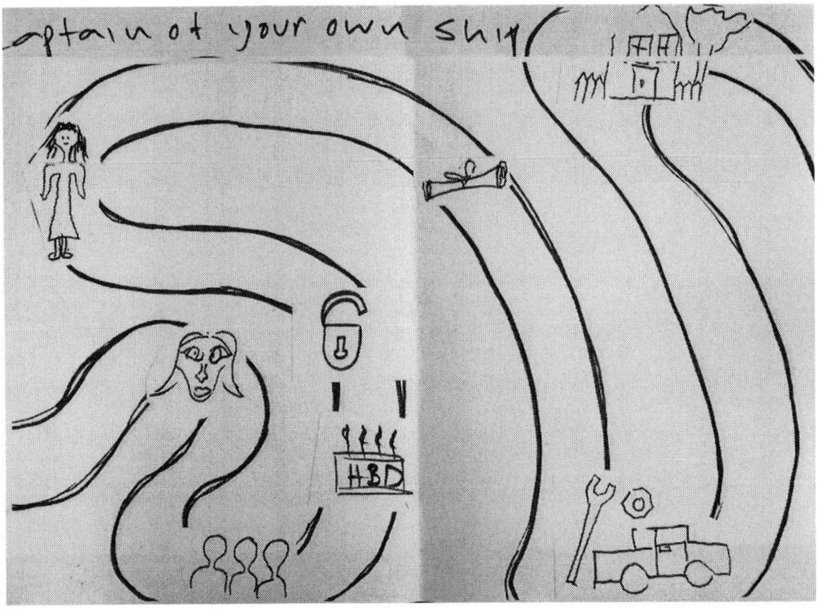

Figure 3.16 Captain of Your Own Ship

was able to use tape and additional paper to complete the corners. He then worked to create a three-dimensional path; one that did not merely meld into the environment but was noticeably differentiated. While he added color to the background he ran into many predictable obstacles such as running out of ink while being faced with a monotonous task (Figure 3.17). He made frequent comments on how it was "difficult" and "tedious." At one point he expressed how "it takes a lot of time and attention," only to exclaim, "I can't do it." Conversely, he identified that he shouldn't "do too much at once" and "the path is more clear and stands out," and, "if I work hard it will pay off" and pointed out that each part of his path was an area of well-being. All in all, it was important that Harris refuse to accept helplessness and instead persevere and integrate his conflicting feelings. Thus, while completing the background, discussion focused on awareness of the realities for a healthy future.

By Figure 3.18 Harris had completed the background and was active in the development of the board game. As such, the next step was for him to choose a game piece and he selected one that said, "I am unstoppable." In subsequent sessions, he would roll a single die and move about the game board discussing the joys of the chosen goal, impending obstacles, and coping skills. Staying within the metaphor Harris would often pronounce his plans, "to stay on the right path, keep doing what I'm doing" and, "not let opportunities pass me by, I need to make things happen, keep moving, rather than waiting."

Figure 3.17 A Tedious Task

Given that Harris introduced obstacles into the verbal discussions it was time to create some visually. The first obstacle created was a black hole (left side of Figure 3.18) and then a brick wall (lower right of Figure 3.18). As he rolled the die one of the impediments was placed in front of the game piece; on his first roll he landed on his college diploma. Harris looked downtrodden as the black hole was placed on the game board but his chagrin was soon replaced with relief when he was told that he could create a chain providing him with safety and strength. On each link of the chain Harris wrote out a total of seven strengths and then he connected the links with tape. An example of his chain can be found just above the black hole on Figure 3.18. In another session the brick wall was placed before his job game piece. He immediately created a grappling hook so he could "climb" over the wall. Additionally, he explored whether he would have "support" while doing this, the strength of the tool itself, how to navigate the wall safely, and the necessity of taking rests along the way.

The differences between Figure 3.16 and Figure 3.18 are as profound as Harris' progress toward self-care and reliance. As the play therapy interventions continued his verbal comments did not deny his past difficulties but did

Figure 3.18 A New Path

not dwell upon them either. His statements focused on his future goals as well as his here and now struggle. To date, Harris continues to focus on the path outlined in his play therapy board game. Some of the goals have been achieved; others will be faced in his future. However, it is the obstacles that he will need to continue to face if he is to attain long-term self-support, integrate balance, and perceive the larger picture.

Good, Bad, or Indifferent

Case Illustration 3

This case involves a 42-year-old medically stabilized, diagnosed schizophrenic whom I will call Ray. Throughout Ray's childhood, he was often described as "quiet and shy," "detached," and/or "timid." Raised in an intact family, he lived in a small suburban town where his mother and father placed high expectations on their first-born child. As Ray neared adolescence, his indifference to forming relationships with others increased and his father distanced himself from his son while Ray's mother projected the parental hopes with unyielding determination. Over time, family disapproval became unbearable and Ray succumbed to his family's entreaties to attend college. On his own for the first time and unable to attend to the vicissitudes of life without his mother's guidance, Ray felt lost and alone. Within a period of six months, Ray suffered his first nervous breakdown and thus began a series of hospitalizations and adult board-and- care home placements that would continue for over 20 years.

Impaired by his experiences, Ray's unusual beliefs intensified into persecutory delusions, which centered on the polarities of perceived danger, punishment, and safety. Often, in casual conversation, Ray would resort to social symbols of protectors to counter feelings of inadequacy and worthlessness. In one such conversation, Ray was spontaneously relating happy times he experienced on a farm with his grandmother and grandfather. As the story progressed, his anxiety began to increase and within moments, he had regressed into fantasy. He stated that his grandmother had gone to Vietnam to save the strawberries and cream and that Buck Rogers and Tweekie the Robot had subsequently been whisked off to the safety of the farm. In addition, Ray would intersperse his comments with, "It's the winds of war, that's what happens, we all have vagabond days."

These isolated and fragmented delusions provided Ray with both an escape from overwhelming anxiety and a model for the invincible protector he so strongly desired. In many ways, the protector he yearned for was a projection of the parental figure. This all-consuming symbiotic need would become increasingly evident as Ray and I began a nine-month therapeutic relationship. For the purposes of this section I have chosen to outline a specific period of directives and exploration based on what Ray loosely referred to as the "Shark's Lagoon."

As Ray's delusional symptoms all surrounded the manifest themes of danger and protection, it was important to move beyond the labeling of "Ray was a schizophrenic." In this vein, the exploration of what Arieti (1976) so aptly stated, we "must try to understand the mechanism that brought about the symptom, the meaning of the content of the symptom, and why the symptom has assumed that particular form" (p. 20), became the focus of the ensuing sessions.

When Ray regressed, he often spoke of "vagabond days;" however, no-one truly understood what was meant by this term as he rarely elaborated. In one of our individual sessions, I asked Ray to *"pick three or four pictures and create a collage about some of the things in your vagabond days."*

Figure 3.19 was Ray's completed collage. In a very methodical manner, Ray spoke of childhood recollections of horseback riding, family picnics with his aunt and uncle, and a high school graduation trip to Colorado. Initially, Ray indicated he had flown to Colorado to visit friends. As the story progressed, he outlined feelings of fear and anxiety which had intensified so quickly, that before he left the airport he called his mother asking for money to return home. She had sent it immediately.

Figure 3.19 Ride the Wild Wave

The last image of a smiling family found Ray regressing into a delusional metaphor. He began talking about a shark's lagoon. He described knocking out the shark with sandwiches and making them drink punch laced with poison. He then stated that his mother was a shark in the "bad" lagoon. In the next breath, he disowned his statement and placed his mother in the "good" lagoon.

In this one declaration, Ray had summed up his pattern of avoiding anxiety through splitting his positive and negative experiences. In terms of Object Relations theory:

> Splitting, which prevents the anxiety associated with negative (aggressive) images from being generalized throughout the ego, usually disappears in the second year of life as positive and negative images are synthesized. If it is excessive, however, splitting interferes with integration of these images and precludes a realistic development of the representational world.
>
> (Nichols, 1984, p. 185)

These good and bad object splits, which formed the majority of Ray's delusional subsystem, expressed his stressful internal experiences in a metaphorical manner. Having established a safe holding environment, it was important that Ray's intrapsychic conflicts were allowed both expression and containment.

Figure 3.20 illustrates the subsequent directive whereby I instructed Ray to "draw a good shark's lagoon on one side, and a bad shark's lagoon on the other side of the paper."

Figure 3.20 is a visual representation of Ray's fragmented and disjointed symbolic constructs. People and objects float in space with no support or grounding, hands are omitted in the metaphor of helplessness, and interaction between these disparate symbols is non-existent. The structure on the upper left side (bad) of Figure 3.20 Ray likened to a "mom and pop store" while on the upper right side (good) he said the male was his twin brother and the female his brother's wife. Ray then related a story of how these two people had told the shark to go to college, and now they have an obligation to help the shark make it through.

As Tauber and Green (1959) stated, "people who speak in metaphors do not experience what they say as metaphors; the symbols they use are regarded not as symbols, but as realities" (p. 36) and for Ray his internal metaphor required expression. As such, the goal for ensuing sessions focused on clarification, expression and containment where Ray's fragile sense of self would not be overwhelmed.

In the next series of sessions, I requested that Ray draw *"anything you please."* This type of directive allows the art therapy client to free associate, "that is, to follow their thoughts as they occur spontaneously, without planning or censorship. This technique is the best way to bring unconscious material

Figure 3.20 The Shark's Lagoon

to the surface" (Nichols, 1984, p. 213). Additionally, the use of a free drawing would empower Ray to make decisions for himself. Figure 3.21 represents a train heading to the shark's lagoon.

During this session Ray superfluously exclaimed that he was "exhausted," and "I can't decide right now," and "something is missing." His numerous difficulties and protestations were unusual for him during the drawing task and this regression was viewed in light of long standing dependency reactions. Eventually, as rescue from this therapist was not imminent, he chose an assortment of colors and drew arms and legs on the person, whom he named Phil, and with a flourish sat back appearing drained. I verbally reinforced his addition, stating that now Phil was able to do things and go places with his hands and feet. Ray simply nodded in agreement. It must be noted that even with the positive inclusion of appendages, not unlike Figure 3.20, a fragmented feeling emerges, one that continues to bespeak of difficulties with integration.

The second free drawing, Figure 3.22, finds the train returning to the lagoon. In this drawing he added a "good" shark and a "bad" lamb on the right hand side.

Spontaneously, Ray related the following paraphrased story: the lamb was kicking water in the shark's face, and the shark was unable to fight back, so he was leaving. The train was coming to take the shark to Minnesota, the land of a thousand lakes, so he would be safe and comfortable. I asked Ray how the conductor knew to rescue the shark. Ray replied, "There is an underwater

Figure 3.21 All Aboard

Figure 3.22 The Good Shark and Bad Lamb

phone in the lake, the shark called his mom, and she sent the train." At this juncture I had the choice to remain in metaphor or to interpret Ray's story. Based upon our long working relationship and that his drawings were showing signs of preconscious material I chose to confront Ray regarding the similarities between this story and his experience of being rescued in Colorado. Ray agreed that the two were similar and in further comments stated that he liked being rescued as well. As we continued with the post-drawing inquiry, Ray returned to metaphor and was adamant that the shark could not fight back and that nothing but escape could save the shark. The lamb was all bad and the shark was all good. Ray's use of the infantile defense of splitting is obvious and as Nichols (1984) has stated, "to the degree that splitting is not resolved, object relations retain a kind of 'all good' or 'all bad' quality" (p. 185).

In his next free drawing Ray returned to his shark theme where he stated he wanted to draw a mean shark. As Ray was drawing the shark (Figure 3.23) he stated, "The teeth look mean, huh?" I agreed. He replied, "He has to be happy!" He then added a curl to the mouth. Next, he drew the eyes and stated, "Oh no, the shark looks mean again." In an effort to integrate the disowned parts of Ray I clarified that this was okay as he was trying to draw a mean shark. Ray did not disavow his "mean" shark; he left it as it was. He then drew a bicycle underneath the shark and talked about how he used to deliver food on a bicycle when he was in college. He then stated, "I'm going to get a job

Figure 3.23 The Mean Shark

when I get out." As the discussion continued, he spoke of a job while serving in the Air Force and stated, "I didn't leave. They made me. Everyone makes me leave. They were baaaaaahhdd lambs." As the session drew to a close, Ray began discussing his future termination and removal to a board-and-care group home. He was both frightened and exhilarated.

As discharge proved imminent, Ray's sessions came to be increasingly reality-based. No reference was made of the shark's lagoon and free drawings continued to predominate as we worked toward increased differentiation. Figure 3.24 was the first image of a man and women, who are interacting, that Ray had rendered.

Ray shared his desire to meet someone in his board-and-care home upon release. He also added that he hadn't had much contact with women or with friends in the past. As for the title, he explained that he was going to "need a hand" to accomplish his dreams. In this drawing Ray has made an attempt at grounding his figures, with functional feet to stand on and a broken baseline. As such, Ray has offered his figures more support and security than in his previous work. Additionally, on the unit he was beginning to initiate contact with a few select peers, and to share his thoughts and feelings in groups.

With just over a month before his discharge, Ray entered the next individual session relating his wonderful experiences in college. I decided to forgo the free drawings and work with what Ray offered me, and asked him to, "*draw the good experiences in college and the bad experiences in college.*" Ray drew the rocket and bunson burner first (figure 3.25). He spoke of high school and how he enjoyed science class. Spontaneously, he drew the figures on the bottom left.

Figure 3.24 I Need a Hand

He spoke of women asking him out while he was in college, and of how he was proposed to twice. He related having a lot of friends also. Considering Ray's lack of social skills and low self-esteem, not to mention his emotional dysfunctions, I viewed his grandiosity within the session as projections of what he wished had happened. Ray then mentioned a girlfriend with whom he had lived at his board-and-care home for five years. They wanted to get to married, but their conservators would not give them the money they needed. He spoke of how sad he was about the event and added that she had passed away. Up to this point, Ray's affect had been appropriate; however, he was soon fidgeting and then he regressed into fantasy. I decided to confront Ray's escape from dealing with problems of loss and frustrated hopes by making observations and interpretations. I asked, "Does loss make you uncomfortable? Sometimes when I lose something I care a lot about, I laugh so I don't cry. Is that what you do?" Ray stopped giggling and fidgeting and nodded in agreement. We then spoke of the loss of people in his life and how that had affected him.

He then drew on the bad experience side (right side of Figure 3.25) the figure of a man and woman eating hamburgers. After drawing a car engine and mentioning his frustrations with his car breaking down, he wanted to end the session. Before he left, I asked Ray about the two figures and he replied, "You get fat at college." After asking for more clarification, he put his marker down

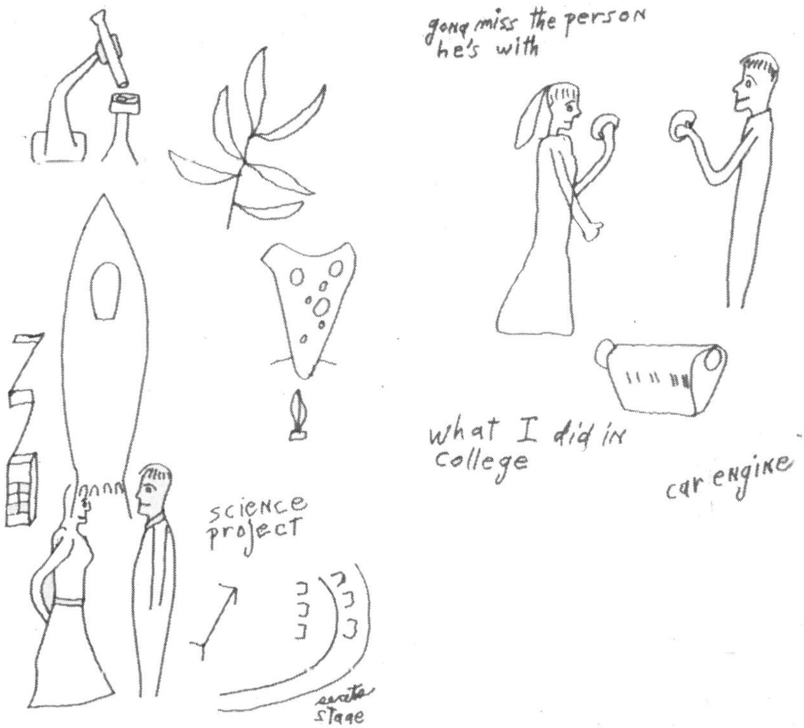

Figure 3.25 College Experiences

and stated adamantly, "People eat when they are lonely. They look sad, huh?" With this simple statement, couched in a metaphor of nurturance, Ray had expressed his need for human attachment.

Though Ray was able to discuss his feelings and was regressing into fantasy less and less, once discharge became evident, anxiety and stress brought the shark's lagoon back in the form of a present. Figure 3.26 was the last drawing that Ray created prior to his discharge.

In order to deal with his feelings of sadness and loss, I asked Ray to, *"draw how you say goodbye to a friend."* Ray initially responded verbally, "Well, you give him a hamburger to make the friend. And you take the hamburger away to say goodbye." Obviously, Ray equated separation with the need to make a punitive gesture. Ray then drew the ladybug (Figure 3.26) and then the man frying a hamburger. Ray related the following paraphrased story: the ladybug has asked for some of the hamburger. The man has refused to give it any and has sent it away. The ladybug leaves, but has no feelings about the situation one way or another. Ray's verbal and emotional regressions had always signaled nascent anxiety and fears surrounding abandonment and separation. This instance was

Figure 3.26 How to Say Goodbye

no different; metaphorically the apathy of the ladybug correlated to his fears of others' apathy (including this writer) and of being callously pushed away.

Ray stared at the then-empty right side of the paper for quite some time before saying aloud, "A present. Yeah, that's it, a present." Ray then drew the wrapped package and placed a woman on the lower left and said, "I know she doesn't have any feet, but I'm gonna leave them off." In other words, Ray wanted to leave the women nonfunctional and unsupported. Considering the fact that Ray had few social skills, keeping this woman immobile was very safe problem-solving. It also bespoke of a regressive and symbolic gesture whereby Ray could hold on in the face of loss.

Upon exploration of what was inside the box, Ray stated that it was the mean shark. Ray has again given a punitive present in response to separation. He then added the plane and said it was going to take the shark to the lagoon. Was Ray hoping that someone would save him? Were Ray's fantasy preoccupations protecting his fragile sense of self? His metaphors certainly drew upon those issues. Ray was facing numerous separations from the unit and from me. It was important to interpret and work though Ray's regression while providing a corrective emotional experience. Thus, for the last few sessions we did not incorporate art or metaphor; instead we explored reality-based issues such as work programs and clarifying feelings as they related to anger and denial. Unlike our initial sessions where Ray would regress to fantasy preoccupations to control his internal conflicts, the termination sessions found him able to discuss reality-based topics without regression. The artwork provided safety and security to explore his regressive tendencies of aggression while the act of identifying his introjects, through the metaphor of the Shark's Lagoon, anticipated his discord and allowed external expression.

And So to Bed

In summary, whether one is incorporating Analytical, Gestalt, or Family Systems therapy, each theory provides established goals, dedicated interventions, and theoretical assumptions based upon interpersonal relatedness. As illustrated in Case Illustration 1, the expression of feelings was not enough to oppose the recurrence of dysfunctional patterns and the accompanying grief. In the case of Harris, Gestalt therapy with a focus on internal support, as opposed to external support, became a crucial objective. In Case Illustration 3, reparative experiences and the building of new internal structures helped Ray to decrease projective defenses. Yet, within each of the therapeutic modalities there was one theme which stood foremost, that of insight through experience.

As such, within each modality, a supportive, therapeutic relationship allows the client a safe venue to further develop his/her natural resources while improving upon inherent fragility; for it is the natural resources of the client which must be taken into account if change, growth, and insight are to occur.

To this end, art therapy has proven useful in lending expression to unconscious feelings where other purely verbal treatment modalities may fail. As outlined in this chapter, the exploration of a personal metaphor can increase understanding as it is in favor of these strengths, while latent defenses can be allayed through trust and acceptance. Overall, it is a powerful tool within any clinical situation.

As Ellen Siegelman (1990) stated, "What is interesting about the metaphor, apart from its respectful indirection, is its comment on both aspects of the situation: both the danger and the defense." (p. 102). Ultimately, the use of non-verbal interventions allows the therapist to process, both literally and figuratively, conflict-laden material while the unearthed symbolism offers each client an equal voice.

References

Adler, A. (1956). *The individual psychology of Alfred Adler: A systematic presentation in selections from his writings* (H.L. Ansbacher & R.R. Ansbacher, Eds.). New York: Harper Colophon Books.
Arieti, S. (1976). *Creativity: The magic synthesis*. New York: Basic Books, Inc.
Battino, R. (2002). *Metaphoria: Metaphor and guided metaphor for psychotherapy and healing*. Wales: Crown House Publishing.

Biedermann, H. (1994). *Dictionary of symbolism: Cultural icons and the meanings behind them.* (J. Hulbert, Trans.). New York: Meridian.

Cirlot, J.E. (1983). *A dictionary of symbols* (2nd ed., J. Sage, Trans.). New York: Philosophical Library.

Gardner, H. (1982). *Art, mind, and brain: A cognitive approach to creativity.* New York: Basic Books.

Gestalt Therapy: *Overview and Key Concepts.* (2007). Retrieved December 1, 2017 from www.counsellingconnection.com/index.php/2007/10/16/gestalt-therapy/

Mason, H. (1970). *Gilgamesh: A verse narrative.* New York: New American Library.

Nichols, M. (1984). *Family therapy: Concepts and methods.* New York: Gardner Press, Inc.

Patterson, C.H. (1980). *Theories of counseling and psychotherapy* (3rd ed.). New York: Harper & Row Publishers.

Riley, S. (2004). The creative mind. *Art Therapy: Journal of the American Art Therapy Association, 21* (4),184–190.

Sarnoff, C.A. (1987). *Psychotherapeutic strategies in the latency years.* Northvale, New Jersey: Jason Aronson Inc.

Siegelman, E.Y. (1990). *Metaphor and meaning in psychotherapy.* New York: Guilford Press.

Tauber, E, & Green, M.R. (1959), *Prelogical Experience.* New York: Basic Books.

Tresidder, J. (2000). *Symbols and their meanings.* London: Duncan Baird Publishers.

4
Metaphors of Communication

> Once in a beautiful forest there lived an orphan girl and she did not have any friends, only the animals that lived in the forest. One day she was walking and a chipmunk told her to seek the red rose. So, for many days she looked and looked, and then she heard somebody say, "Hello." She turned around and saw the beautiful red rose just as the chipmunk had said. They talked for a long time. The girl told the rose that she wanted to have parents and the rose said, "Okay." Suddenly a nice lady and a nice man appeared. They took her home. They fed her and gave her lots of presents. The girl was full of happiness and her parents too. They put the flower in a beautiful jar and they all lived happily ever after.

Myths, fairy tales, and fables are the literature of history and the prose of progress. These stories, with the sky, wind, earth, and mountains, have become entwined with humans, animals, beasts, and the stars to form a personality of life. The characters of fairy tales, though defined as typical people, most certainly are not. They live in castles, speak to animals, and the animals respond in kind. They are not given usual names, but instead are often referred to as their role in the family or society. The fairy tale often depicts the youngest and "simplest" child as the hero who ultimately overcomes the odds and succeeds where others have failed. They focus on children's fears in relationship to parents and siblings. These struggles are either familiar to the child or equivalent to familiar ones.

Conversely, myths, with their naïve explanations of the mysteries of existence, ask the time-honored question: Who are we within this larger world? It is the myth which provides the growing youth with fantastical answers by confronting the reader directly with conflicting inner tendencies. Gone are simplistic first names. Instead myths tell of people with distinct identities and family histories. In this manner, myths parallel the child's growing maturity as he/she becomes increasingly aware of his/her world, his/her place in it, and its relationship to the future.

In this chapter, the therapeutic use of storytelling will be explored through children and adults' metaphoric communication. Utilizing the work of

Richard A. Gardner, storytelling is not a passive form of narrative, but instead one that can communicate meaningful insights when applied properly. Its goal is the expression and resolution of fundamental conflicts; its process that of a give and take between client and therapist. This technique allows the client to express conflict-laden feelings in a safely disguised form, and "from the stories children tell, the therapist is able to gain invaluable insights into their inner conflicts, frustrations, and defenses" (Gardner, 1986, p. 17).

In the world of a child, fantasy is utilized as the primary means of adjusting to emotional states. It is within this adjustment that fear fantasies reside, sibling jealousy abounds, and monsters become symbols of the unknown. However, through the method as originally devised by Gardner, the utilization of dolls, drawings, clay, or other media is believed to restrict the story. However, it is my contention that instead of restriction it offers another dimension toward the symbolic constructs in the quest for resolution.

In the early 1960s, Gardner utilized a tape recorder and a much formatted "script," while the child was presented as a guest of honor on a make-believe television show where stories are recited. The child was introduced, and made to feel comfortable with the process through a series of clarifying questions such as their age, the name of their teacher, what grade they were in, etc. Once the child was at ease and the story began, Gardner would identify one or two important themes. He would then create a story of his own, using the same characters in a similar setting. This story was related back to the client with the addition of a healthy resolution or alternative to the fundamental problem. I feel it important to stress that when incorporating the Mutual Storytelling technique, the characters and settings remain constant. The only thing to change is the addition of a healthy story ending.

As the years passed, Gardner continued to refine the technique to remain in line with technological advances. In this way, by the late 1960s the children were taking an audio tape home and listening with their families. In the 1970s Gardner began videotaping the process and as VHS recorders became prolific within the home, these tapes were then sent with the child. In today's climate of computer technology there is no end to what a clinician can accomplish.

As stated prior, Gardner's introduction to the client is quite structured. In the examples that follow, due to the addition of the art media, very little has been taken from his suggested framework as it relates to an introduction. This is because when one is incorporating clay, art, or puppets into the therapeutic hour, the client has been made aware of the ongoing nature of the project and tends already to be at ease with the creation of "characters" or drawings as it relates to the narrative.

Let's Get the Show on the Road

As the therapist, your role, beyond deciding upon a theoretical approach, is to recognize the individual defensive functioning which serves to protect the affect-laden memories. In repression, desires, impulses, thoughts, and strivings incompatible with the individual's conscious self are pushed into the unconscious. The experiences of shame, guilt, or humiliation are particularly apt to be repressed. With the defense of reaction-formation, unacceptable impulses are permitted by the expression of the impulse in its opposite form. In this way, feelings of rejection and hostility may be disguised by politeness or demonstrative expressions of gratitude; insecurity could appear as aggressive demands; submissiveness may cover up unrecognized aggressive drives. In the case of displacement, an emotional feeling is transferred from its actual object to a substitute, while symbolization employs an object or idea to represent another.

In all, the art production coupled with storytelling can allow the client to break through these well-honed defenses and provide the emotional release toward a mature adaptation. It is to this end that the art experience offers its invaluable service. The ability to vent emotions through the process of art allows for both distance and perspective. As Judith Rubin (1984) points out, "In the doing part of art therapy, patients do not talk about feelings or relationships from a distance, but they get into them and feel them" (p. 140). Thus, art therapy allows the therapist and client to embrace defensive measures by making them part of the treatment plan.

In art therapy one accepts as basic to treatment the psychoanalytic mechanisms of repression, projection, identification, and sublimation (Naumberg, 1953). These mechanisms, used unconsciously, are incorporated to defend against feelings of anxiety that have become uncomfortable, humiliating, or shameful. Removed from the ego, experiences may be isolated, but never forgotten. They creep into our relationships and have the power to both protect and stifle. This repression, however, "will make itself felt sooner or later in some manner if it is at all vital to . . . development" (Whitmont, 1969, p. 107). As a result, it is the client's repetition of behavior and language that serves to vent uncomfortable experiences through symbolization. In the therapeutic hour this defensive structure of the ego is played out within the act of creating the characters (if you are employing art therapy) and providing a narrative. Yet, recall that these displaced symbols have not yet re-grouped. Thus, the themes of stories or art productions are generally not pleasant or oriented toward mastery. Instead, they encompass the impairments of the fantasy that is insufficient to surmount the situation.

It is at this juncture where the themes, details, plots, and characters of the story require interpretation. As with all non-verbal therapy, interpretation is most effective when it directs itself to issues closest to the client's preconscious awareness. In the case of storytelling, often the client's narrative is filled with multiple plots and themes which can easily confuse and muddle the interpretive abilities of the clinician. Table 4.1 offers the mental health professional a quick guide to the important issues that will aide in interpretation.

Additionally, if one applies what I call the *symbolic abundance of ideas* (Moschini, 2004) to the interpretation, the act of content analysis is significantly eased. Through this method of interpretation, I believe that the client's

Table 4.1 Steps to Interpretation

Steps to Interpretation
Knowledge of the client, their issues, history, etc.
Identify the symbolic significance of each character
Viscerally experience the setting
Pay close attention to the moral of the story
Ascertain one theme and provide a healthier adaptation
Incorporate initiative and hard work toward maturity rather than magical cures

stories reveal verbal repetition on both a primary and secondary level. In a study on children's fantasies through storytelling, eight main themes were identified: "aggression, death, hurt or misfortune, morality, nutrition, dress, sociability, and crying" (Gardner, 1986, p. 181). Beyond themes, there are story elements that must not be ignored. These archetypal story elements play an integral role in our personal stories. From hero to monster, these six designations, as outlined by Mills and Crowley (1986), have proven very helpful in my work as the elements of a metaphorical story are unswerving:

1 Establish an overall theme of *metaphorical conflict* in relation to the protagonist;
2 Personify *unconscious processes* in the form of heroes or helpers (representing the protagonist's abilities and resources), and villains or obstructions (representing the protagonist's fears and negative beliefs);
3 Personify *parallel learning situations* in which the protagonist was successful;
4 Present a *metaphorical crisis* within a context of inevitable resolution by which the protagonist overcomes or resolves his problem;
5 Develop a new sense of *identification* for the protagonist as a result of his victorious "hero's journey";
6 Culminate with a *celebration* in which the protagonist's special worth is acknowledged (pp. 65–66).

Still, should I become overwhelmed with story details and confused with a general direction toward a healthy alternative, it is the moral of the client's story which offers bearing. Through the moral, I can identify the singular issue and provide the *one* healthy alternative. Do not be tempted to heal every storyline, theme, or character. To do so will confuse the client and make your story ineffectual. Additionally, it is important that the narrative reinforces the client's abilities and hard work. To provide magical cures keeps the client mired in fantasy production rather than reality-based pursuits.

A quick reference guide is provided below to assist the therapist in his or her quest to heal the story:

1 While listening to the client's story, pay close attention to the *metaphorical conflict* and find the one that matches the client's fundamental problem.
2 The characters in the story personify *unconscious processes* especially as new characters are presented and move closer to the central character.
3 As the protagonist copes with the environment, incorporate new and effective skill development as a *parallel learning situation*.
4 Have the protagonist overcome the *metaphorical crisis* through his/her own skills and abilities as learned in step 3.
5 The protagonist reaches the end of his/her journey. This corresponds with Erikson's stage of industry over inferiority and identity versus identity diffusion.
6 Have the characters, as created by the storyteller, *celebrate* the protagonist's new-found success.

Let Me Bend Your Ear

The following story was told by an adolescent male who had been living in residential care due to his mother's inability to provide shelter and food. Prior to placement, he had lived in a series of hotels or abandoned cars with his mother and sibling. After one and one-half years of placement, his mother had acquired a steady job, found suitable living arrangements, and was attending weekly family therapy sessions. The client was awaiting his release date and was often heard expressing negativistic thoughts ("they won't release me," "I'm going to live here forever"). Here is this young man's story:

> Outside of a bank there was a baby blue Jaguar car parked. In the trunk was money, hand grenades, guns, and pistols. The men in the car were there to rob the bank and they stole $5,000,000. When the cops showed up, there was a fight and the bank split in half. People got shot and were lying dead on the street and the couches. The 12 robbers took off in the car and stopped at a Hotel 11. Eventually the cops found the robbers and killed them. The moral of the story is never stop at a hotel.

At the conclusion of his narrative, I directed him to draw his story (Figure 4.1). The drawing style was typical for this male. Moreover, he frequently added words to his drawings and in this rendering he wrote, "Stop in the name of the law" two separate times. These details should not be overlooked as they can provide subtle clues toward interpretation.

Figure 4.1 Hot Pursuit

While he was completing his drawing, I was developing my healthy story response. My first thought was to mentally review the select phrases that stood out. In some areas of his narrative he had added copious verbal details (the color of the car, what was in the trunk); yet in the fight scene, his story held only numbers. The use of numbers is important when analyzing a story and in this case the number 12 correlated to the exact number of peers living in his cottage. Yet the hotel was given "Hotel 11" which correlates to someone missing (perhaps the client). I knew in his history he had lived in multiple hotels or slept in cars. I also knew that he was removed by the police prior to Children Services taking over the case. Consequently, I viewed his cops and robbers story as one predicated on separation and loss from his family of origin. Just as the bank split in half, so did his family. Just as the "robbers" eluded the police, they were eventually caught and punished with permanent separation.

In the end, this story would require a thoughtful approach as it was based on true-to-life events couched in a fantasy crisis. It would be impossible for me to provide the "happy ending," so my story would need to contain reality-based issues surrounding loss. In my story, I purposefully stayed away from the mother's responsibility for the client's "release from jail," as I wanted him to understand that he cannot change others, only himself.

My story as told to the client:

> One day there was this guy who found himself in all sorts of trouble. Nothing seemed to be going right. People in his life got into all kinds of scrapes and he always felt like he had to set things straight. He was a smart guy, but no-one would listen to him so in desperation he decided to rob a bank to solve all his worries. On the way he gathered up 11 other guys and now they were 12. He didn't particularly like all of them but they were all he had at the moment. He pulled up to the bank in his fancy car and that's when he showed his cohorts his stash of weapons. There were a lot of weapons. In fact one of his robbers asked, "Why do we need so much fire power?" But no-one ever answered him. After robbing the bank for millions of dollars, the cops showed up and a fight began. Neither side wanted to give in because they thought they were both in the right. So as the fight went on the bank split in half and the robbers tried one last desperate escape in their car. When they found themselves surrounded at the Hotel 11, the guy with all the troubles knew he had to face the consequences of his actions. He still didn't think it was fair because it wasn't his fault he was in this trouble, but he yelled out, "Okay, okay, I guess I give up." The cops arrested him and took him to a holding cell with his 11 cohorts. Eventually, the guy watched as others got released from the cell, but not him. He just seemed to get angrier and angrier. One day he asked why he couldn't leave and the jailor told him he had a few things to do before he could be released. As time passed (it felt like forever), the jailor came to him and said, "you did everything you needed to. It appears you learned to make good decisions in the face of difficult circumstances." With that, the guy happily left and vowed he would never return. The moral of the story is: Fighting and thievery may look tempting but in the long run, hard work pays off.

If you recall the client's story, it could be easily broken into three parts: 1) the robbers in front of the bank, 2) the chase scene, and 3) the capture. It is clear that Figure 4.1 relates to the chase scene. Here the "group" is on the run and still hoping for successful evasion. I found this drawing to be a healthier choice than any of the other plot lines available (i.e., confrontation of a victim with a weapon or a permanent separation through death). With this information (the drawing of the chase scene) the client still possesses optimism regarding future "pursuits." And it is in this manner that I chose the healing aspect of acquiescence, coupled with acceptance of the consequences for actions.

However, if he had chosen to draw either of the other two story plots, my focus would have changed accordingly. As an example, if his drawing had encompassed the armed robbery plot with his "gang of robbers," I would have adjusted my story to one of the robbers questioning the plan and a positive change of action would have occurred. If he had drawn the death scene, my story would have focused less on an actual death and more on a metaphorical death. Therefore, instead of having the robbers truly get shot and die, I would have placed the robbers in the Hotel 11 "scared, worried, and lying on the couches as if they had died." I then would have had the authority figures (police) talk them out calmly, and also would have verbally stressed feelings (i.e., "the cops disliked this part of their job immensely. It always made them feel sad when people refused their help. They knew if the robbers just gave up and spoke with them, that everything could work out fine. Sure they would have to pay a consequence for their actions—we all have to do that—but the robbers would be allowed to move on and make a better life for themselves. But how could they get them to understand this? These robbers were a stubborn lot.").

Ultimately, the use of the art media, employed after the client's story, offered a richer direction, while providing the extra bonus of time for me as I created my narrative. To this end, I wondered if I could employ the same process in the group therapy hour.

The group I ultimately chose encompassed eight adolescent males with diagnoses that ranged from developmental delays to significant abuse issues and traumas. In early sessions it became apparent that these teenagers exhibited little capacity to share information, recognize behavioral patterns toward the development of empathy, or interact in an effective and beneficial manner.

As a result, the primary goal of the group was to promote interaction and expression while encouraging problem-solving and negotiation. I had tried numerous art therapy interventions ranging from the safety and comfort of collage to the perfectionistic quality of pencils. However, the result that I was striving for never materialized and after two months (with little move toward empathy development) I both asked and answered my question with a simple observation: these guys just did not listen to one another. They were either so busy arriving at a witty response (the high functioning peers) or occupied with following the flow of group (the cognitively impaired ones) that my directives appeared to be beyond each of their capacities. Thus, after more than four months, I introduced storytelling to the group hour.

In the next session I asked the members to raise their hands if they thought they were good listeners. Almost every hand was raised. I then asked who was a good leader and got an equally enthusiastic response. At this point I explained that we were going to be telling stories and while the narrator was speaking, the group members were to draw what was being described. I then challenged the group members by saying that all the "good listeners" will have their opportunity to show their abilities right now. A member was chosen to begin the story and the directive was underway.

Here is the story that the adolescent related:

> There once was a tree man who saw a boy playing at night. His mother told the boy to come into the house and take a shower but he said, "No." His mother gave him three chances to go inside the house. She asked him once, and he said, "No," she asked twice and he said, "No." The third time the tree man grabbed the boy and turned him into a tree. The tree man said, "if you don't talk for ten years I will turn you back into a boy, but you have to listen to your mom." So after ten years he hadn't talked and the next day his mother asked him to go inside the house and he listened.

While the storyteller related his narrative, the other peers were frantically drawing his verbalizations. After the story, I gave our narrator a chance to draw and Figure 4.2 was his response.

Here the boy is playing outside after being released by the tree man. Another peer has drawn the boy being snatched by the tree man for his insolence (Figure 4.3).

In other drawings the boy was either playing happily or being snatched, so I prepared my story accordingly. In all, the goal of having the group members listen to one another was undoubtedly achieved and I certainly did not have to

Figure 4.2 The Tree Man

Figure 4.3 A Boy Captured

relay a story, yet the belief that it would add another dimension of awareness and insight spurred me forward.

I viewed the metaphorical crisis to be twofold: 1) the act of being removed from his family due to his wrongs, and 2) the excessive punishment meted out at the hands of others. With this in mind, I wanted my story to revolve around mischievousness rather than wickedness, care rather than punishment, and choices rather than passivity.

Here is my response to the initial story:

> Once upon a time there was a boy who was outside playing. He was having so much fun that when his mother called him to come home and take his shower (yuck, how boring) he pretended he didn't hear her. She asked again and he said, "No." When she called him a third time, he decided to hide from her. So he ran around to the base of a big tree and laid down. As he waited for his mother to call again, he felt a hand grab him and some weird tree creature saying, "If you don't listen to your mother and go home right now I will keep you here with me. And I won't let you go for ten long years. Do you hear me? Ten long years." The boy was terrified. He squirmed and fought the tree creature but kept hearing, "ten long years." Finally, he broke free and then awoke with a start. There in front of him was his mother saying, "Goodness are you going to sleep for

ten long years?" He was so happy that there was no tree creature that he ran inside the house and took his shower. The moral of the story is sometimes it's just easier to do what you are told the first time.

As weeks passed the telling, drawing, and re-telling of stories became a group favorite. As Yalom (1983) identified, paramount in group therapy are two factors: that of interpersonal learning and group cohesiveness. However, this task is made increasingly difficult due to the fact that the majority of groups encompass a wide range of clinical populations with varied therapeutic goals and abilities. In those instances, it is the therapist's task to ascertain how best to treat a variety of populations in the most effective manner. And, though Gardner's work focused on single clients, the incorporation of storytelling into the group setting can prove healing on a multiplicity of levels.

You Said a Mouthful

The following example was taken from a group containing four adult males. This group met one time weekly and had been newly formed with the focus on theme-based work. In this way, I explained to the group that our first "theme" would be to both write and illustrate a short story. The initial reaction to this directive was disbelief. The members as a whole felt they could not accomplish such a task and immediately rejected the statement. While the group processed their fears and insecurities I continued to focus on their competency and assuage their anxiety. Ultimately the group settled into the first phase of this multi-layered project by "drawing a person."

If we believe, as Karen Machover (1949) has postulated, that the drawing is essentially a projection of the self, then the directive to "draw a person" can be viewed as a symbol, illustrating an individual's personality. Thus, each group member's drawing was a window into their unconscious values, beliefs, defenses, and conflicts. In order to decrease confusion, I will refer to the clients by the names that they gave their characters and supply a brief history of the individuals within the group.

Sergio: This young adult had a juvenile record as well as several convictions as an adult. In the living space he tended to lurk in the shadows and utilized his verbal skills to manipulate staff members as well as peers. Figure 4.4 is his drawing of "Sergio," the character. Notice the identification with a masculine, powerful, confident, body image. His sense of self obviously intertwined with that of a gang member while his verbal statements point toward his identity confusion, "when people are around me they see me as someone that has tattoos, that used to belong to a gang, and they test me on assumptions of my past before they even get to know me."

Bo Arthur: This depressed, young adult often spoke of "riding the rails" (hopping freight trains) and his travels throughout the United States. He had a

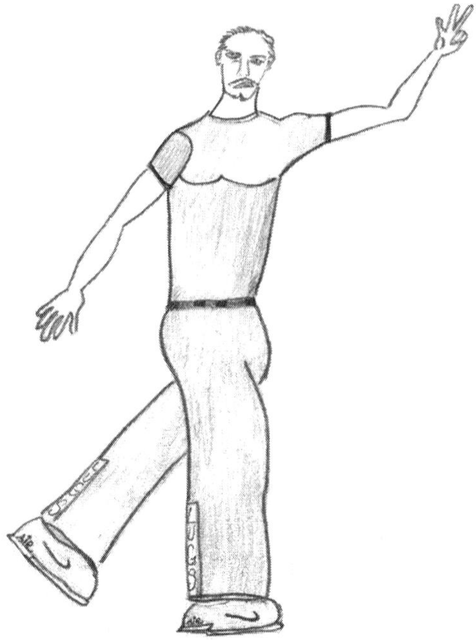

Figure 4.4 Sergio

history of visual and auditory hallucinations whereby he believed that demons were after him. Subsequently, he employed prayer as a coping mechanism; however, he had a tendency to go to extremes and then became delusional with regard to his religious preoccupations. Overall, Bo Arthur the client and Bo Arthur the character exhibit issues related to feelings of insignificance which can be noted in the final size of Figure 4.5 as well as the overcompensation of muscles, coupled with an intimidating stance and derisive stare.

Mike Doe: This 34-year-old male had a history of aggressive acts toward woman beginning at the age of 17. He had spent the majority of his youth and adulthood in jails or prisons. In talking with him, he was brusque, candid, and made no excuses for his past or present. Additionally, he exhibited no motivation and had a tendency to look upon others with disdain. His character (Figure 4.6) was described in much the same manner. He stated, "Mike Doe is well liked, but he wants to be left alone." Of importance is the name he gave to his character, "Doe", a non-descript name—one that is given to orphans with no background, family, or relations. This was an early indicator of his strong desire to remain anonymous.

"M" Chocolate: This client, a 29-year-old male, had a chronic history of substance abuse. Within the recent past he had attempted suicide, as well as

Figure 4.5 Bo Arthur

suffered the onset of auditory hallucinations. At one juncture, during an initial interview, the client stated, "I can see others laughing and talking and I don't fit in with them." As you can easily sense, Figure 4.7 represents that feeling both graphically and physically.

At the completion of the drawing exercise, the group members were instructed to write a biography for their characters. This was instituted to elicit associations toward personalized meanings through an indirect "interview," as well as to begin the process of feedback at the end of each group session.

The character Mike Doe was described as "laid back and easy going," while Sergio "dislikes trouble and too much pressure." The ever-striving Bo Arthur was described as "a hard worker who gets upset when pushed," while "M" Chocolate, "looks like a ball. He pleases people. He doesn't knock before entering people's houses. He howls in the middle of the night." Within each of these descriptions, the conflicts, desires, and personalization that categorize the unconscious process can be discovered. In all, each group member had identified projections of the self, a self that was transposed upon their fictional characters.

As the sessions moved forward, the group was divided in half with one pair creating the villain, and the other pair creating a guardian. In this exercise, Sergio and Bo Arthur created the guardian angel (left side of Figure 4.8) while Mike Doe and "M" Chocolate created the villain/Mike Dow (right side of Figure 4.8).

Figure 4.6 Mike Doe

Figure 4.7 “M” Chocolate

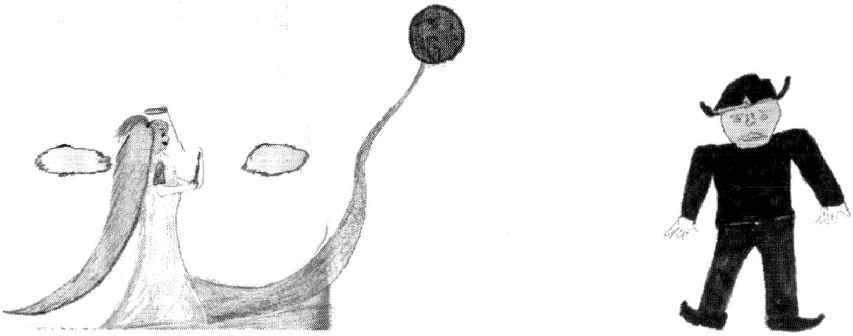

Figure 4.8 Guardian and Villain

The group again processed their drawings and introduced the new characters to one another. Again, it is interesting to note that the villain (as created by Mike Doe and "M" Chocolate—though Mike Doe did the lion's share of work) is named Mike Dow. This choice is a close derivative of the protagonist's name, Mike Doe, and further expresses not only the duality of the creator's personality, but a subtle reference to the disdainful attitude surrounding the task.

As the group progressed, they were faced with defining the obstacle as well as the story goals. After much discussion and debate, the story goal (of going to a rodeo) was decided while the obstacle was the villain's jealousy.

Returning to the work of Richard Gardner (1986), a microphone and tape recorder were brought into the group circle for the telling of the story. As such, the therapist's role is, as "Master of Ceremonies," the person who lends the supportive ego as needed. As with most clients, performance anxiety swells when faced with a microphone and the task of creating a story. Therefore, to acclimatize the group, the recorder was passed around with each gentleman providing a brief biography of their character. Once comfort was achieved, the story began (with the therapist taking a role also).

The outline below is a transcript of this session. The italic notes behind select passages were added to describe the process or provide further information as needed. It should also be stated that the name Mike Doe was changed to John Doe as the group found the resemblance of protagonist and antagonist to be too confusing. When this was decided, the client who named the two characters so similarly simply shrugged.

TAPED TRANSCRIPT

SERGIO: Bo Arthur is a friend of Sergio, "M" Chocolate, and John Doe. The four of them have plans for the future and something is coming about.

THERAPIST: One night Bo decided that he wanted to go to Cheyenne Wyoming for the rodeo, so he got a hold of John who . . .

JOHN DOE: listened patiently to Bo's ideas. After Bo was done, John thought, "Hey, that's a good idea." Then he said, "We're going to have to save up some money, rent a nice car (*appearances are of utmost importance*), and tell the other fellas about the trip."

"M": After Bo agreed, they gave a call to "M" Chocolate, who was happy to hear about the trip. He quickly figures out the gas mileage, because he wanted to be in charge of the transportation (*need to belong*) at the same time he was pacing (*anxiety relief*) while he waited for a call from . . .

SERGIO: Sergio. It didn't take long for the phone to ring and Sergio told "M" that he put together a plan to make money to get down there. "M" agreed to the plan, and when John Doe was called, he agreed too. But there was one other person they had to talk to before all this went down.

(Bo was unable to complete the statement and passed the microphone to me/therapist):

THERAPIST: Had we mentioned that Bo was a famous cowboy *(provide Bo with confidence around his role)* and in his younger days he made his living riding the bulls? But there was another cowboy in the rodeo named . . .

JOHN DOE: Mike Dow and he was a bad man. He was a shiesty character, didn't do much, was 6' 5", weighed about 230 pounds and did a whole lot of drinking in the Okey Doke Saloon. When John heard Mike was going to be at the rodeo, he immediately called Bo. *(This is the beginning of John Doe passing tasks off to the other group members.)*

THERAPIST-AIDED TRANSITION: Now Bo didn't scare easy, but he had a lot on his mind so he told John to call "M" and "M" would handle it. *(Increase feelings of industry, method, and competence.)*

"M": "M" was busy looking for his wallet when the phone rang, so he ended up being in the middle of two things. He felt like he was losing his mind. "M" was contributing to the conversation because he was, wasn't ready for it, but he had to say his share . . . *(Beginning to decompensate due to stress. Intermingling his present situation/feelings into his character.)*

SERGIO: Later on that evening, Sergio received a call from "M" telling him he was having some troubles. Sergio hated trouble. The only thing he could do about this was to act smart, but he couldn't do it alone. So he called one other person. Bo Arthur.

BO: Now Bo has Christian faith so he got a hold of his Guardian Angel. And the Angel said, "I'll talk to Mike Dow and try to calm him down." *(Bo begins to participate but resorts to religion for protection and problem-solving.)*

THERAPIST: By and by all four drove off to Cheyenne feeling pretty confident that their Guardian Angel would look over them and convince Mike Dow to be less sinister and shady. *(Remaining with magical thinking to appease anxiety, it would have been better if I had reinforced reality-based achievement rather than magical thinking.)* As they were driving down the road they were met by . . .

JOHN: none other than Mike himself. Mike leaped from his truck and said, "You have no business going to the rodeo and if I see you guys there, there's going to be trouble." John stared at Mike for a long time and finally said, " 'M' will handle all this."

"M": "M" quickly suggested that they should find out what Mike was really after. Mike asked the four, "What I want to know is do you have money? And are you going to gamble?" "M" figured Mike wanted them to go to one gambling place, but thought they should go somewhere else so they wouldn't fall into his trap.

SERGIO: By this point, Sergio figured not too many things were going well, the Guardian Angel couldn't convince Mike Dow to back off, so secretly while "M" and Mike were talking, Sergio spoke to Bo about getting this guy off to a saloon somewhere. *(Note convoluted problem-solving when taking matters into his own hands.)* Sergio figured they could secretly get him drunk and he would pass out which would be one more trouble out of their way. *(Note repetitious use of word "secretly.")*

BO: The four were a few hundred miles from Cheyenne at a bar in Rocksprings and Bo was able to get Mike Dow so drunk he fell asleep.

(In the final proof this was edited out. Instead the group added the following sentence.) But they did call him a cab so he could get home, which, by the way, Sergio complained about the rest of the trip. *(The last sentence was added emphatically by Sergio, who was against the disclaimer. His words were, "Let the story be, he's (Mike Dow) trying to stop us, tie him up, cut off his head . . .")*

THERAPIST: The four raced down the dusty roads all night to get to Cheyenne. Once they got to the rodeo, Bo rushed to get ready for his ride.

John Doe skipped his turn

"M": "M" Chocolate was especially excited looking at the bulls all lined up and while he petted them, he imagined himself as a bull rider.

SERGIO: Sergio was very happy to be there. Sergio was also having daydreams of riding the bulls, but that was in the future.

BO: Bo stayed on the bull for 8 seconds and came in second place. *(Note he placed himself in second instead of first.)* After his ride, Bo was talking to Sergio and told him all about high school rodeo.

THERAPIST: Sergio was hopeful that he could learn and while the two spoke, they heard the announcer say, "Now in the gate is our most ferocious bull 'Killer' and aboard is a new cowboy named 'M' Chocolate." John, Bo, and Sergio's mouths dropped open.

JOHN: As "M" jumped onto the back of the bull, John Doe leaped into one of the rodeo cans and waited for Bo's assistance. *(Note statement of hiding in a rodeo can, not to provide assistance himself, but to pass it off to Bo if it is required.)*

"M": The bull rode off strongly as "M" called out, "Yippee." He was having more fun than he could believe. He was also very afraid of falling too hard but he made sure he was on there like glue. *(Verbal expression of fear revolving around trying new tasks.)*

SERGIO: Sergio, excited at seeing his friend jump on the bull, was cheering loudly. He was still dreaming that someday he might be able to jump on a bull. *(Metaphor for tackling fears, problems, head on rather than through deceit or secrets.)*

BO: "M" Chocolate stayed on for 8 seconds also and got first place. Bo was very proud of his friend for doing such a good job and thought that his Angel had something to do with giving the four advice on how to stay away from Mike Dow. *(Continues to rely upon external forces for problem-solving and delusional beliefs to navigate his environment.)*

THERAPIST: So the moral of this story is . . .

JOHN: When you're feeling good with your buddies and decide to go to a rodeo and Mike Dow finds you, get him drunk so he'll pass out and you won't have any problems. *(John too relies upon external forces; trickery, and drunkenness, to problem-solve and navigate his environment.)*

Once the story was completed, I typed out a transcript for each group member and we reviewed it to see which parts would remain and which they wanted removed. As a group, they decided that the portion they most wanted corrected was the moral. They felt John's story lesson was too negativistic. However, John became increasingly assertive with regards to keeping his moral as the group sentiment. The group members continued to debate while I sat quietly by and watched the process of negotiation unfold. Ultimately, a compromise was struck whereby each member agreed to write their own moral at the end of the book. To that end, Bo Arthur's moral was, "Good communications with friends and using your head!" "M" Chocolate wrote, "Having fun with friend's together." As stated, John Doe resolutely refused to change his moral and felt it summed up the story well. Sergio ended with his story lesson, "Complications are taken care of easier as a group."

In the ensuing sessions the book was compiled (text only) and the members decided upon the necessary tasks to illustrate the book.

Prior to binding the completed book, the group continued their negotiation as they sought out a title. In the early stages of deliberation, the titles had little to do with the story, and instead focused on the places within the story. Eventually, the group was able to problem-solve and a consensus was reached to focus on the theme. They titled their book, *Glory takes Sacrifice.*

Figures 4.9 to 4.13 represent the completed, bound book.

In the final group session, a bound copy was presented to each member. In this way, the group took with them not only a transitional object of the task, but a concrete example of what can be accomplished through cooperation, communication, and affiliation. As such, it was the art media, and the act of

Figure 4.9 Cover and End Notes

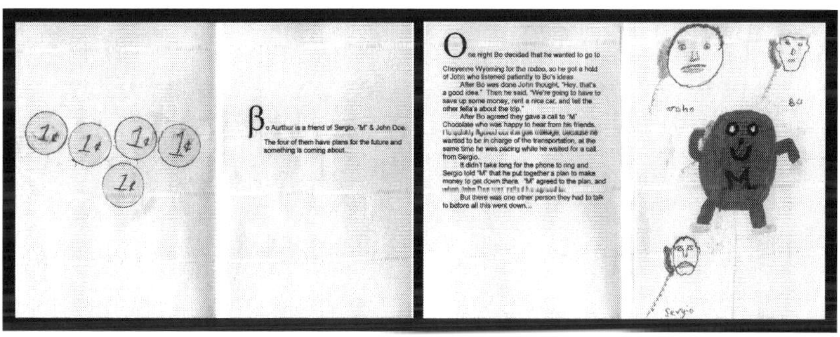

Figure 4.10 Pages 1–4

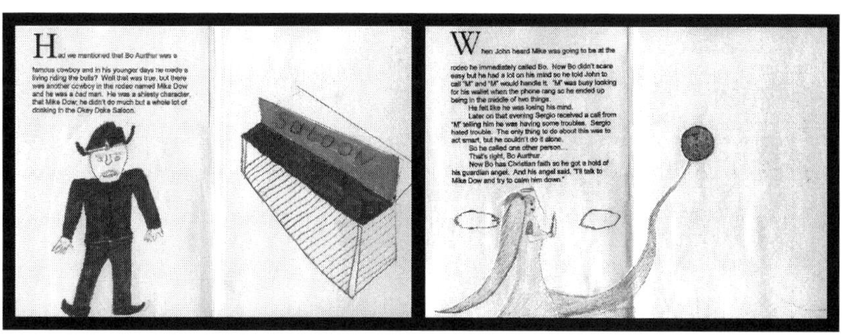

Figure 4.11 Pages 5–8

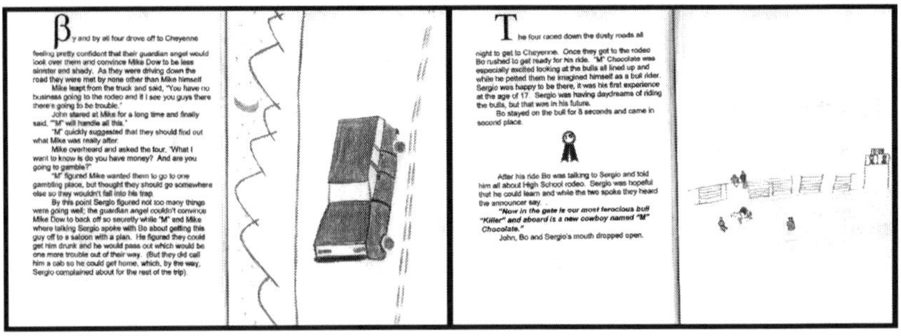

Figure 4.12 Pages 9–12

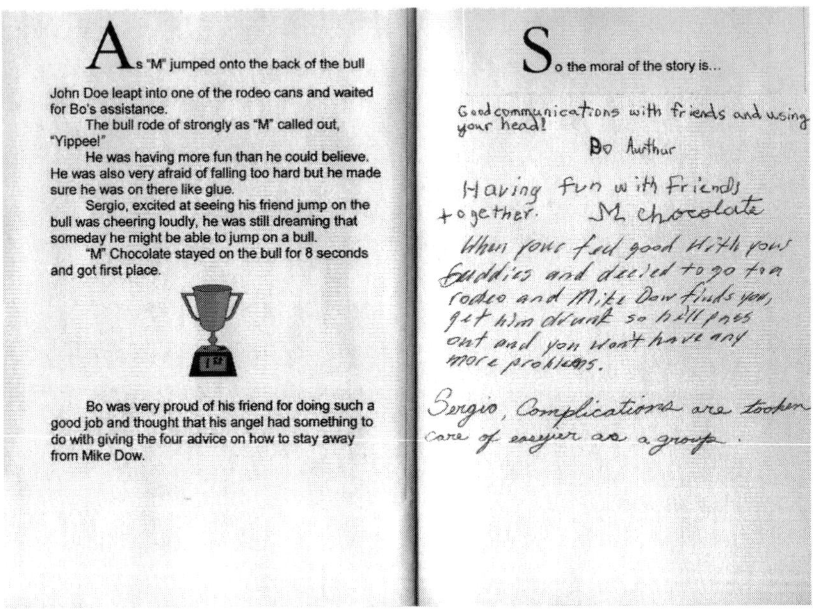

Figure 4.13 The Moral

creation/making things together, that encouraged interaction and expression among a group of peers who routinely ignored the other.

Between the Devil and the Deep Blue Sea

The following case illustration involves a 17-year-old male, whom we will call Billy. In this example, I have remained closer to the structure of Richard Gardner's Mutual Storytelling technique than in the prior illustrations.

Billy had been adjudicated on a series of crimes ranging from breaking and entering to grand theft auto and was subsequently placed in residential care. These crimes were committed to support his rising drug habit which had recently taken over every sphere of his daily living. Dually diagnosed with Cannabis Abuse and Conduct Disorder, this was the first time he had been separated from his family.

Billy's father was a hard-working, tough-talking man, who had little time to spend with his family and even less time to spend with his only son. His mother over-compensated for this fact and had a tendency toward enmeshment. These behaviors, instead of endearing her to him, were met with cruel indifference on Billy's part.

An incident that had taken place just prior to the initiation of the Mutual Storytelling Technique revolved around a weekend visit. Billy's father had promised that he would arrive for a visit and they would go to a local restaurant. The father never showed. The following week Billy's father apologized profusely and adamantly insisted that it was not his fault and that he would take Billy to a restaurant that very weekend. Billy put on his best clothes, gathered up reports from the school and residential section that outlined his improved behaviors and accomplishments, and waited for two hours in the lobby. The only phone call Billy received that day was from his mother making excuses for the father's rebuff. This situation, unfortunately, was not an isolative one, and with each false promise Billy retreated further within himself.

Prior to beginning the narrative, I asked Billy to *"draw three characters and then we will be telling a story."* Once he was done, I put on the role of "Master of Ceremonies" as Gardner specified:

THERAPIST: We are here with Billy who is going to be telling us a story today. He is a master storyteller and we are delighted to have him on our program. Before we begin, let's first introduce the three characters he has drawn. The first character has "Korn" written on his shirt, two devils on his shoulders, and a halo. He's a pretty big guy (Figure 4.14). The second character is a . . . (*pause here*)

BILLY: A pot smoker (Figure 4.15)

THERAPIST: Right, a pot smoker with a leaf on his shirt and his hair in his face. Lastly, the smallest of the three is . . . (*pause here*)

BILLY: Named Jim (Figure 4.16). He's the one with the red hair, Bo is the pot smoker, and Bob is the one with "Korn" on his shirt.

THERAPIST: I now introduce to you, Billy, the storyteller of the hour.

BILLY: These guys are pretty crazy; they like to run around and do some damage, get wasted, go out and jump guys. They have a good time while they're blazed. They like to raise hell all around town. Basically rob stores, rob cars, and be radical.

THERAPIST: Can you tell us a story about them?

Figure 4.14 Bob

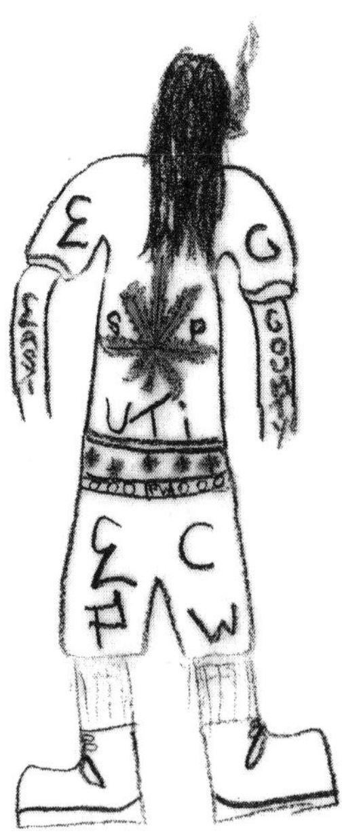

Figure 4.15 Bo the Pot Smoker

Figure 4.16 Jim

BILLY: Okay . . . well they were walking down the street, they were all wasted, and one of them was looking around and saw a group of guys in front of them. So one said, "Let's go jump those guys." So they all said, "All right." They pulled out their brass knuckles, knives, spikes, and they went up to them and started talking shit and beating the crap out of them. The big guy, with "Korn" on his shirt, decides he's going to stomp on one guy, so he grabs him and slams his face on the curb and stomps it. So now his jaw is broke open and he's in some serious pain. The other guys are beating the crap out of them. And they live happily ever after and go home and get wasted and drink some more and tell stories to each other about what each one of them did.

THERAPIST: And the moral of the story?

BILLY: There is no moral.

As with all stories, there are numerous directions that can be taken toward the healing of the metaphorical crisis. In this story, Billy is so angry and became extremely excited while relaying the fight scene that it was obvious that the story's plot and theme were giving sway to pent-up emotions.

As I began to apply the symbolic constructs to the characters, I interpreted Figure 4.14 as the client's ego. As you look at the image, notice the two devils sitting upon Bob's shoulders. This characterization often represents the maintaining of harmony between the urges of the id and the aspirations or demands of the superego. Moreover, this is the only character that has both hands and feet, giving this personification mobility and the capacity to reach out within their environment. I interpreted Figure 4.15 to be the representation of Billy's inner desires. This character was immediately introduced as "a pot smoker" with hair running down his face, gang epigrams running the length of his body, and no hands; the picture in-and-of-itself representing the primitive impulses that allowed Billy a cathartic release. Lastly, Figure 4.16 was immediately given the name of Jim. However, Jim is the smallest of the characters, lacks both hands and feet, and yet is the only one with facial features. In this vein, I viewed this figure as the embodiment of Billy's ill-formed superego.

With this analysis I understood that each character symbolized an aspect of Billy himself. Yet, missing was an ego-ideal. In the story, the secondary characters become overrun by Billy's primitive aggression with no guidelines for emulation. The rival gang that Billy struggles with was viewed as his father. This was reinforced by Billy's excitement when relating how "the big guy . . . slams his face on the curb and stomps it. So now his jaw is broke open and he's in some serious pain." If you recall in the overview, Billy had been lied to numerous times by his father and what better way to stop the lies than to break someone's jaw?

Again, we are presented with a metaphorical story that parallels reality. It would be imprudent of me to pretend that the rival group did not deserve punishment, but an action must be applied to why they are being assaulted. In this story, I will have the rival gang tell lies, offer false promises, and ultimately disappoint. This will link in the client's unconscious to his father's mode of interpersonal relationships. I will remove the jaw-breaking exercise, as this is where Billy needs to find alternative methods of expression. Equally, I have chosen to remove the act of escaping issues through substance abuse.

Following is my story:

> Okay, now I would like to tell a story to you. One day, three guys were walking down the street. This group was really close, but they couldn't have been more different. The first one, and he's the biggest, was named Bob. Bob knew the score. He understood things his friends didn't. He was a really nice guy when he wanted to be, but do not cross Bob. He doesn't put up with liars very well. The other guy, Bo, he lived for the moment. He loved getting high and hanging out with his friends. They never expected anything of him, just that he would get high. The last guy was named Jim. Jim sometimes got lost in the crowd. He was a smart guy too, but often the others wouldn't listen to what he had to say. Well, these guys were walking down the street and the first person they see is this guy who is the

> biggest liar in the world. I already told you Bob hated liars so when he saw this guy it was all he could do to not smack him in the face. Of course the guy started right in with his stupid lies while Jim stood in disbelief and wondered why someone would lie so much. Bo looked around just hoping to get out of there and go get high, and Bob began to imagine hitting the guy so hard his jaw would break open. Somehow Jim knew what Bob was thinking and he whispered in his ear, "Don't do it man, it's not worth it. He's just a liar. We all know it. Just take what he has to offer and let's move on." Bob really wanted to bust this guy wide open, but instead yelled, "I'm sick to death of your lies, and frankly I'm getting tired of trusting you only to be disappointed!" With that the three walked away. Bob just walked with an angry scowl on his face wondering why he was placed in that situation. Jim whispered in Bob's ear, "Hey you listened to me this time . . . cool."

The metaphorical crisis that I decided to address in the telling of this story was related to the father's lies and the need for Billy to unite the organization of his personality. This, of course, would never be achieved in one sitting, but the symbolic communication of Billy's story offered an insight into his struggle with the integration of the pleasure principle and ego-ideal toward the development of a total personality.

You Can Bet Your Boots

This final case illustration involves a 14-year-old male, whom I will call Joel. In this example his personal narrative has been combined with illustrations to carry a message of revenge, coupled with loss and deprivation. This young man was first introduced in Chapter 2 (Figure 2.4) and his communication style was both aggressive and dependent. Joel had been abandoned by his father at the age of 8, while his mother was unavailable and ineffective. The resultant all-powerful compensation is evident in Joel's comic book entitled, "The Nemesis Returns" (select pages from his final book can be found in Figures 4.17 to 4.21).

Figure 4.17 Antagonists Have Destroyed the Calm of Mogine

The story begins with a planet called Mogine, which was "a quiet place" until two rapid-fire explosions brought anguish and death upon the once peaceful community, only to be followed by the swift arrival of multiple antagonists called Pyro Punk and Roeken.

While these imposing antagonists are "so big they can destroy dragons," they also inhabit the parental traits of callousness, coupled with devious cunning and uncaring neglect. The survivors of Mogine are scared, but then, "the man of the world arrived" in the form of our superhero protagonist. Figure 4.18 offers two interpretations of our protagonist. The figure to the left is described by his protective armaments—"he had two guns, a sword, and a bullet proof vest." The figure on the right focuses on important adolescent attributes, "He is cool. His name is 'Super J'. He uses his fists most of the time. He likes wrestling." Note how Joel names his hero, "Super J," after himself. This identification is what Sarnoff (1987) was referring to when he stated, "When the child expresses his drives through fantasies, identification with characters, internalization, and introjection of certain components related to that character, he becomes himself like the character" (p. 335).

Stereotypically, Joel's protagonist displays traits of loyalty, fidelity, and capability; the polar opposites of his adversaries. Consequently, as the story unfolds, Super J falls in love and gets married; for an individual both needs to know that they can be loved and in turn love; a belief which can transcend the personality. Figure 4.19 illustrates our protagonist falling in love (left side) only to leave his wife (right side). Joel's text states, "He left her at the house to fight.

Figure 4.18 Two Views of Our Protagonist

She was sad that he left." While his wife's dialogue balloon says, "Go get them Joel. I will always love you. Then when I have our kid I will tell him about you my husband. But come back."

The next two panels have Super J, "beating all of the guys, but before he died he wrote a letter . . . Dear Stacey, say 'Hi, I love you son,' I love you too baby. My last saying before I go son, I love both and love b--." Joel made a point to outline that his character was unable to finish the letter as Super J had died. While the son grieves, the story text outlines, "The next day Super J died. It is a bad thing to happen in life when the baby grows up and he never saw his parents. He was so sad. One day they gave the boy a picture. He is depressed for the rest of his life. Then he was adopted by beautiful parents." Figure 4.20 holds the separation of feelings that Joel was experiencing both in reality and in his "fictitious" comic book. The left side of Figure 4.20 displays one villain apologizing to the hero's son from across a gap in two buildings, which metaphorically expresses Joel's needs and wants of a parental apology; an apology that would never materialize and thus was rendered just out of reach. While the right side of Figure 4.20 is a drawing

Figure 4.19 Love Transcends All

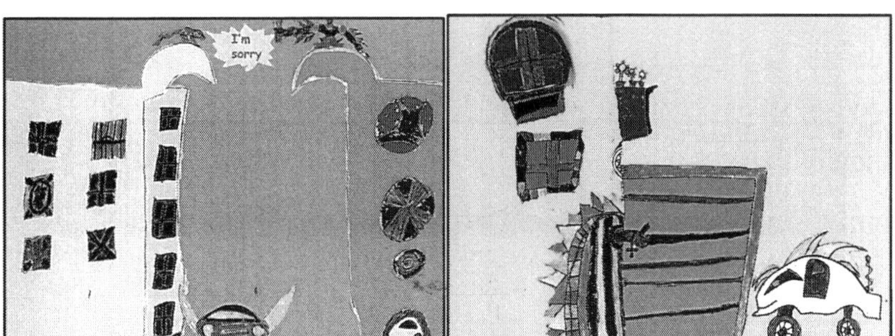

Figure 4.20 Sorrow and Gratitude

representing the safety and protection of his new-found "beautiful parents." It would be within this much needed gratification where Joel would be able to find the hope for stability and integration.

Unfortunately, a hopeful resolution, the discovery of unconditional love, would be interrupted by the villains' return resulting in yet another battle. As the story began to wind down it became increasingly difficult to distinguish between the villains and heroes; both blending together until it culminated in a swirl of color. In this way, Joel's difficulties proliferated as he continued to face the metaphor for the parent-child relationship.

The left side of Figure 4.21 shows the return of the final villain daring the hero's son to fight while the right side panel has the child exclaiming, "No, no, no I can't!!!" After initially being taunted, the challenger implores him to just try, and it is here that "The Nemesis Returns" abruptly ends. This fragmentary denouement, a metaphor for Joel's incomplete individuation and separation process, typifies his inability to integrate his feelings.

In the end, how can Joel finish a story, which for him remains ongoing? Instead, to combat reality, Joel retreats to fantasy, whether it is through the incorporation of stylistic drawings or his social interactions in his daily life. Instead of awareness, he carries painful thoughts and feelings emblematically like the dragons that an adversary can easily destroy, but are insurmountable for our hero or his son.

And So to Bed

If one accepts the premise that we experience life through each of our senses; visual, auditory, tactile, and kinesthetic and as such our minds give meaning to each of these perceptions, then it is the metaphor which binds each of those emotional experiences. Intrinsically, metaphor through storytelling can be a daunting process to any therapist and it can take many trials and errors before

Figure 4.21 Revenge and Loss

feeling comfortable with the healing aspect of interpretation. This is due primarily to the fact that a client, at any given time, can supply in a single story a multitude of themes, plots, sub-plots, and directions that can confuse even the most attentive clinician. However, as James Denny (1975) stated, "The art therapist is a full participant as well as an observer in the therapeutic process, helping the client to experience *who* he is and might become rather than *what* he has produced" (p. 133). In this manner, the therapeutic use of storytelling is not a passive form of narrative, but instead one that can communicate meaningful insights when applied properly. Its goal is the expression and resolution of fundamental conflicts; its process that of a give and take between client and therapist.

As such, the objective of this chapter was to explore how the use of storytelling can be assimilated into the therapeutic hour. For me the incorporation of evocative therapy has proven indispensable. Consequently, my use of art therapy is frequently combined with Gardner's approach as an ancillary method of intervention and interpretation. However, unlike Gardner's approach, I believe an integration of art, with the story, adds another layer of analysis. An undeniable advantage of the art production is not merely the contribution toward the development of healthier resolutions and mature adaptations, but the lasting quality of the illustrations.

References

Denny, J.M. (1975) Techniques for individual and group art therapy. In E. Ulman & P. Dachinger (Eds.), *Art therapy in theory and practice* (pp. 132–149). New York: Schocken Books.

Gardner, R.A. (1986). *Therapeutic communication with children: The mutual storytelling technique.* Northvale, New Jersey: Jason Aronson Inc.

Machover, K. (1949). *Personality projection in the drawing of the human figure.* Springfield, IL: C.C. Thomas.

Mills, J.C., & Crowley, R.J. (1986). *Therapeutic metaphors for children and the child within.* New York: Brunner/Mazel.

Moschini, L.B. (2004). *Drawing the line: Art therapy with the difficult client.* Hoboken, New Jersey: John Wiley & Sons.

Naumburg, M. (1953). *Psychoneurotic art: Its function in psychotherapy.* New York: Grune & Stratton, Inc.

Rubin, J.A. (1984). *Child art therapy: Understanding and helping children grow through art.* New Jersey: John Wiley & Sons.

Sarnoff, C.A. (1987). *Psychotherapeutic strategies in the latency years.* Northvale, New Jersey: Jason Aronson Inc.

Whitmont, E.C. (1969). *The symbolic quest: Basic concepts of analytical psychology.* New York: G.P. Putnam's Sons.

Yalom, I. (1983). *Inpatient group therapy.* New York: Basic Books.

5
The Wonder Box

> If you would like to hear a story please, please, say Rudolph the Red Nosed Reindeer. Do you know what Rudolph did? This is going to be a funny one. He turned into a chicken. There was magic in him. And then, guess what? The reindeer turned into different animals like wolves and then they turned into jellyfish. Guess what the snow turned into? The ocean. Then it turned into a beach. And then guess what? And then the Christmas trees and ornaments guess what they turned into? They turned into dolphins. You know what? Things are magic around here. And that's the end.

In the story above a world of wonderment existed in this child's ever-changing story symbols. As such, his dreamlike perception of reality influenced each fluctuating representation. The metaphorical meanings of these symbols may never be ascertained as his story was personal. Much like sandtray therapy, where miniatures represent a non-verbal flow of communication, the therapist did not interrupt his process to ask why the wolves turned into jellyfish or the ocean became a beach. His choices were brought forth from his being; his imagination; his reality in the moment. Were they random? Were they seated in his unconscious? Were they merely a function of his developmental age? An ego identification? Or simply a recitation of natural things in contrast to the glamourous decorations that surrounded him as the holidays approached.

As Bradway and McCoard (1999) stated, "Symbols enter the ego's awareness in many forms. They can appear in dreams or in fantasies. Symbols may appear as sudden inspirations or intuitions" (p. 33). As such, the sandtray environment and its figurines, when viewed in this fashion, represent our world, how we interpret situations, and how we understand ourselves as we walk surrounded by others.

There is nothing more experiential, covering each of the sensory preferences, as sandtray therapy. The tactile quality of the sand allows body communication; the figurines provide a visual and tangible stimulation; the post-tray inquiry provides the auditory experience; while the choice and physical placement of the figures, in the tray, is kinesthetic. In addition, each miniature when employed on a metaphorical level represents personal symbols whereby a client's inner expression and experience can proceed unimpeded.

Without Further Ado

One would be remiss to explore the world of the sandtray without reviewing some of the major pioneers who each, in their own way, have become synonymous with the method. It must be noted that I will not be outlining an exhaustive list of each innovator, who adapted and advanced Margaret Lowenfeld's original approach. They are, instead, the central figures that I have incorporated when applying interpretive methods to the assessment of sandtray worlds.

The originator of the World Technique, Margaret Lowenfeld, was inspired by H.G. Wells' book *War Games* (1911) where he described imaginative play with miniature soldiers, wood, and other objects while playing on the floor with his sons. In 1928, Lowenfeld began utilizing toy miniatures and other miscellaneous items which she initially characterized as *The Wonder Box*. By 1929, she would eventually introduce two trays of sand and through its continued implementation the children in her clinic began referring to the trays as *The World* (Turner, 2005; Mitchell & Friedman, 1994).

Lowenfeld attributed specific qualities to the tray, from its size, to the blue interior coloring reminiscent of the sky and water, as the children in her clinic worked with the medium coarseness of the sand (Mitchell & Friedman, 1994). Additionally, the cabinet that held the miniatures was described as a "multi-drawered design (instead of open shelves or other display arrangement) . . . because she believed that the child should not be overwhelmed with numerous miniatures displayed on open shelves" (Mitchell & Friedman, 1994, p. 11).

Figure 5.1 is a picture of my first sandtray cabinet. A combination of closed and open shelving allowed clients to explore in much the same manner as they explore the creations they fashion in the tray. "With choices spanning the full range of life and fantasy, the selection of a figure, or of combinations of figures, is always a unique and remarkable event" (Turner, 2005, p. 155).

Over the years, Lowenfeld would perfect the World Technique which permitted the children to compose, discover, and express themselves without censure. Though she offered a two-step introduction to the tray, it is her final statement, simplistic in its complexity, "Make a picture in the tray" (Mitchell & Friedman, 1994) which I incorporate into my work.

As such, my preferred method for introducing the tray is to stand next to the client and while presenting the technique, I feel the sand, moving it around to reveal the blue underneath and say, "Choose as many of the miniatures as you

Figure 5.1 My First Sandtray Cabinet

please and make a picture in the tray." After smoothing out the sand, I retreat behind and to the side, to sit on a stool, which allows me to be elevated and out of the peripheral vision of the client, so that I may record their creations. I do not ask questions or communicate with the client while they are working; this permits their non-verbal expression to continue without interruption.

While the tray is being created there are certain aspects that should be evaluated. Mitchell & Friedman (1994) outlined five main considerations based on sandplay literature: how the tray is created, the content, developmental perspectives, the verbalizations or story, and the therapist's visceral response to the tray. The first consideration focuses on the manner in which the client approaches the tray. It is important that the mental health professional observe the totality of the interaction; from the client's engagement level, to the pace of their work from choosing the miniatures to how they are placed into the tray. Where they stand while working can easily be overlooked as an essential consideration; just because the client places themselves on one side of the tray, as they position the miniatures, does not mean that this should be considered the "front" of the tray. I have always placed the tray on a rolling wood base so that it can easily be maneuvered around the room. In this way, if a client points out that the front of a tray is not where they are standing; it can simply be turned in order to view it while inquiring about the "story."

As an example, Figure 5.2 was created by an adolescent female. The therapist's feeling response, another of the five considerations, is of significance because it is not a reasoned sensation, but instead intuitive and spontaneous. When reviewing Figure 5.2, what is your visceral reaction to these two trays? What catches your eye first? Which tray feels mores immediate? Foreboding? What is the client trying to convey? The tray on the left was the client's final construction which she described as strength and protection from hidden dangers.

Two other considerations focus on content and the developmental perspectives of the tray. Developmentally, when reviewing a series of trays, one looks both at each session's tray as well as the sequences for balance or disorganization, empty trays or fluid creations, repetitious characters coupled with ongoing themes, and movement or stationary indicators. Content focuses on the combination of factors already discussed and the symbolic communication inherent in the act of making the final production. Metaphorically speaking, the act of creating the tray is the language while the miniatures are the words. What is the collective and personal symbolism in Figure 5.2? What was the client saying as her sandtray production unfolded?

The last consideration, verbalization, revolves around the story. Often in the act of creating the tray a client will spontaneously talk; at times this will be to address the therapist and at other times just to speak aloud as they drop into process. At the end of each tray, after determining which side is the front, I will stand beside the client and ask, "Tell me what's going on?" Dependent upon the client I may also ask, "If you could zoom in on any portion of the tray where would that be?" Metaphorically, this allows me to ascertain what they would like to get closer to. Conversely, I sometimes ask, "Which part of the tray would you move away from?" Generally, I do not prompt the client to explore their tray any further than those questions. Within this post-tray discussion an ongoing story metaphor, based on a

Figure 5.2 Which Way Is Front?

series of trays, can be ascertained by way of the symbolic content, themes, emotional reactions, and resolution.

Often the post-tray discussion and subsequent documentation issues can prove daunting when the mental health professional is left to assess the sandtray productions. However, between the post-tray discussion and recording the completed trays the question arises of how to break down the final creation. Viewed as a symbol for communication the tray can be interpreted as a personal metaphor; thus, it is imperative that the tray remains assembled until the client has left the session. "Clients can actually provide themselves symbolically with what they need in the sandtray" (Bradway & McCoard, 1999, p. 35). As such, one never wants to deconstruct a tray, a representation of the self, while the client is observing. Additionally, it is imperative that the therapist replace the figurines on the same shelf, in the same place, after each session, thus providing the client with consistency, structure, and safety.

While the client is working in the sand the therapist should be recording the miniatures that were chosen, returned, superfluous comments, and the manner in which the figurines were positioned. Table 5.1 illustrates eight central questions that I record both during and after each session.

Table 5.1 Sandtray Documentation

1 What was the order of miniatures chosen? (list them)
2 How were the miniatures selected (thoughtfully, quickly, haphazardly, and/or indecisively)?
3 How was the sandtray created (carefully, quickly, static, in motion)?
4 While creating the tray:

   What was the client's primary focus?
   Were any items put back? Which ones?
   Were any items raised above the others?

5 Organization of the tray (empty, full, chaotic, balanced, aggressive)?

   Any groupings of miniatures present?

6 Was a story told?

   Theme:
   Resolution:
   Main Character:

7 Were any items omitted in the discussion?
8 What was the therapist's initial reaction?

   What was prominent?
   What did the client "zoom in" on?
   What did the client "zoom out" from?

In all, Lowenfeld viewed the World Technique as a vehicle for communication and expression, an approach which permitted the release of conflicts without the need for interpretation, a technique which provided a balance between environmental and inner realities, whereby healing comes through an increased sense of self (Mitchell & Friedman, 1994).

A second innovator, Charlotte Buhler adapted Margaret Lowenfeld's work as a diagnostic test for cognitive and developmental process and called her method the *World Test* which is performed without sand (Buhler, 1951a; Turner, 2005). Though initially supportive, by 1950, Lowenfeld was not a devotee of Buhler's diagnostic test due to its emphasis on pathology rather than a technique applied within the therapeutic relationship.

For the purposes of this chapter, we will review Buhler's research which standardized the tray constructions along developmental norms. However, rather than a diagnostic tool, her findings will be incorporated as a way to provide clinical insight. Buhler (1951a, 1951b) divided her developmental indicators, or signs, into three main categories: *Aggressive World* signs, *Empty World* signs, and *Distorted World* signs.

Figure 5.3, viewed from above, typifies the *Aggressive World* with its overabundance of soldiers, encircling both aggressive animals and humans attempting to hold off an all-consuming assault with inadequate weaponry. The use of antagonistic soldiers tends to project individual aggression; while weapons can be viewed as a protective measure from external threats (Buhler, 1951a).

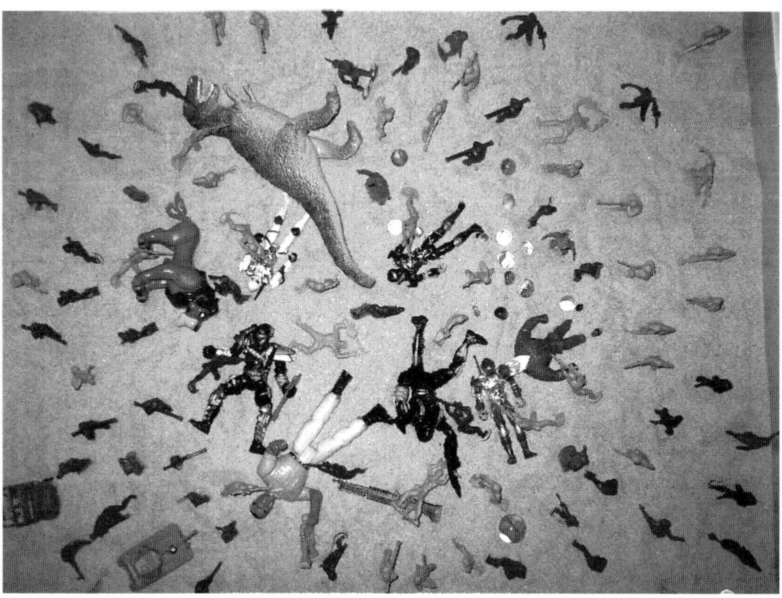

Figure 5.3 Aggressive Signs

In contrast, Figure 5.4 is an example of Buhler's *Empty World*. As the name implies, these trays generally contain a paucity of miniatures. However, it is important to keep in mind the age of the client as young children often create empty worlds (Buhler, 1951a). In Figure 5.4 the fantasy figure of a mermaid looks upon a desolate landscape while a hospital is placed in a far corner. It is important to note that, according to Buhler (1951a; 1951b), empty trays indicate emotional, not intellectual deficiency. In this example the feeling of loneliness, depression, and escapism are palpable.

Buhler's third sign, the *Distorted World*, has three subsets. In the first group, a closed world contains numerous walled areas. Metaphorically speaking, these types of worlds could be said to fence people in and/or keep others out. This need for protection is shown in Figure 5.5 where an adolescent female composed not one but six separate fortifications. These barriers so apparent in her sand tray were also apparent in her interpersonal relationships with family, friends, and staff members where her excessive need for protection kept her isolated from others.

Figure 5.6 is an example of a *Distorted World* that Buhler (1951b) titled disorganized. Made by an adolescent male and his mother, in a family sandtray session, few words are needed to describe the chaotic and aggressive arrangements, confusion, disconnect, and overall pandemonium within this family system which is illustrated in the tray.

Figure 5.4 Empty World Signs

Figure 5.5 Distorted World/Closed

Figure 5.6 Distorted World/Disorganized

The last sample is a rigid, *Distorted World* whereby schematic arrangements are over-exaggerated in their symmetry (Buhler, 1951a). In Figure 5.7, rows of soldiers line up and face one another. Metaphorically speaking, this type of compulsive rigidity is an attempt to organize and systematize the environment; a way to manage anxiety through meticulousness, and manage excessive fears.

Another central figure, Dora Kalff (2003), began her analytic training with Carl Jung where symbolic dream work, with adults, was the principal emphasis. However, as Jung (1971) stated:

> Symbols . . . do not occur solely in dreams. They appear in all kinds of psychic manifestations. There are symbolic thoughts and feelings, symbolic acts and situations. It often seems that even inanimate objects co-operate with the unconscious in the arrangement of symbolic patterns.
>
> (Jung, 1971, p. 55)

It would be within sandplay therapy that Dora Kalff would begin her work with children and ultimately study with Margaret Lowenfeld, in 1956, after attending a lecture, years before, on the World Technique (Turner 2005). As a trained Jungian analyst, Kalff's process of working in the tray differed in many ways to Lowenfeld's as she applied her early training incorporating both archetypal patterns and Eastern Philosophy to the interpretation of the tray. Kalff also distinguished herself by working not only with children but also with adults, additionally she utilized the trays only in individual sessions, and most notably she never interpreted the tray to the client. Kalff (2003) has stated, "It is not necessary to communicate the therapist's insights to the child in words, as we are

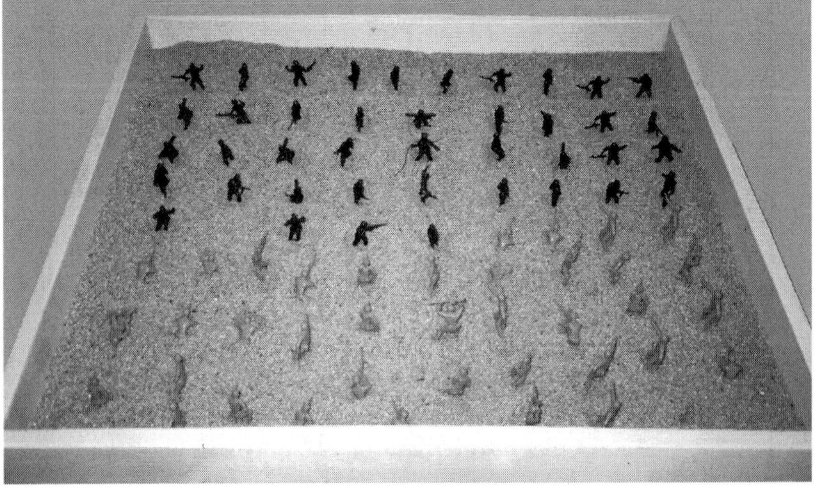

Figure 5.7 Distorted World/Rigid

dealing with the experience of the symbol in the free and sheltered space" (p. 9). As such, Kalff "practiced 'delayed interpretation' and witnessing of the creation of a sandplay with no verbal interventions" (Steinhardt, 2012, p.181).

Whether one calls it delayed interpretation or delayed review (Bradway & McCoard, 1999) the incorporation of a post-sandtray discussion, after numerous years have passed, can be an exceedingly powerful moment. Time and distance allows for knowledge and insights that are rarely revealed with the tray's initial creation.

The following sandtray was completed over 14 years ago by a married woman with a small toddler. When she was first presented with Figure 5.8 she exclaimed, "Oh my gosh, look at that, I didn't remember the water in the middle. That is fascinating to me. That circle of life with the shells is amazing." Throughout her review she would return to this center section to discuss the turtles and other sundry items found in the middle of her tray. Allowing her the time and space to work her way through her memories she added:

> I remembered the upper left with the pavilion and the horses. I do remember that. And the bottom left corner. I didn't remember the bottom right with the butterfly. The water was the biggest surprise. I love the turtles in the water it's what I really like about it. I put motion into this, there is motion there. Water is life and the turtle going into the water. I like the center, and the turtles with the center of life being around it.

Figure 5.8 The Circle of Life

Figure 5.9 It's Almost Like a Metamorphosis

As she made a conscious effort to recall the order in which she had made the tray she settled on the lower right corner where themes of "comfort" and comments about "idyllic" scenes were repeated. Beginning with Figure 5.9, she stated:

> I remember the tunnel and in a weird way it is almost like a metamorphosis, it is very naturey, its very comforting the wood and the tunnel with the butterfly and the trees and the relaxing kitty. The concept of nature is very comforting. It is a very idyllic setting. It's very comforting and the geode in the background it is very calming to me when I look at that scene.

Continuing her way counter-clockwise around the tray she began to talk mostly to herself as she outlined the miniatures placed in the rear right corner of Figure 5.10:

> There is the castle with a tree and a pathway and the pavilion with the horses, very cute. I love the colored rocks leading up to the castle and two kitties and some pretty little rocks and a kangaroo. Is that a kangaroo? It's a very ideal home situation. A sense of home, comfort and security. It makes me feel happy to look at that. It feels like a good home.

Figure 5.10 Is That a Kangaroo?

Even though 14 years had elapsed, I recalled that what struck me in the initial tray was the addition of a kangaroo to the rear right and the "fussy" horse located in the rear left corner. As the client noticed, yet skipped over the kangaroo, I silently wondered if she would eventually return to the figurine. I did not have to wait long.

As she moved to the left rear of the tray (Figure 5.11) she again noted the idyllic qualities:

> It's like a little sitting area with trees, it's interesting I put two rocks there, that yellow one that didn't match, I don't know why I did that? That's not like me. I don't know why I did that? I love the two horses. Again, it's an ideal setting. The two horses to me that's a couple, they're mates, that's how I see it.

She then zoomed in on the two horses by switching to the next slide. Moving on to Figure 5.12, she became growingly contemplative:

> Well again I see them as a couple, I mean (*here she paused for a very long time*) looking at the long shot all I saw was two horses, but when I see up

> close its like what's that one horse doing? I don't know if I cared when I picked out the horses, so I might not have cared, but now that I look at this it's like the one on the right is the female and she's going to the guy "what the hell are you doing?" Look at the look on her face. "What are you doing there, guy? You obviously have a problem of some kind". Which says a lot about my relationship at the time too.

At the time of this sandtray, the client was having relationship issues with her husband. Wondering how everything fitted together she would fleetingly discuss her interpersonal issues but never with any true sense of trouble or separation.

While she pondered Figure 5.12, I recalled her previous comment about the yellow rock "that didn't match." Before I could ask her a question she added:

> Something I didn't say, but I was thinking it so now I am going to go back to it. The corner with the castle (*Figure 5.10*) it's like the kitty and dog and then I said what is that other animal back there and again it's like the odd man out . . . . I'm obviously the kitty. What is that creature doing in there? Why would there be a kangaroo in the backyard? Isn't that freaky? Why would I do that? And that's a weird looking kangaroo too . . . . The kitty and the doggie are so cute and in the backyard is this kangaroo. Something isn't right there.

Figure 5.11 I Love the Two Horses

Figure 5.12 What's That One Horse Doing?

After her perceptive comments increasing amounts of insights came forth as she moved to the front left of the tray. As Jung (1971) has stated, "When we attempt to understand symbols, we are not only confronted with the symbol itself, but we are brought up against the wholeness of the symbol-producing individual" (p. 92).

By Figure 5.13, she initially returned to reciting content, "A single horse and a nest and cute little birds with the nest." But soon she noticed that select objects seemed out of place.

> Just one horse? Huh? It's funny the horse from the previous scene is by itself and watching the cute little bird family. Looking at it now this horse wanted a family and the horse is thinking this is the kind of life I could have had . . . . It's all idyllic. The horse is watching this scene. Wishing . . . . Or more observing . . . . It's definitely seeing a perfect working family situation . . . . The horse looks lonely. Not lonely, the horse is just single. The horse is single.

After another long pause she quietly looked over Figure 5.8 as she attempted to put her insights into order; an order that would organize her experience.

> When I first started looking at this, I thought well I'm going to start in the lower right hand corner and go counter-clockwise but now looking I see all these different phases of my life. The center. That is life itself for me. The front right (*Figure 5.9*) is how I always viewed my life. By myself.

> Maybe what happened is I started in the bottom right corner and went clockwise (*Figure 5.13*) and I became the horse, the one horse looking at the bird family and I said 'I want that', then I found the lame horse (*Figure 5.12*), okay I have my family in my castle (*Figure 5.10*) but I have this weird creature in the backyard.

Her final comment was simply this, "It's almost like a mandala with the decorations around it."

An astute observation as the four corners of her sandtray could be said to represent, as Edinger has stated, "Quaternity, mandala images emerge in times of psychic turmoil and convey a sense of stability and rest. The image of the fourfold nature of the psyche provides stabilizing orientation. It gives one a glimpse of static eternity" (as cited in Steinhardt, 2000, p. 139). Thus, this client's "mandala" sandtray, with her affinity for the center area, or her own innate center, Jung's the self, metaphorically embodied a soothing effect to the tumult and confusion that surrounded her and was subsequently symbolized in each of her sandtray corners.

If we return to Dora Kalff she interpreted her client's trays from a Jungian perspective. To differentiate her work from Margaret Lowenfeld's, and with her blessing, she termed her technique Sandplay Therapy. Bradway and McCoard (1999) define the differences as follows, "In 'sandtray' work *expression* is

Figure 5.13 Just One Horse?

emphasized, whereas in 'sandplay' therapy *experience* is emphasized" (p. 37). Thus, with its influence based on Carl Jung's work, sandplay therapy places its focus on collective and individual archetypes, personal metaphors, symbolism, and the innate power of the individual psyche to find wholeness.

In contrast to Charlotte Buhler's developmental indicators, Kalff incorporated Erich Neumann's theory of ego-development. She believed, "the details and composition of the pictures give the therapist an indication of the path to follow in the treatment" (Kalff, 2003, p. 9). As such, she purported that Neumann's three stages corresponded to the phases of children's play and consequently revealed progression and/or delays.

In combination with Charlotte Buhler's indicators, I incorporate the stages developed by Jungian analysts John Allan and Pat Berry. Allan and Berry (1987) define their process stages as, "chaos, struggle (organized fighting), and resolution in recurring stages" (Mitchell & Friedman, 1994, p. 103). Consequently, initial disarray eventually transforms to order which subsequently corresponds with developmental progression.

By way of example, Figures 5.14 to 5.18 were created by a 12-year-old adopted female who exhibited aggression, regressed social skills, and poorly developed inner controls. Her biological mother was diagnosed with Schizophrenia, and her biological father had a history of Bipolar disorder. Additionally, in the year prior to the undertaking of sandtray therapy she had undergone multiple

Figure 5.14 Chaos

losses and separations from her home, her friends, her adopted family, and was subsequently placed in residential programming.

As outlined by Allan and Berry, Figure 5.14 offers an example of the first stage, titled *chaos*. These trays are generally typified by the absence of order, animal, plant, and human life. In this tray order was forsaken for baskets filled with disparate figurines coupled with objects scattered about the sand in disarray.

Figures 5.15, 5.16, and 5.17 illustrate three different trays that each typify the increasing phases found within the *struggle* stage. In Figure 5.15, "good and bad" horses fight to protect a home where shifting alliances create mistrust and fear.

Successive trays (Figure 5.16) have figurines battling for supremacy. The tray becomes increasingly crowded as cars, foliage, and creatures both magical and evil make an appearance. Dangers arise from all sides as the horses continue to fight toward a resolution.

By Figure 5.17 the struggle for supremacy turns toward organization and balance as the castle fortress of earlier sandtrays is replaced with appealing dwellings, winding walkways, and alliances representing fidelity and protection. The horses not only escape carnage but emerge symbolically in a safer world even though danger still existed. The final stage, *resolution*, can be seen in Figure 5.18 where a prominent bridge "carried all of the friends home" while the systematized creation of the tray provided layers of protection from the possibility of future harm.

Figure 5.15 Struggle Toward Annihilation

Figure 5.16 Struggle for Supremacy

Figure 5.17 Struggle Within Organization

Figure 5.18 Resolution

Over the course of a year, this pre-teen was able to express past wounds and present fears through the use of the miniatures; something she had found difficult to explore utilizing traditional talk therapy. The symbols of herself emerged though her eventual incorporation and use of an enchanted unicorn, which looks over the crossing in Figure 5.18, and the staid horses now united in friendship. Both of these symbols served to protect her need to believe in the magic of a childlike world while remaining grounded in the reality of encroaching maturity. As Kalff (2003) has stated, "Symbols speak for the inner, energy-laden pictures of the innate potentials of the human being which, when they are manifested, continue to influence the development of man" (p. 6).

Eloquent Silence

In the example above, the sandtray pictures when viewed as a tool for healing gave each of the client's *worlds* its own "voice" where she was free to display anger, loneliness, and vulnerability into one expression where safety was developed at her own pace and in her own time. Healing is a personal endeavor, it is not cognitive nor is it intellectual, it is an unconscious process that arises from our psyche. Bradway and McCoard (1999) have stated, "In sandplay we can just let the connections 'work:' we can let them remain at an unconscious level where they can do their work. Early interpretation, or consciously making connections . . . can rob the patient" (p. 29).

If we return to Figure 5.7, this young adult was preoccupied with factors related to right and wrong, his anxiety overpowered each decision and therefore he would become immobilized. An assessment using Buhler's stages yielded a distorted and rigid world as the last tray, in a series of five sessions, where inflexibility eventually produced a purpose. In this way Buhler's assessment, taken as a single tray, would have left the viewer seeing this client's creation from a rigid world. However, Allan and Berry's stages identify a struggle toward a resolution.

The first tray, Figure 5.19, is replete with items of both protection and destruction populated with venomous snakes, spiders, and beetles while a single, armored, and embattled figure, looks over the struggle. The client created this tray in complete silence. When the tray was finished he chose not to answer any questions and merely left the room with a slight nod. In much the same manner, Figure 5.20 and 5.21 were created in silence with many of his first tray figurines making repeat appearances. However, the poisonous animals by Figure 5.20 had been replaced with an army seemingly fending off external threats in a progressively organized struggle. In Figure 5.21 these unseen foes make an appearance and give the impression of facing off as the struggle escalates into a battle for control.

In Figure 5.22, his fourth session, the client spoke throughout the creation of his entire sandtray. He discussed a multiplicity of topics; his impending

Figure 5.19 A Beleaguered Struggle

Figure 5.20 A Struggle Against Unseen Foes

discharge from treatment services, his fear of re-offending once he returned to the community, numerous loss issues as he explored his grief of having family members in jail, and the fear that there was little social support ready for him upon his discharge. With each vulnerability expressed he placed yet

Figure 5.21 A Struggle Where the Foes Appear

Figure 5.22 A Poisonous Struggle

another bug methodically into the sand in rows moving ever outward, once again, toward external threats.

By the fifth session, returning to Figure 5.7, both sides of the tray contain soldiers clearly delineated with no hidden adversaries lurking in the shadows. This tray could be viewed as a rigid and distorted world, but also as the beginning stages of a resolution to the fears which this young man carried with him silently. Again, throughout the session, he spoke but this time it was to explore attending community college in order to attain his General Education Diploma (GED), accepting living arrangements in a community that allowed him distance from his family while still maintaining a connection. It was this decision, to return to a community that held little advancement for him or to remain outside it to move toward reaching his personal potential, that plagued him. As he stepped back from his tray and I asked him to tell me what was going on he stated, "Let them win this battle." In that singular statement he expressed acceptance while also releasing the constant need to fight and overpower. Ultimately, it would be this young man who would win by changing his reactions toward his family system and false beliefs of destruction and disappointment toward healthier more industrious choices.

If we review this case from a humanistic perspective this young adult arrived at his own insight, based on inner conflicts, and found his locus of control rather than following that of his family or even the providers in his residential placement. By choosing, or even expressing a desire in attaining his GED he took control of his life while expressing his feelings in the here and now.

The following series of sandtrays illustrates another male struggling with issues related to loss and protection. This teenaged male harbored excessive anger against a father that abandoned the family when he was five and a mother who was negligent due to struggles with substance abuse until the client turned 11 years old. Throughout his early years he spent most of his energy protecting his younger siblings and is resentful that his mother, who is in recovery, now wishes to claim the parental role. In all, this young man views limits, no matter how insignificant, with disdain while rebellion allows him to separate from his family without self-condemnation.

Figure 5.23 is replete with innocent wants, parental desires, and unmet needs. The basic family, unavailable to this young man is expressed by way of a closed world. In the rear left corner, a cow, often a maternal symbol, is encircled by wild mustangs and wandering farm animals. The middle and far right of the tray show numerous idyllic family scenes while parents and protective figures watch canoes as they set out on a languid journey, with a father holding a small child on his shoulders for better viewing. A magical sandcastle stands in the center of the tray dividing the front and back surrounded by two soldiers at the ready. Lastly, the front fenced in area encompasses a baby's crib flanked by a series of police vehicles. In its totality, the entire sandtray has all figures facing backward. Nothing gazes upon the viewer leaving one feeling secluded and withdrawn.

His next tray, Figure 5.24, retains the same themes of protection and separation. However, this tray, clearly broken into three defined worlds, much like

Figure 5.23 A Desire for Family

the dyad of parents united with a child, speaks of power and struggle. Unlike Figure 5.23 he spoke much of the self in Figure 5.24 where he makes an appearance in every subdivision. Additionally, the figurine of the man with a child on his shoulders returns in the largest section as they watch a lion square off with a dinosaur.

> When we see trays with dinosaurs and other ancient creatures, we must similarly consider the role of history in the client's wounding. It could be that the psyche is addressing a wound that occurred very early in the client's development.
>
> (Turner, 2005, p. 158)

The client stated that the lion, a symbol of courage and strength, was him while he is being encouraged to fight a dinosaur, emblematic of primitive power. In the far rear of the tray the black jet, at the front of the formation, was identified as the client in a show of physical strength and control. The largest section in the sandtray is a mixture of primal symbols and those of soldiers (the identified symbol for himself); while a war rages in the far right corner he describes fighting over land to protect what belongs to those who are weaker, perhaps representative of a personal struggle to survive. In all, passions abound as each division exhibits power, struggle, and a desire for control.

Fighting becomes prominent in Figure 5.25 as the three subdivisions now become two. The client spoke about a struggle between the two distinct sides while the left hand side, where the client is located, is going to lose as they are

Figure 5.24 The Self as Powerful

Figure 5.25 Three Becomes Two

killing their own men. Gone are any signs of idyllic family moments instead these are replaced with a battle for supremacy which is out of reach as the self turns upon itself.

Figure 5.26 Two Becomes One

By his last tray, Figure 5.26, the fence disappears and a barrier is created with soldiers and foliage. Monsters make an appearance and are attacking the army which is protecting the client who is now on the winning side. He stated he was the man in the car because he had the "most powerful weapon." In the role of hero, the client begins to combine power with success rather than just the embodiment of struggle.

When considering the interpretation of the tray many factors can be reflected upon: a common theme such as power, aggression and dependency needs, the integration of boundaries that did not require fences such as Gestalt therapy, or a humanistic approach which allows the client to find their own potential for self-actualization. One could also incorporate the psychosocial stages of Erikson whereby in Figure 5.23 motherly and nurturing figurines are united with despair representative of the trust versus mistrust stage. Figure 5.24 symbolizes the desire for autonomy contrasted with shame and doubt where uncertainty proliferates. By Figure 5.25, feelings of guilt are supplanted with initiative as the client, even though in a struggle against deception, has direction and purpose. The last sandtray, Figure 5.26, represents feelings of industry and competence triumphing over inferior feelings.

Lastly, viewed through a Jungian lens, the psychic experience of people could be described by way of archetypal images which shape the personality and where actualization begets harmony and wholeness. In Figure 5.23 the client's anima, the feminine component of his psyche, remained unconscious and primitive thus the incorporation of the feminine symbols of the cow and water. By Figure 5.24, the lion, with its ferocious and animalistic passion takes precedence, in conjunction with fighter jets and soldiers all symbols of strength, masculinity, and power; each identifying with Jung's shadow archetype, as it relates to survival, and its capacity to be accepted into the structure of the client's ego.

"For Jung, the lion, in its wild state, is broadly speaking an index of latent passions; it may also take the form of a sign indicating the danger of being devoured by the unconscious" (Cirlot, 1983, p. 190). The shadow with its precarious, and precocious, nature appears in Figure 5.25 as well. Here threats and vulnerabilities abound where the community of fighters, all possessing dark and threatening attributes, begin their deception, where supports turn upon one another and hostile reactions ensue. It should be noted that betrayal, in the sense of archetypal imagery, is not as foreboding as one may believe, for within a betrayal is a lesson to be learned not just about external duplicity (as in Figure 5.25) but how we can unconsciously damage and harm ourselves.

Wholeness, as Jung explored it, passes through phases until the individual reaches maturity and self-realization. This is a laborious process and in no way does Figure 5.26 signify achievement. However, what it does indicate are the beginning steps toward an understanding of the power of the self. Moving beyond his repressed shadow's struggle this client's awareness begins to increase as he recognizes that he can moderate the direction of his life instead of living within his ongoing battles represented by mistrust, doubt, and destruction. As Jung has stated:

> So to the self is our life's goal, for it is the completest expression of that fateful combination we call individuality, the full flowering not only of the single individual, but of the group, in which each adds his portion to the whole.
>
> (Jung, 2014, p. 240)

Actions Speak Louder than Words

In the prior examples, the individual psyche came to life through Kalff, Lowenfeld, and Buhler's unique interpretative methods. In this section the communal psyche of group sandtray therapy will be explored. Whether one refers to the work of Theresa Kestly's (2001) school based sandtray "friendship" groups or to De Domenico's (1999) dynamic Worldplay sessions using a singular tray, within a group, group sandtray promotes joint, rather than parallel play, enhances the dynamics of the relationship by highlighting conflicts, negotiation, and resolution, and promotes a group identity over an individual identity whereby shared needs can be acted out as the relationship takes precedence. Like individual sandtray therapy, the group sandtray will also show: chaos, aggression, barriers, disorganization, balance, and/or rigidity.

If we explore the phases of group sandtray therapy as identified by G. S. De Domenico (1999) what we find are distinct levels of cooperation. Initially, members are assessing how they fit in, what is safe to share, and the norms of the group. Members tend to work in their own area until group cohesion develops whereby contact with other members grows and metaphorically connections develop through the use of bridges, thoroughfares, and vehicles for transport. In the end, cooperation and self-expression becomes prominent.

Figure 5.27 is an example of an elongated tray made specifically for these sandtray therapy sessions. This 4-foot-long tray allowed numerous clients to work in tandem while giving the provider an opportunity to create physical boundaries, which increases structure and manages interactions, until client to client cooperation could be achieved.

This group of eight adolescent males worked in a non-directed manner and as such their play was spontaneous as the group silently determined the theme. Beginning with the back of the tray (Figure 5.27), a chaotic struggle is apparent where a dinosaur consumes an army which in turn fights for dominance but instead finds annihilation. The middle of the tray sees a castle being overrun with a well-placed bridge located behind the struggle. The front of the tray, far more organized though still destructive, illustrates figurines which are buried, ineffective methods of escape are in abundance, and a client's self-drawn line separates two-thirds of the tray from the front.

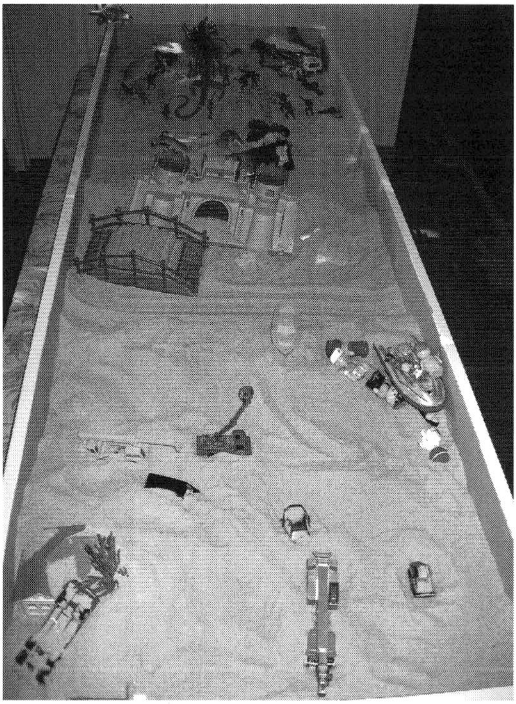

Figure 5.27 Group Sandtray Therapy

During the course of Figure 5.27, some of the members moved about the tray's length while others, mainly in the front of the tray, would glance but never joined. Subsequent trays continued in this vein until roughly four weeks later a gradual organization of the tray ensued as egocentric thinking declined and the clients exhibited collaborative thoughts where reciprocity and self-expression became customary. After each tray a discussion followed where the group processed issues surrounding who led the experience? Who followed? What was enjoyable and what they would change if they so wanted?

Figure 5.28 is an example of this group's tray as they moved from their first, where safety and cohesion were being born, to the group's fifth tray which correlates with De Domenico's (1999) working stage. At this point the clients had developed a sense of boundaries and rules, and themes began to emerge around security through strength (power) and wisdom (knowledge to secure goals). Additionally, as they built their tray they collectively talked about the added items in a more systematic manner. Though aggressive scenes with hidden dangers persisted into the succeeding sessions vulnerabilities were met with rescue from outside authority sources and their storytelling took on themes of protection and freedom as the member-to-member interaction exhibited more empathy and not just catharsis.

Figure 5.28 A Story of Rescue

If we return to Chapter 1 of this book, R. R. Dies (1992, 1996) outlined five distinct stages of group development, with adolescents, which are similar to De Domenico's (1999) though Dies' life cycle was not referencing sandtray therapy. In Figures 5.27 and 5.28, as the group convened they each monitored one another as a way to identify behavioral expectations from the group as well as the provider. Dies' (1996) group life cycle calls this the *initial relatedness* stage. As the group's differences emerged and awareness increased he titled this *testing of limits*. De Domenico's (1999) working stage correlates to Dies' (1996) resolving authority figures, and once cooperation and communication increased this was titled, *work on the self*. Lastly, as healthy stories emerged, in conjunction with cooperation, Dies (1996) called this *moving on*.

In much the same way, Yalom's (1983) therapeutic, or curative factors, "provide a useful construct in that they span the entire field of the group therapies. These factors represent the core of therapy" (p. 40). Whether one focuses on directed or non-directed group work treatment concerns related to collaboration, envy, and hostility as well as problems with interpersonal relatedness need to be addressed and corrected. Thus, hope, universality, and cognitive reflection are foundations for social development.

The following Figures 5.29 to 5.33 illustrate an example of semi-directed group sandtray therapy sessions, with four female teenagers, who lived together in residential programming and as such had long standing relationships. In directed play the therapist assigns themes or topics which reflect the needs of the group. However, in these sessions I knew the clients required boundaries lest their propensity for adolescent grandiosity overwhelm the standard size tray. Therefore, I decided to give them some ground rules to follow but overall allowed them to create in a non-directed manner. The limit I asked each of the girls to follow was that using the sandtray miniatures they were to make an environment and choose no more than two characters per person.

For the purposes of the following trays I will call the four individuals Lori, Dana, Anna, and Mary. Lori was the most infantile and regressive of the four having suffered a severe brain injury, in latency age, due to a traumatic fall down a flight of stairs. Dana was a controlling and defiant youth having been exposed to sexual and physical abuse coupled with neglect. Anna, the unspoken leader, had a diagnosis of depression, and Mary exhibited significant obsessive-compulsive traits with predominate shame and doubt tendencies.

As Bradway and McCoard (1999) stated, "Children are apt to make a 'movie' rather than a single scene . . . . Adults may change the position of some of the objects, but they seldom act out a drama" (p. 54). Even though these clients were adolescents, and not children, their creations were not static as their play immediately commenced once the environment was created and Anna in an authoritive tone announced, "Now we play," to Mary's hesitant question, "What are we doing?"

Figure 5.29's composed and well-organized tray repudiates what was truly occurring. The creation of the environment was a relatively cooperative effort. Very little discussion occurred until Mary's question emerged; at that point each of the girls took on their customary roles. From Lori's attempts at organizing the play by stating aloud her intentions, to Dana's protestations to "follow the rules" and form a caring and cohesive family based on the chosen figurines, these four girls exhibited moments of inclusion to moments of possessive and territorial fears.

Viewing Figure 5.29 through Dies' (1992, 1996) group life cycle this tray typified the first stage of initial relatedness whereby the group members steeplechased for domination with factions forming and attempting to be formed.

The following week's tray (Figure 5.30) had the four constructing the environment with far more discussion and planning yet as play began there was a noticeable sense that each of the clients required a heightened amount of acceptance and validation from one another. Early in the process, Anna decided she would choose a malevolent character (Dracula) and the clients promptly began to weave a communal story with a plethora of good figurines being added to counteract the evil, even a hospital with a gurney made an appearance to control the dangers that bordered both the tray as well as

Figure 5.29 Organization Belies Interpersonal Difficulties

Figure 5.30 A Story of Strife Unfolds

the imaginative play. Dana and Mary got into an argument over "rules" and were largely attempting to ignore Anna's contributions. In time, Dana and Lori eventually hid the characters from the evil of Dracula as alliances moved to and fro and Mary employed her logical inclinations explaining to the others how to kill Dracula with a stake through the heart. Just before the session ended, Lori regressed into play crying and exclaimed, "I'm scared" which was met by Dana's instructions to "go to bed . . . don't worry your Dad's got a knife" which was Dana's manner of providing protection and security.

Anna's symbolic choice of Dracula, imbalance versus stability, dark and depressive qualities versus light and joyful reactions, is an interesting one given the metaphorical connotations when one interprets good versus evil as an emotional dilemma leaving us with choices and the subsequent consequences that can lead to pandemonium and struggle over order.

When one compares the second sandtray to the third it is easy to see the regressive qualities found within Figure 5.31. In this session Dana immediately took control from Anna and stated, "I got a good idea. This is the safe side and this is the outside." Unfortunately, by the end of the tray there was no safe "side" despite Dana's hoped-for familial closeness and Lori's receptive agreement of "fairness" coupled with the other peers' shared agreement. As the story unfolded cars and school buses appeared to transport the children and parents. By the end of the "day" neighbors visited, on the opposite side of the tray, for

Figure 5.31 Finding a Safe Side

a cordial meal. As kindness flourished Dana became increasingly aggressive and controlling as her "play" significantly impacted the theme of the story. The school bus was driven manically by Dana into other homes and characters as she knocked down the miniatures; she was chastised by her peers, quickly apologized for her destructive actions, but ended with throwing the self-proclaimed drunken father figure face down while shouting, "This is your last chance, if you do that again I am divorcing you." After the group climbs in a car to take a ride she states to Lori, "Your Dad is gone. There is only me to watch you now."

Incorporating De Domenico's (1999) theory, Figure 5.30 could be likened to his second stage as members worked in their own areas of the tray without encroaching upon the other peers' figurines. By Figure 5.31 the tray was verbally split into "sides" though more to organize the story than it was to exclude cooperation. Notably, Dana's personal history of abuse and neglect clearly took forefront within the group's story. During the early course of the creation Dana interjected infrequently until the mid-point where she could no longer restrain her own projections onto the miniatures. Noticing Lori's distress, at the father being tossed callously aside, she attempts to calm her apprehension with what was, in her experience, a caring retort. In all, Dana's actions, born out of early traumas, typified her difficulties with attachment. As such, these types of interactions directed inward manifested themselves as depression and outward as aggressive responses which were both protective and hostile in nature, a dichotomy which had structured her exchanges in all areas of her life.

Figure 5.32 Themes of a Cohesive Family Life Appear

Despite the fact that in Figure 5.32 the miniatures are toppled over, due to play rather than hostility, themes of family life continued to prevail as the group's story now revealed cohesion with less fragmented and egocentric relations. Homeyer and Sweeney (2016) when reviewing De Domenico's theory stated, "Stage 3 is marked by individuals selecting miniature figures, but then discussing the emerging story. As the story unfolds, more figures are added to increase cohesiveness in the story. This is what is typically labeled as the working stage" (p. 83).

From the very start, Mary, whose history was to be plagued with doubt and shame, rebuffed Dana's attempts to provide her with a figurine and unequivocally decided that the tray required a doctor "in case anybody gets hurt," and as she proceeded she added, "This is our world. Our streets." Lori replied, at the first sign of Dana's attempt to begin a play argument, "We're sharing . . . . These are the ones I'm sharing. These are for my babies and your babies. Everyone share the stuff okay?" This assertive statement, made by the group's most passive member, was met with the ultimate in compliance as Anna, who engendered a stabilizing presence, interjected in her familiar confident yet apathetic manner while facing Dana, "That's a good idea." For the remainder of the session a story unfolded based on friendship and fidelity for the "children" of the varied families with feelings being accepted and honored in both the tray as well as with one another.

Figure 5.33 Cohesion Drifts Further Away

For the last tray, Figure 5.33, only three of the four peers were present. Due to this, Anna's absence created an imbalance in the group dynamic and as such Dana reverted to controlling her peers by choosing their miniatures, deciding on the theme of the tray, and chastising others at every opportunity. Dana's interactions could be viewed as an attempt to return the relationships to homeostasis, a stability that was both familiar and comforting. Her attempts at control were met by periods of self-assertion from Lori and Mary and though they utilized their combined strength without the catalyst of Anna's presence it did not hold much sway.

Even though the collaborative improvement of Figure 5.32 did not endure through Figure 5.33 the unconscious communication patterns in this session symbolized each member's family issues. "Without exception, patients enter group therapy with the history of a highly unsatisfactory experience in their first and most important group—the primary family" (Yalom, 1985, p. 15).

Grasp the Nettle

One of the advantages of group sandtray therapy is that rigid and fixed roles can be projected onto the miniatures thus allowing the mental health professional to not only assess the shifting alliances but also assist the clients as they experiment with new interactional behaviors through the metaphor of play. When sandtray therapy is utilized, in conjunction with families, the process of joining can be a powerful promoter of change. If one looks at Bowen's theory, which postulates that families are centered on two opposing forces one which can bind a family in togetherness that can also be immobilizing and those that seek differentiation and individuality (Nichols, 1984), the entire system requires relational improvement.

If we return to Figure 5.6, this adolescent male, and his mother, created an early series of trays which personified their chaotic relationship as well as their disconnect. This family had been intact up until three months before they began therapy sessions. The mother, having been diagnosed with Bipolar disorder as a young adult, also suffered from anxiety attacks and recent divorce proceedings had accentuated her emotional need for closeness to her son. The father, who was disengaged from the family both emotionally and physically, had a history of Attention Deficit disorder, while the son's impaired social skills and infantile reactions distanced him on an emotional level.

The goals of therapy focused first on reducing the emotional reactivity and improving communication skills between mother and son. Throughout the first session (Figure 5.34), the son, whom I will call Tony, took the lead while his mother, whom I will call Mary, requested permission from Tony prior to adding any miniatures. As he added his items he spoke aloud while talking about "death bridges" and being "dropped" from excessive heights. In response, Mary added ladders and other escape routes while stating, "I was rescuing the poor people that Tony was killing. I like happy endings."

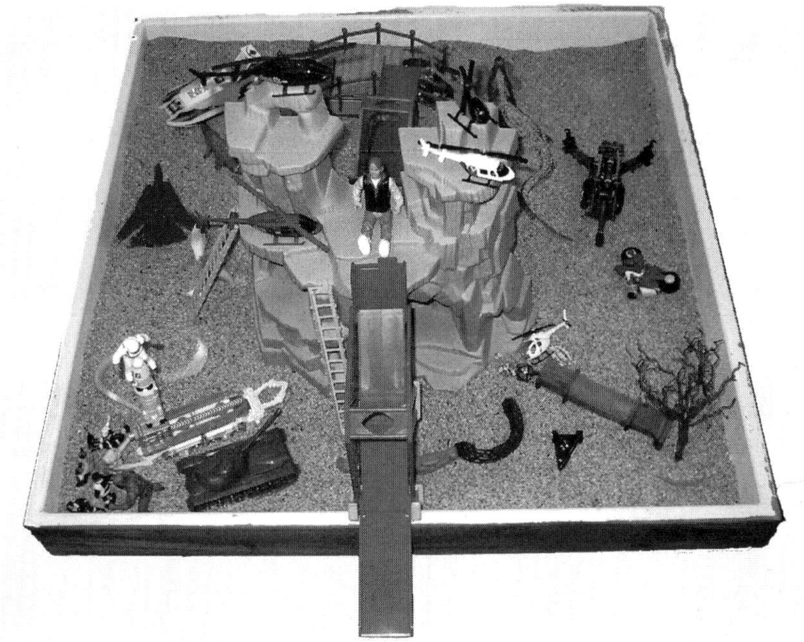

Figure 5.34 I Was Rescuing the Poor People

After each session ended I met privately with the mother as a way to develop a closer relationship, normalize and reduce the emotional reactivity, and emphasize improved communication skills with Tony. By educating her on key Bowenian concepts of triangles, emotional fusion, and differentiation I hoped to lower her anxiety and promote understanding for future sandtrays.

In their second session, Figure 5.35, Mary took the lead while leaving the center of the tray entirely for Tony, metaphorically making him the center of the world. With every comment by Mary about how "it shouldn't be violent . . . I like things pretty, happy, and natural" Tony would pile on increased amounts of combatants and dangers.

In our post-session discussion issues related to fusion were explored and triggers identified within Mary to determine alternative responses to Tony's anger. The most important discussion centered on Mary's over-involvement with Tony which had created a triangle leaving the father on the outside. Thus, forming a stronger, healthier connection with Tony was paramount. In all, once the father had left the system, Tony's hostility and rage had grown into a two-person, unstable system and Figure 5.36 illustrated this far better than any amount of words ever could.

Take a moment and look at Figure 5.36. What is your visceral reaction to this tray? What is your assumption of what occurred and why? The emotional turmoil

Figure 5.35 I Like Things Pretty, Happy, and Natural

Figure 5.36 Emotional Turmoil

that is so palpable was foisted upon Mary as she worked, for the first time, autonomously from Tony. As she placed her focus on differentiation she spent her time dodging the constant piling on of Tony's figurines. For his part Tony's anxiety flooded both himself and the boundaries of the tray. With each frustrating and hostile response Mary's decreased anxiety and ultimate acceptance of his reactions, began a person-to-person relationship rather than one that was fused.

At the end of the session, in consultation with Mary, the discussion focused on her feelings of apprehension while Tony metaphorically expressed his hostility and frustration. In all, emphasis was placed on Mary making changes within herself rather than attempting to change Tony.

If you return to Figure 5.6, the disorganization and chaos found in that sandtray replicates the same emotional turmoil of Figure 5.36. In Figure 5.6, Tony continued his attempts to resolve his own anxiety by increasing his mother's. However, in the midst of the aggressive reactions, Mary (figure 5.36) added a small fish inside a shark's mouth and exclaimed with pride to Tony, "How do you like that! I did something vicious?"

In the upper left hand corner of Figure 5.37 is a close up of Mary's symbolic example of de-triangulation which allows individuals to respond without simply reacting and in the process redirects conflict and anxiety. With more stability in the mother/son relationship subsequent trays revealed less chaotic anxiety and increased connection.

Figure 5.37 I Did Something Vicious

Figure 5.38 Crawly Bugs Inhabit the Home

By the fifth session (Figure 5.38) people, families, and the interior of a home make an appearance. Gone are the threatening alligators, snakes, heaps of miniatures, and overall disorder of the prior sandtrays. In Figure 5.38 an organized tray saw mother and son working collaboratively to add "crawly" bugs in the front left. Here Mary and Tony took turns adding a variety of caterpillars and approaching spiders around a sleeping male figure. Though one could look at the choice of caterpillars and spiders as destructive; these symbols could also be viewed as encouraging signs. Caterpillars "sometimes a symbol of lowliness and ugliness" (Chiron, 1986, p. 33) also give birth to new life; spiders suggest the possibility that one could be caught in a web of aggressiveness or conversely, the power of the spider's web could be viewed as life itself (Cirlot, 1983). To the left of this scene is a family sitting in a living room with a screaming figure center stage. Was this a symbol by and for Tony? A silent scream that expressed his rage and fears non-verbally? Were roles within the family beginning to shift so that individual needs, flaws, and longings could be attended to without concomitant angst? If so, all of this could point toward improved emotional interactions and growing differentiation for both parties.

By Figure 5.39 Mary and Tony continued to work collaboratively. However, as Mary added a pirate ship in the back left corner Tony reverted to dropping throngs of medieval men inside and around her ship. Mary's response was an amused, "Oh. Why'd you do that silly?" To which Tony picked up each of the fallen men and stated, "Does it look better now?"

Figure 5.39 Why'd You Do That Silly?

The following two trays (Figure 5.40 and 5.41) were created, for the most part, independently of Tony. When mother and son entered the session, Mary did just as she had for the prior six weeks and went to the cabinet to begin collecting miniatures. Yet, Tony who was busy assembling track soon realized its entirety would not fit into the tray; he then completed the session working on the floor with the remainder of the train track.

Figure 5.40, Mary's first autonomous sandtray, is replete with nearly every dolphin miniature in the sandtray cabinets, as well as other sea animals, with an imposing fortress situated in the rear of the sandtray. As one looks at the symbolic significance of the dolphin, "its peaceful personality becomes obvious. There seems to be no conflict with other sea creatures, nor humans. In this regard Dolphin can be regarded as a diplomat who builds cooperative bridges between humankind and nature" (King, 2017). As such, it could be said that each of Mary's communal symbols pointed toward her developmental desire to move toward functional patterns of communication, interaction, and reduced emotional activity.

In the last session, Figure 5.41, Tony returned immediately to the train tracks except this time he worked in the tray before retreating to the floor. The train track motif, a journey, or feeling that you are on the right "track" was not what one would say transpired in Tony's addition to the tray. Here, disconnected and partially buried track is cut off from any assured destination.

Figure 5.40 A Proliferation of Dolphins

Figure 5.41 It's Okay That You Work Separately

For her part, Mary did not attempt to pull Tony into the tray and instead when Tony moved to the floor she stated, "It's okay that you work separately."

Ultimately, her acceptance of his budding individuality allowed the structure to change, roles to realign, and thus the behavioral problems which had maintained the family's emotional tension was given permission to move beyond the confines of interdependency. From the initial stages of this family's tray where fusion and anxiety governed to the last tray where each member worked together, yet independently, an unstable system learned to convey their anger safely and without reproach.

And So to Bed

Throughout this chapter, whether individually, in group, or through the lens of the family, sandtray therapy gave expression to spontaneous, nonverbal, imaginative, and metaphorical communication; an unconscious process where healing originated through increased control to counter anxiety, empowerment to counter rebuff, and safety by means of the therapeutic relationship which invited detachment into the light of day. Thus, when a therapist observes a sandtray's creation they are also viewing the intrapsychic life of the people themselves.

As Bradway and McCoard (1999) outlined:

> Sandplay therapists bring different expectations or "set" to sandplay, depending on which professional affiliation they come from. Social Workers and Marriage, Family and Child Counselors have been trained to pay close attention to the details of family inter-relationships and to have the freedom to interview collaterals, both family members and teachers. And sometimes they look at sandplay pictures as another way of clarifying their understanding of those family inter-relationships.
>
> (Bradway and McCoard, 1999, p. 28)

Consequently, when incorporating theoretical constructs into sandtray therapy sessions the inter-relationship between client and professional cannot be separated when seeking wholeness. Whether one is working with children, adolescents, adults, families, or groups; whether one interprets utilizing Jungian symbolism, humanistic processes, family systems modalities, or developmental stage theories, the physical creation of the tray, in the here and now, allows the therapist to see through the eyes of the client while enabling growth and awareness which is so necessary for self-actualization. The identification and exploration of a personal metaphor provides an enriched experience for the client through the incorporation of their natural resources.

Individual therapy is a personal endeavor, one where healing is not found intellectually but instead unconsciously; one that connects behavior to inner feelings. Cognition and social development are improved through self-expression and cooperation. Beyond individual sandtray, group sandtray can be incorporated to promote insight and empathy, cooperation, relationship building, and group identity skills. As Yalom (1985) outlined, group therapy is often a recapitulation of the client's family and therefore points toward unresolved family of origin attachments which over time tether the client to rigid and dysfunctional relationships. As Bradway and McCoard (1999) have stated, "Clients can actually provide themselves symbolically with what they need in the sandtray, whether it be food, a caring mother, or energy to combat a hostile figure" (p. 35).

In the end, sandtray therapy allows free expression to long standing emotional issues allowing the client to seek their own solutions, in their own time, in their own way. As stated in the beginning of this chapter, with sandtray, things truly are magic around here.

References

Allan, J & Berry, P. (1987). Sandplay. *Elementary School Guidance and Counseling, 21* (4): 300–306.

Bradway, K., & McCoard, B. (1999). *Sandplay: Silent workshop of the psyche.* New York: Routledge.

Buhler, C. (1951a). The world test: A projective technique. *Journal of Child Psychiatry, 2* (1), p. 4–23.

Buhler, C. (1951b). The world test: Manual of directions. *Journal of Child Psychiatry, 2* (2), p. 69–81.

Chiron Publications (1986). *The herder dictionary of symbols: Symbols from art, archaeology, mythology, literature, and religion.* Wilmette, Illinois.

Cirlot, J.E. (1983). *A dictionary of symbols* (2nd ed., J. Sage, Trans.). New York: Philosophical Library.

De Domenico, G.S. (1999). Group sandtray-worldplay: New dimensions in sandplay therapy. In Sweeney, D.S. & Homeyer, L.E. (Eds.). The handbook of group play therapy: *How to do it, how it works, whom it's best for* (pp. 215–233).

Dies, R.R. (1992). Models of group psychotherapy: Sifting through the confusion. *International Journal of Group Psychotherapy, 42* (1), 1–17.

Dies, R.R. (1996). The unfolding of adolescent groups: A five-phase model of development. In P. Kymissis & D.A. Halperin (Eds.), Group therapy with children and adolescents (pp. 35–53). Washington, DC: American Psychiatric Press.

Homeyer, L.E., & Sweeney, D.S. (2016). *Sandtray therapy: A practical manual* (3rd ed.). New York: Routledge.

Jung, C.G., (1971) Man *and his symbols.* New York: Doubleday.

Jung, C.G., (2014). *The collected works of C.G. Jung: Complete digital edition.* New Jersey: Princeton University Press.

Kalff, M. (2003). *Sandplay: A psychotherapeutic approach to the psyche.* Cloverdale, CA: Temenos Press, (Original work published 1980).

Kestly, T. (2001). Group sandplay in elementary schools. In Drewer, A.A., & Carey, L.J. (Eds.). *School based play therapy* (pp. 329–349). Hoboken, N.J.: John Wiley & Sons.

King, B. (2017). Retrieved from https://whatismyspiritanimal.com/spirit-totem-power-animal-meanings/mammals/dolphin-symbolism-meaning/

Mitchell, R.R., & Friedman, H.S. (1994). *Sandplay: Past, present and future.* New York: Routledge.

Nichols, M. (1984). *Family therapy: Concepts and methods.* New York: Gardner Press, Inc.

Steinhardt, L. (2000). *Foundation and form in Jungian sandplay: An art therapy approach.* London: Jessica Kingsley Publishers.

Steinhardt, L. (2012). *On becoming a Jungian sandplay therapist: The healing spirit of sandplay in nature and in therapy.* London: Jessica Kingsley Publishers.
Turner, B., (2005). *The handbook of sandplay therapy.* California: Temenos Press.
Wells, H.G., (1911). *Floor games.* London: Frank Palmer.
Yalom, I. (1983). *Inpatient group therapy.* New York: Basic Books.
Yalom, I. (1985). *The theory and practice of group psychotherapy* (3rd ed.). New York: Basic Books.

III
From Start to Finish

6
The Art of Anger Management

> Once upon a time there was a snail named Francis. And Francis moved very, very slowly. While she moved, at times her thoughts were long and involved and complicated. Francis didn't have a mouth and so she had no way to communicate. So all she could do was think, and think, and think. One day Francis was walking slowly across a path filled with danger. On either side of her were two islands. She looked to her left and she looked to her right and she had no idea which way she should go. So she decided to let the wind blow her anywhere that the wind felt like blowing her. When a big gust of wind came it blew her to "lonely island." Once Francis landed on "lonely island," she could see no one because it was surrounded with hundreds and hundreds and thousands of gallons of water. She was not better off. So she sat on "lonely island" and thought her thoughts like a blob.

The Snail Named Francis was created in an individual session by an insecure and negativistic adolescent female by means of the Scribble Drawing Game developed by Donald Winnicott (1968). This scribble story could not have represented her feelings of helplessness any better if it had been written strictly with that goal in mind. Winnicott purposefully fashioned this intervention as an unstructured interaction between therapist and client, which in Figure 6.1 I have subsequently modified. These six drawings were completed in turn with the first person making a scribble (in this case myself, the therapist), then the client created an original picture from the scribble and gave it a title. The second image was created inversely (client scribbled, therapist completed and titled) and so on and so forth until all six images were finished. After the sixth drawing Winnicott would focus on the themes, as after each titling the client and therapist would discuss the image. However, in this modified version the client generated a story based on the titles. By incorporating a story after all the drawings were completed, feelings of shame, fear, and doubt were able to find spontaneous expression while remaining in metaphor.

Figure 6.1 The Scribble Drawing

Metaphoric communication, in the group setting, is just as prevalent as it is in individual work. However, group therapy can be far more complicated. Instead of looking into the eyes of one, you peer into the depths of many. And each participant brings with them their experiences, their family traumata, their personal stories bound within the past, present, and future; individual identities that crowd the room and can easily overwhelm the process.

A national survey of art therapists (Patterson, Debate, Anju, Waller & Crawford, 2011) found that the majority of art therapists preferred a non-directive approach when working with the severely mentally ill. However, as with any group therapy experience, varying opinions prevail and it is my belief that a directive style is advantageous and it is in the following two guidebooks that such a methodology is undertaken. Each of these theme-centered groups relate directly to the needs of the members by centering on both supportive discussion and relational healing. Fundamentally, a structured art therapy group can provide both the opportunity to learn cooperation, as well as deal with emotional issues through collaboration with others. Found within each carefully chosen directive is an exchange which provides direction and connectedness, as each participant begins their journey from autonomy to interdependence. In the resultant group connection, self-exploration as well as communication becomes overriding. Placed end-to-end, communication is more than what we say; it is not merely a search for the self, but a search for each person's place within their immediate environment.

At Your Fingertips

To that end, *The Art of Anger Management* is a guidebook designed for mental health professionals who wish to incorporate the techniques of art therapy with clients who have exhibited anger management difficulties. Though written with the group therapy client in mind, the directives (interventions) can easily be modified for treatment with individuals. Whether your client is an adolescent or adult, whether they function at a low or high level, the following guidebook will assist with the expression, management, and understanding of anger and consequent feelings. As such, the directives can be used singularly or as a complete treatment technique.

Table 6.1 outlines the Table of Contents for the guidebook, *The Art of Anger Management*, and provides a choice of skills to accommodate both short-term therapies (from 8 to 12 weeks) or long-term groups (more than 40 weeks) at the therapist's discretion.

The therapist should complete the directives from Table 6.1, in the order outlined, as each directive is designed to slowly build and link upon the preceding skill. However, it is not necessary to complete each skill within each content area.

Before we review the two guidebooks it is important that a framework be established; one of the first things that the mental health professional should do is to create a folder (preferably no smaller than 12" × 14" and no larger than 18" × 20") for each group member. This helps to keep the artwork both safe and organized. Though not specifically outlined within the Table of Contents, it is helpful for the mental health professional to incorporate physical relaxation techniques, such as mindfulness exercises, which provide a mind-body balance. Relaxation techniques can take the form of deep breathing, acknowledgment of items that are in the immediate area, yoga, or simple stretching. The goals of such exercises are to focus the group members and reinforce the principles of stress management before each group session. Also, many of the directives, especially within the middle to late stage of therapy, may require more than one session to complete. Therefore, if you are working with a time constraint, please keep this in mind.

Another issue to be aware of, in the group art therapy hour, is the incorporation of client pictographs which often serve to distance members from

Table 6.1 The Art of Anger Management Table of Contents

What is Anger?

Skill 1: Violence: 1
Skill 2: Violence: 2
Skill 3: This Just Burns Me Up
Skill 4: My Week
Skill 5: When Anger Hurts
Skill 6: In My Past
Skill 7: How I Express Anger
Skill 8: I Statements

Anger is a Valid Emotion

Skill 9: How My ____ Looked
Skill 10: Advantages and Disadvantages
Skill 11: My Band-Aids
Skill 12: My Story
Skill 13: Living with Anger
Skill 14: Mask Making

Anger is a Choice

Skill 15: Change
Skill 16: What Comes Next?
Skill 17: Taking Responsibility
Skill 18: Controlling Your Anger

Judgments and Blame

Skill 19: In Their Shoes
Skill 20: When I Say No
Skill 21: But I Expect
Skill 22: It's So Big
Skill 23: Face to Face
Skill 24: Pass to the Left

Oh, My Aching Back

Skill 25: Close Your Eyes and Relax
Skill 26: Pick a Feeling
Skill 27: Physical Warning Signs
Skill 28: My Body

Me and My Provocations

Skill 29: Focus Your Response
Skill 30: How Annoying
Skill 31: Finding a Direction
Skill 32: Taking Action

Identify the Problem

Skill 33: Through Their Eyes
Skill 34: Needs and Wants
Skill 35: Things I Can Do
Skill 36: The Real Problem

Communicating Expectations

Skill 37: I Expect
Skill 38: Pick a Word
Skill 39: What I Said
Skill 40: Where I Stand

How I Feel

Skill 41: You Never _____
Skill 42: From the Past
Skill 43: I Am Still Hurting
Skill 44: Around and Around We Go

Healthy, Wealthy and Wise

Skill 45: I Expect
Skill 46: I Can Handle It
Skill 47: I Can Cope
Skill 48: Where I Stand

the experience. If you recall in Chapter 1, Edith Kramer (1971) outlined five main classifications, with the fourth categorization labeled "pictographs." She defined these drawings as "pictorial communications which replace or supplement words" (p. 54). This primitive style of drawing is frequently utilized as a graphic means to counter client angst. When a mental health professional notices this type of picture, not only should they acknowledge its propensity to reduce anxiety, but also recognize that it is best to deal with this form of self-protective emotional release in a proactive manner. If left unbridled, the remainder of the group members may have an inclination to follow suit and the process of self-exploration, due to fears of judgment, could come to a halt. In these instances, deviating from the outlined Table of Contents for the guidebooks may be necessary. Oftentimes a simple modification of the directive coupled with a media change will suffice. If you notice, after the first session, that group members are using pictographs as a defensive reaction, the mental health professional can repeat the same directive and adapt it by using clay instead of drawing. An example from Table 6.1 would be taking the first Skill and asking the members to recall the prior week's art and state, "Now I would like you to use the clay provided and create what comes to mind when you hear the word violence." Frequently, this type of intervention, combined with a post-drawing exploration, allows members to feel safe and emotionally process, without the fear of judgment.

Lastly, you will notice the use of a collage box in some of the directives. A collage box is made up of pre-cut and torn images from magazines. I have found that the use of pre-cut images deters the clients from reading the magazine articles and allows them to focus on the task at hand. Finally, it is my recommendation that the pictures chosen are not of famous or easily recognizable people as this impedes an unconscious projection which ultimately can encumber expression.

To conclude, I am providing an example from my practice, when I was just beginning as an intern, which will hopefully offer you my most important message for the group experience. The following directive, "*draw all the things you think about, but never say,*" was given to a group of adult males who resided in a State Hospital. As the group settled into the directive (Figure 6.2), working off one extremely large piece of butcher paper, a client approached who generally refused to attend groups. This gentleman, whom I will call John, had many diagnoses, one of which was echolalia, and he generally spent his days roaming the halls repeating conversations. While the group staked out their "territory" on the paper, John followed suit and copiously wrote only my statements made to the other members (bottom right of Figure 6.2). Much of it says, "*Ah, pretty, how nice, yeah, who wrote hands off? I'm sorry what did I ask? I know you are.*" It also offered phrases like, "*I don't hear you, you must speak up . . . a lot of you got to speak up . . . clean up the materials, yeah? I didn't see him coming back.*" As the group neared completion I said things like, "*Can we talk about what everyone drew? Yeah? Excuse you?*" As the group began the process illumination, my comments explored feelings, "*That's how you feel about it or about him? Someone added color to your drawing? How does that feel? Yeah? Is that your airplane?*"

Figure 6.2 Thank You John

What this group offered me was a permanent example of not only how nervous I was in groups but also how much talking I did which decreased the member-to-member interaction. After seeing, and more importantly reading, the final group creation I realized clearly how the thought of silence was anxiety-producing *for me*. It was I who required a running dialogue to ease my own sense of anxiety. In much the same manner as egocentric speech, I was repeating words for the pleasure and security of talking, with little thought of talking to anyone. This did not serve the others. And in many ways was no different from John's pathological echolalia. In the end, I am proud to say that, more than 20 years later, I have never forgotten this experience. I now embrace silence and when I do speak, it is not out of insecurity, but out of a need to promote interaction, group cohesiveness, and most importantly illuminate the process. Thank you, John.

The Art of Anger Management Guidebook

The first section, titled *What is Anger?* provides clients with an opportunity to understand their individual anger reactions while establishing the need for anger management skills. Thus, the first two skills begin by helping the group members define the types of violence in their environment, the reasons for violence, and the effects that violence has had upon them.

Skill 1: Violence 1

1) Discuss with the group members the types of violence that they see around them. Explore why people use violence (i.e., intimidation, blame, manipulation, physiological excitement, to cover emotions).
2) Write the word "violence" on a board or large sheet of butcher paper and cluster their responses around the word. Move on to 3 once the clients have verbally discussed the answers.
3) Provide each group member with one sheet of paper. Ask them to *"draw what you think of when you hear the word 'violence'."*
4) While discussing the drawings as a group, don't forget to explore all aspects of violence, the emotional side as well as the physical.

Figure 6.3 illustrates the varied responses that this directive elicits. The left side of Figure 6.3 was completed by a regressed male who has depicted a person whose head has just exploded; while the right side shows the intensity of emotion that the client ultimately chose to resolve by tearing the final drawing in half immediately upon finishing.

Skill 2: Violence 2

1) Review the drawings from Skill 1.
2) Discuss with the group how violence affects the environment and those who live there.
3) Provide each group member with one sheet of paper.
4) Ask them to *"draw how violence impacts you."*
5) Discuss the drawings as a group.

Figure 6.3 Violence

Skill 3: This Just Burns Me Up

1) Provide each group member with one sheet of paper.
2) Instruct them on one side to *"draw what makes you angry."* Once this is completed, move on to 3.
3) On the opposite side, *"draw what you do with your anger."*
4) While discussing the drawings, focus on utilizing "I" statements. It is important to pay close attention to the discussions from Skills 1 and 2. As such, note any similarities around what makes the group members angry. Additionally, do not forget to normalize anger as a universal feeling with positive benefits, as well as negative consequences.

Skill 3 begins the process of letting another person know, in a constructive manner, about their feelings of anger. The left side of Figure 6.4 demonstrates an adolescent male's dichotomy of feeling, whereby a mad and happy sun share a fiery alliance. As an active participant in the group it is important that when looking at a client's drawing, your visceral feeling is also taken into account. What do you think when you look at this illustration of anger? Whatever your response, do not hesitate to incorporate this into the process illumination during the group feedback. The second image (right side) is a depiction of a local skate park where this same client goes to relieve his anger kinesthetically. Notice the haphazard lines within the park crossing over and upon itself, illustrating the restlessness of perpetual motion.

Skill 4: My Week

1) Review the concept of violence as both physical and emotional. Review the past week with the group and their feelings of anger.
2) Provide each group member with one sheet of paper. Instruct them to draw a line down the center of the page.

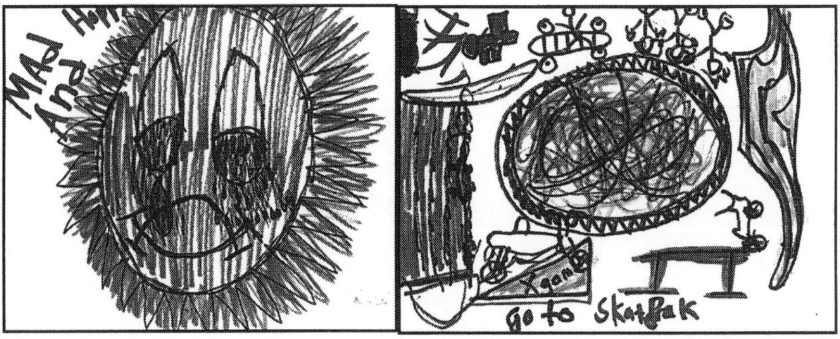

Figure 6.4 This Just Burns Me up

3) On one side have them *"draw how you handled your anger positively in the past week."* Once this is completed move on to 4.
4) On the opposite side have them *"draw how you handled your anger negatively in the past week."*
5) While discussing the drawings focus on utilizing "I" statements.

Many people choose to symbolize their anger by drawing a volcano as a metaphor for sudden outbursts of emotion. Figure 6.5 offers two examples of this powerful metaphor whereby a young adult stated, "a volcano has all that pressure and it has to erupt right away; that's me." His second drawing (right side) was also of a volcano, as it lay dormant. In the discussion phase he was so resolute in his opinion that calm prevailed, he added the words, "happy and calm" just above the volcano opening. However, the heavily drawn, wavy lines indicate the pressure that lay just below the surface. Due to this, it was important to discuss both the internal as well as external pressures during the process illumination.

Skill 5: When Anger Hurts

1) Have the group begin by thinking of a time in their past when they were visibly angry at another person. Ask them to use "I" statements and explain it briefly to the group.
2) Provide each group member with three sheets of paper.
3) On the first sheet have them *"draw what the harm was to the other person mentally."* Once they have completed that drawing, give them a second sheet of paper.
4) On the second sheet have them *"draw how you think the victim's family and friends felt."* Provide them with the third sheet.
5) On the third sheet have them *"draw how you felt."*
6) Discuss the drawings as a group.

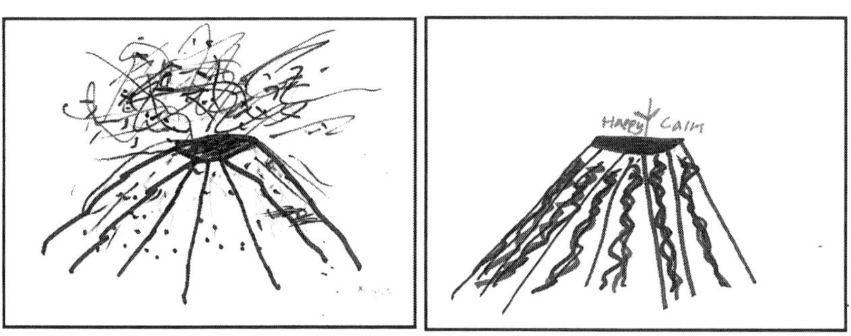

Figure 6.5 My Week

Skill 6: In My Past

1) Discuss with the group members how the past often sets the stage for the present. Have the members explore what they believe you mean by this statement.
2) Provide each group member with one sheet of paper. Instruct them to draw a line down the center of the page.
3) On one side have them *"draw how you have dealt with anger in the past."* Once this is completed move to 4.
4) On the opposite side have them *"draw what you have lost because of your anger."*
5) Discuss the drawings as a group.

Past relationships take on an important role within every person's present interactions; they dictate whether these exchanges will be healing and can therefore support future relational conflicts or will instead focus upon the interactional frustrations of an external expectation counter to an often unspoken internal desire. Figure 6.6 personifies the isolation experienced due

Figure 6.6 I Lock Everyone Out

to aggressive outbursts where an adolescent male drew himself boxed-in and explained, "I lock everyone out. That's how I deal with my anger."

While another peer, in the same session (Figure 6.7), deals with his rage by choosing to "sit in my room and close my eyes and pretend I'm flying in the air." In the ensuing group discussion, these solutions, ever so similar in nature, allowed a member-to-member interaction where ineffective problem-solving was explored from a feelings perspective. It is at this juncture that the group members generally begin to notice the universality of their experiences.

Skill 7: How I Express Anger

1) Building upon the prior week's post-drawing inquiry, have the group members discuss what makes them angry and what they do with their anger. While they speak, encourage the use of "I" statements rather than "you" or "they" statements.
2) Provide each group member with one sheet of paper.
3) Ask them to *"draw a time when you were angry. Make certain to add the person you were angry with in the drawing."*
4) When this is complete, instruct them to *"write what you said in this situation. Below this write what you could have said using an 'I' statement."*
5) Discuss the drawings as a group. Remember to focus on "I" statements as outlined in 4 above. If a group member did not incorporate "I" statements, explore their drawing as a group and have the client receive support and assistance from the other members.

Figure 6.7 I Fly in the Air

Skill 8: "I" Statements

1) Provide the group members with the following incomplete sentences:

I hate it when . . .	I like it when . . .
I wish that . . .	I want . . .
If I could only . . .	I need someone to know . . .

2) As a group, have them choose two of the sentences. This is not an individual directive, but a structured member-to-member intervention where the group must not only negotiate but cooperate. Pay attention to how the group navigates this process.
3) Once the group has agreed on two sentences, give each member one sheet of paper. Instruct them to draw a line down the center of the page.
4) On one side have them illustrate the first sentence chosen.
5) On the opposite side have them illustrate the second sentence chosen.
6) Discuss the drawings as a group and explore how they felt while arriving at a group decision. Ask them whether they felt they communicated assertively, whether they asked for what they wanted or preferred to follow, and whether they felt heard or ignored. Would group members do anything differently if the directive was beginning again?

In the second and third sections, *Anger is a Valid Emotion* and *Anger is a Choice*, the guidebook turns toward the essential elements of anger; its advantages as well as its disadvantages. This polarization is an indispensable concept if one is to accept anger as a valid emotion which does not merely dictate destructive moods and reactions but can be harnessed to energize and therefore be managed.

Skill 9: How My ______ Looked

1) Discuss with the group members how anger is often a learned behavior which can be unlearned. Have the group provide ideas of where, in the past, they could have learned their anger reactions. As the discussion progresses, have them identify a family member who was often angry.
2) Provide each group member with one sheet of paper.
3) Instruct them to *"draw how your father or mother (or other significant person in the client's life) acted when they were angry."*
4) Discuss the completed drawings as a group. Focus on what the group members learned about anger, how they learned to express their feelings, and most importantly what they would like to change.

Skill 10: The Advantages and Disadvantages

1) Provide each group member with one sheet of paper. Instruct them to draw a line down the center of the page.
2) On one side have them *"draw the advantages to anger."* When this is completed, move to 3.
3) On the opposite side have them *"draw the disadvantages to anger."*
4) Discuss and compare the drawings as a group. Explore with the members how anger can be disruptive, protect our feelings of pride (rather than feeling anxious), can lead to aggressive acts, scare others in the environment, and can leave us feeling lost and alone. Balance out the discussion by considering how anger can energize, express tension, and can also be used as an internal signal to begin the coping process.

Skill 11: My Band-Aids

1) Discuss with the group members how anger's negative aspect often hides our present feelings of fear, loneliness, and anxiety. Ask them to recall a time in which this happened to them.
2) Provide each group member with one sheet of paper.
3) Recalling the discussion, ask them to *"draw a specific fear that has been covered up either in the past or presently."*
4) Discuss as a group how their feeling was covered, why they chose to cover it up, and what feelings they replace with their anger reactions.

Figure 6.8 was completed by two adult males. The left side illuminates a young adult's feelings surrounding the loss of his uncle, "who was the black sheep in

Figure 6.8 The Fear of Loss

the family just like me." He outlined his fear of abandonment and discussed how he honors his uncle by continuing criminal pursuits. Notice the three suns with varying expressions. The sun is often expressed as both a "heroic and fierce character" (Cirlot, 1983, p. 318). In contrast, the right side was completed by an elderly male, who during the process illumination began to cry as he spoke of multiple losses; that of a beloved pet, the present loss of his family members, and his own "healthy" attributes as his mental illness became prominent. He went on to outline that he covers up his feelings through isolation which is clearly depicted in this stark and empty drawing.

Skill 12: My Story

1) Refer to Skill 11 and how our anger often helps to protect our true feelings by covering them up.
2) Provide plasticine clay to the group and have them *"create your anger out of the clay. Give it a form, shape, body, head, anything that you can think of to express to the group what your anger looks like."* This skill could take multiple weeks to complete.
3) When the group members are done, have them share their creations.
4) After the process illumination, provide group members with art and craft materials (construction paper, tissue paper, cellophane, boxes, etc.) and explain to them, *"using any of the materials available, cover up your anger. Disguise it, bury it, and make certain it is no longer visible."*
5) Discuss the completed projects as a group. Discuss with the members if "covering" the anger has removed the expression. Ask the members what they feel will eventually happen to the anger. Process ways in which the group members feel they could express their anger without violence.

As a variation to Skill 12, Figure 6.9 demonstrates how to incorporate these directives in an individual session. Completed by a young adult over three meetings, the left side of Figure 6.9 shows a ball of black clay (which he ultimately stated represented a fist) encased in the tactile experience of clear cling wrap which he wound multiple times around the clay ball while stating that this embodied the tight and restricted "clothing" that others can see through. Lastly, toothpicks which he painted red, were thrust into the ball and defined as the pain of anger.

In the next session, deviating from the directive, he was asked to choose another feeling and he settled upon "anxious." The right side of Figure 6.9 shows a twisted figure that represented the knots of anxiety, which quickly changed to a flat "wave." He then added staples symbolizing being "stuck" and returned to a clothing metaphor of "sweat pants" and a "hoodie" that were baggy and epitomized a lack of care and wanting to hide like a fog that hung closely over the "figure," clouding what makes him happy. In all, this young

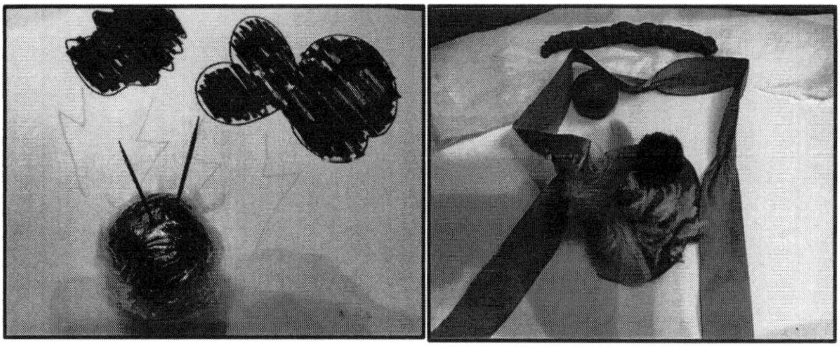

Figure 6.9 Anger and Anxiety

man's language was one of metaphors; as each feeling expression was created, a heightened awareness of the self began to take shape.

In the third session, before the client could be given the directive, he began expressing feelings of anger. Using this as an opportunity to segue into a post-drawing inquiry surrounding the natural propensity to "cover" feelings, the two creations were placed before the client and he was asked if he could "explain the connection between the two." With this he remained impassive. The therapist then chose to place the anger encased ball over the flattened symbol of anxiety. With this he became responsive. He shared that this was how his anger used to be, but that he could not recall having anxiety as a child. When asked to describe his experience with anxiety, he stated it was scary, confusing, and frustrating. Ultimately, he asked what to do with these feelings, and the therapist engaged him in a role play surrounding the expression of anxiety rather than oppressing the emotions.

In all, the power of this directive provides clients with a greater understanding in a language that is inherently their own. Offered new patterns of relating they are capable of exploring past conflicts rationally rather than emotionally.

Skill 13: Living with Anger

1) Begin the group by reviewing the cause and effect of violence and anger outbursts. Make a point to review Skill 9 and how the clients felt when they experienced a family member who raged.
2) Provide each group member with one sheet of paper.
3) Ask them to *"draw what it was like to live around an angry person,"* or *"draw what you imagine it would be like to live around an angry person."*
4) While discussing the drawings, make certain to explore issues related to living isolated from others as well as assertiveness skills (rather than aggressive reactions) to stop someone from taking advantage or being abusive (i.e., setting limits, verbal confrontation, end the relationship).

Figure 6.10 Weathering the Storm

Figure 6.10 requires few words to grasp the emotional stress of living in close proximity with someone who rages; a barrage of dangers approach from all angles, while the title "Weathering the Storm" bespeaks of the client's preference to suffer attacks rather than resolve relational conflicts.

Skill 14: Mask Making

1) Provide each group member with a pre-made papier maché mask or if this cannot be purchased or made, the use of a white lunch bag can be substituted.

2) Ask the members to create *"the face you present to new people you meet on the outside of the mask (or one side of the bag)."*

3) After this is competed, ask them to create *"the face you would like to present on the inside of the mask (or on the other side of the bag)."*

4) Explore each of the sides, making certain that the group members use "I" statements as well as assertive problem-solving.

Skill 15: Change

1) Challenge the group members to recall a situation, from within the last 72 hours, when they became angry or upset. Discuss how they dealt with the situation, whether it was with further aggression or mindfulness. Process the decisions that they made in the moment as well as consequences of their decisions.
2) Provide each group member with one sheet of paper. Ask them to draw a line down the center of the page.
3) Ask them to *"recall a recent event that you didn't handle well. On one side of your page draw the event."*
4) When this is complete, ask them to *"draw on the other side what you could have done differently."*
5) Discuss with the group the situations they illustrated making certain to explore not merely their thoughts, but also their feelings of control, stress, guilt, or shame. Begin to focus discussions on problem solving issues as well as negotiation and resolution.

During the post-drawing illumination, one young adult (Figure 6.11) expressed his tendency toward apathy as a solution for both of the directives. As he spoke,

Figure 6.11 Learning Assertiveness

he related his tendency to speak before thinking regardless of the consequences. His solution, as he explained to the group, would be to "hush." At this point the group was steered toward exploring assertive skills as problem-solving rather than withdrawal or passivity.

Skill 16: What Comes Next

1) Provide the group with your pre-made collage box. Make certain that the images in the box are of open-ended situations (i.e., people with expressive faces, either alone or with another person).
2) Have them take one sheet of paper and fold it in half. Ask them to *"choose one picture from the collage box and glue it onto one-half of the sheet of paper."*
3) On the other side of the paper, ask them to *"draw what action could follow on the other side of the page."*
4) Once this is done, have them fold the paper in half so only the collage image is showing.
5) Have each group member, one at a time, show the collage image to the other participants and allow them to say what they think might come next.
6) Reveal the group members' solutions/actions and discuss.

No matter how many times I utilize this directive, the images chosen and subsequent drawings tend to concentrate upon the client's formative years, mothers and fathers, sisters and brothers, all focused upon early attachment issues. As Grothe (2008) postulated, "We don't grow old in a vacuum, but in a web of relationships with others—and often with one very special person." (p. 228)

The left side of Figure 6.12 shows a collage picture of a child gloomily refusing to eat with the ensuing drawing showing the parental figure furiously scolding

Figure 6.12 Early Attachment Predominates

the child. In contrast, the right side of Figure 6.12 shows a child tugging for attention, as the woman looks on impassively and unreceptive. However, the resultant drawing shows a smiling figure lovingly bending over to greet the expectant child.

Both of these projections, though dissimilar, point toward a vital need to explore the unconscious process surrounding expectations. Thus, it is the mental health professional's responsibility to work toward process discussions and not merely remain on content issues; for it is the process, the feelings underneath, that propels therapy. Content discussions simply disguise and derail the therapeutic progress.

Skill 17: Taking Responsibility

1) Review Skill 16 and process whether any group members utilized mindfulness in their interactions since the last session.
2) Provide each group member with one sheet of paper.
3) Ask them to *"draw the person who you tend to be angry with the most."*
4) When this is complete, give them another sheet of paper and ask them to *"draw what you are afraid to acknowledge or insist on with this person."*
5) This is a very difficult next step to explore so it is important to provide enough time for the clients in the group to discuss their anger reactions and perhaps hesitancy to employ problem-solving.

Skill 18: Controlling Your Anger

1) Provide each group member with one sheet of paper. Section the paper into four by folding it twice.
2) Ask them to *"recall an angry incident that is recent."*
3) When this is complete, ask them to *"draw your emotions in the first square."*
4) Once this is completed, ask them to draw in subsequent squares *"your physical sensations, your frustrated needs, your response."*
5) Focus the discussion on what the clients perceived the other members' needs to be. What alternatives to anger they could have utilized?

This skill could take multiple weeks especially if the group is above eight. Functionally, the provider is asking each group member to complete four separate directives on one piece of paper. As such, time for the process illumination may be impacted. A solution to this issue is to break the skill into the first two directives in one week and the second two directives in the following week. This allows ample time to discuss each member's artwork without feeling rushed.

Figure 6.13 Anger and Its After Effects

Figure 6.13 characterizes an adult female whose response to the directive was to focus on the bags she drew under her eyes rather than the feelings behind her anger reactions (anxiety, worry, sadness). This drawing provides a natural bridge into the next two sections of *The Art of Anger Management Guidebook*. As such, *Judgments and Blame* and *Oh, My Aching Back*, turn toward understanding the thoughts that trigger anger reactions and the recognition of how our sensations, beliefs, and emotions communicate those reactions. In this way, the client can begin the process of learning how to hold painful thoughts and feelings in balanced awareness rather than over-identifying with them.

Skill 19: In Their Shoes

1) Have the group members retrieve their drawings from Skill 18. Referring to this anger incident, have them *"draw what you believe the other person wanted."*
2) This discussion may overlap with the post-drawing inquiry from Skill 18, but the mental health professional should concentrate on how the clients got their needs met, whether their methods were successful, and what fears, worries, or problems may have influenced the other person's responses. What fears, worries, or problems influenced the client's choices?

Skill 20: When I Say No

1) Provide each group member with one sheet of paper.
2) Ask them to *"draw your needs."*
3) Discuss as a group.
4) When this is complete, give them a second piece of paper and ask them to *"draw a time you had to say no to another person's needs."*
5) Explore in the post-drawing discussion why everyone's needs are equally important.

Skill 21: But I Expect . . .

1) Ask the group members if they have ever attempted to get another person to change because they wanted them to. Discuss the responses from both a content and a process perspective.
2) Provide each group member with one sheet of paper.
3) Ask them to *"draw a time where you used power and control over another person."*
4) Discuss as a group the feelings that this provoked on both sides of the relationship. Focus mainly on issues related to power and control. End the exploration by asking how the group members get their needs met presently.

This male (Figure 6.14) drew two images of power and control. The left side depicts him giving money to a friend which kept control over their relationship, while the right side shows him using violence when his needs were thwarted.

Figure 6.14 My Needs

Skill 22: It's So Big

1) Provide each group member with one sheet of paper.
2) Ask them to *"choose one marker and draw a picture that contains at least two people and one other object and/or thing."*
3) When this is complete, give each member an 8½" x 11" sheet of paper and have them fold it in half. Instruct them to cut a small (stress the word "small") square out of the center of the paper (at the fold) using scissors. This should make a frame.
4) Have them unfold the paper and move this "frame" around the drawing they just completed. When they find a detail they like, give them a second piece of paper and have them *"draw that detail as large as you can."*
5) Discuss both drawings as a group and ask the clients which drawing they prefer and why. Explore the differences between the two drawings. Ask the members to pretend both drawings were a "problem." Which one would be easier to handle? Why?

Skill 23: Face to Face

1) Discuss with group members how facial expressions reveal feelings.
2) Provide each group member with one sheet of paper.

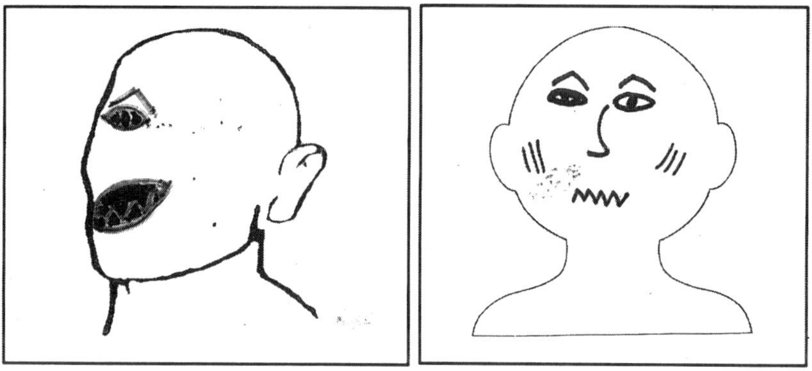

Figure 6.15 Face to Face

3) Ask them to *"draw how you look when you are fighting. Make your drawing as large as possible."* In some instances it may be best to provide the members with a pre-drawn outline of a head. These can be found on the internet.
4) When this is complete, give them another sheet of paper and ask them to *"draw how the person you are fighting with looks."*
5) On the back of the papers have each group member write down the experience of fighting from the viewpoint of a victimizer and a victim.
6) Discuss.

Figure 6.15 was completed by an adult female, using a pre-drawn head. She described the left side by stating, "I wasn't angry at the time. It didn't feel like much of an experience. But I'm surprised at the face I drew. Pretty monstrous." When exploring the right side of Figure 6.15, she said, "This was like a 3rd grade angry face. I wasn't angry on this one either. The experience was placid."

Skill 24: Pass to the Left

1) Offer each group member a piece of paper. Tell them *"you have three minutes to draw anything you like."*
2) When the three minutes are up, have each member pass the drawing they are working on to the member on their left. This can prove very uncomfortable for some clients and as such, they may not want to pass the drawing. If this occurs, allow the group to manage the situation on its own. In my experience the issue will resolve itself without the provider's "interference."
3) Every three minutes, continue to pass the drawings around until each member has his or her original drawing back.

4) Have the group members title the newly completed drawings.
5) Process the feelings that passing the drawings engendered.

Incorporating the pass-around directive often brings up a myriad of feelings as control gives way to cooperation. The power of this directive is unparalleled as "every step of the art production allows each individual to focus on the self—and on the interactions in and among the group members—and provides the impetus for the processing of the here-and-now interactions" (Moschini, 2004, p. 258).

Skill 25: Close Your Eyes and Relax

1) Ask the group members to close their eyes and relax. When they are ready instruct them to *"open your eyes and look at the markers. Let a color pick you and draw anything you want on the paper."*
2) Explore with the group the importance of recognizing and paying attention to how our body feels and reacts. As the group shares their drawings, discuss the colors chosen, and how they can represent our mood, feelings, thoughts, and sensations.

Skill 26: Pick a Feeling

1) Continue the discussion from Skill 25 and explore with group members how colors can represent moods.
2) Provide the group members with a list of feelings:

Sad	Angry	Happy	Hate
Love	Joy	Anxiety	Jealousy
Fear	Worry	Confident	Frustration

3) Have the group members choose, as a group, at least four feeling words from the list above. This assists the group with decision making and allows the mental health professional to notice strengths and weaknesses when members must negotiate their needs. A variation, though less impactful for the members, is that each client chooses their own four words.
4) Offer each group member one sheet of paper and have them section it into four.
5) Ask them to *"write one feeling word in each section and draw what it looks like."*
6) When this is complete ask them to *"write where in your body the feeling 'lives'."*
7) Discuss as a group.

Skill 27: Physical Warning Signs

1) Provide each group member with one sheet of paper.
2) Ask them to *"draw your body when you are tense or frustrated."*
3) When this is complete, give them another sheet of paper and ask them to *"draw your body when it 'screams'."*
4) On the back of the papers have the group members write down the experience.
5) Discuss the completed drawings, focusing on problem solving and coping skills.

Figure 6.16 represents two different responses to the first part of Skill 27. In this example, both of these young adults approached the bodily sensations of frustration from very opposite perspectives. The drawing on the left, with its visceral wavy lines, undulating through the upper torso, bespeaks of anxious restless drives. In the discussion phase this young man verbalized that he experiences "constricted energy." Conversely, the young adult on the right side articulated his anger through a literal depiction of a kinesthetic experience. In the discussion phase he stated, "It was good to release my loneliness with this drawing." This insightful comment reveals the power that anger yields as a replacement for other, more painful, affective responses such as loneliness.

Figure 6.16 When I Am Tense

Skill 28: My Body

1) Discuss with group members how tension can affect the body physically. Link this to where individual group members feel they carry their tension (i.e., hands, head, shoulders, stomach, etc.).
2) Provide each group member with copies of Figures 3.5 and 3.6. Allow them to choose which outline they would like to work on.
3) When this is complete, ask them to "*write down four feelings on the side of the body outline.*"
4) After this is done, ask each member to "*choose colors from the markers that represent the feelings you just wrote down. Using those colors, draw where you carry each of those feelings on the body outline.*"
5) Once each group member finishes, discuss what it feels like when tension can no longer be controlled. When anger cannot be controlled. When fear cannot be controlled. When worries cannot be controlled.

The following section, *Me and My Provocations*, promotes identification as well as alternative methods to anger responses, and the *Identify the Problem* section aims to help the client practice problem solving skills, while exploring the feelings which influence their reactions.

Skill 29: Focus Your Response

1) Provide each group member with one sheet of paper. Instruct them to choose one image from the collage box (make certain your collage box contains images of people only).
2) Ask them to "*glue your image down and write out how that person is feeling and why.*"
3) When this is complete, ask them to "*think about why that person is upset. What would you say to him/her to get information on why he/she is so upset? Write out what you would say.*"
4) Discuss the completed projects. Ask the members if they have ever stopped to wonder why another person is upset. If not, what stops them? If so, what do they do with the thought? Continue with the process illumination by asking whether questioning the person has escalated or de-escalated a situation. Complete the group discussion by asking the clients how they use this in their lives.

Skill 30: How Annoying

1) Provide each group member with three sheets of paper. This directive could take many weeks.
2) On the first sheet, have them "*draw how you look when you are frustrated.*"

3) On the second sheet have them *"draw how you look when you are annoyed or irritated."*
4) On the final sheet have them *"draw how you look when you feel you are being treated unfairly."*
5) Have each individual decide which of the three drawings tends to trigger their anger the most. Share these as a group.

Skill 31: Finding a Direction

1) Discuss with the group the benefits of assertively expressing feelings when they are upset, frustrated, or annoyed.
2) Provide each group member with one sheet of paper. Have them divide the paper in two.
3) In the first section ask them to *"draw a recent situation where you were angry."*
4) In the next section have them *"draw what you wanted from the situation."*
5) Ask the clients how they feel when they express their anger assertively rather than aggressively.

Skill 32: Taking Action

1) Provide each group member with one sheet of paper.
2) Ask them to *"draw all the things that upset you the most."*
3) Discuss the completed drawings.
4) Once each client has shared, have them choose the "most upsetting" representation and focus on problem solving and coping skills.

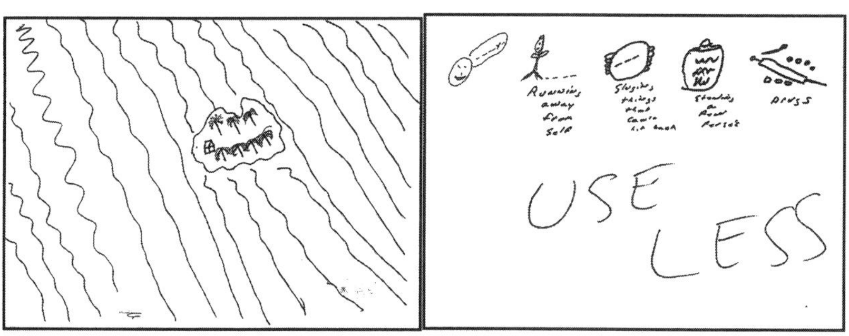

Figure 6.17 What Upsets You?

Rather than drawing all the things "that upset you the most," an adolescent male (left side of Figure 6.17) drew only one thing—an island adrift in an endless sea. In the process discussion, he explored how he felt alone and deserted, but was unable to arrive at any solutions to his emptiness despite plentiful group feedback. This situation is not surprising as "in loneliness we feel left out, cut off, lost, bereft, forgotten, unwanted, unneeded, or ignored. These feelings are so bitter because they run contrary to what we expect" (Sadler & Johnson, 1980, p. 38).

On the right side of Figure 6.17, an adult male explored past issues where he used drugs, stole from people, "slugging things that can't hit back," and "running away from self," all summing up to a feeling of uselessness. In the discussion phase, he focused on how he is haunted by the knowledge that he hurt others that were weaker than himself. As Tillich (1980) states:

> We cannot make anybody else responsible for what has happened through us. We cannot run away from our guilt; we cannot honestly cover it up. We are alone with it; and it is this loneliness which permeates all other forms of loneliness, transforming them into experiences of judgment.
>
> (Tillich, 1980, pp. 550–551).

Skill 33: Through Their Eyes

1) Provide each group member with one sheet of paper. Instruct them to choose two images from the collage box which contains images of people only.
2) Ask them to *"glue your images on the bottom of the page and, on the back of the paper, write out a conflict that these two are having."*
3) Once this is done, ask them to *"turn the paper back to the collage images and above each person's image, write what they are thinking about the conflict, and how they can solve it assertively."*
4) Discuss the completed projects. For select drawings, ask the clients what would have happened if these people had chosen revenge instead of problem-solving.

Skill 34: Needs and Wants

1) Provide each group member with one sheet of paper. Instruct them to divide the paper in two.
2) In the first section ask them to *"draw the things you need."*
3) In the next section have them *"draw the things you want."*
4) Discuss the completed projects by asking which was the most important need or want. What were some of the problems when needs and wants were at odds?

Figure 6.18 Needs and Wants

Figure 6.18 was completed in one group session by two different members. On the left side, an older male with significant dependency issues has drawn needs surrounding affection and love. On the right side of Figure 6.18, a female group member has drawn the same basic desires. The need to belong is universal; however, these two, though similar in content, could not be more divergent. The male's drawing on the left understands love as something to receive passively from those in his environment. His post-drawing illumination described nothing related to the need for connection. Instead, his drawing provided a cursory image of two people with a floating heart, while the other figures were reported to represent exercising and sleeping. His want was a simply drawn cruise ship devoid of people. Conversely, on the right side, the female has created a plethora of images with people encircled, families preparing for community outings, and dinner, while her want was to be closer to God. In all, fulfillment and devotion, understanding and acceptance permeate this woman's artwork illustrating her ability to both give as well as receive love; an expression of needs and wants all within the metaphor.

Skill 35: Things I Can Do

1) Discuss with the group members problems which they tend to worry about. Process how they worry, how they handle the anxiety, and the outcome of excessive worry.
2) Have each group member retrieve their project from Skill 32 and review the one thing that upset him/her the most.
3) Provide them with another sheet of paper and ask them to *"draw what is most likely to happen."*
4) On the back of the paper have them *"draw the worst thing that could happen."*

5) Discuss the completed projects. Ask the members, if the worst did occur, what they could do to handle the problem, or solve the problem. Are there things they could have said or done that would have changed the "worst scenario" outcome? How can this type of problem-solving apply to their lives?

Skill 36: The Real Problem

1) Have the group members think about a problem that they are experiencing in the present. Discuss among themselves.
2) Provide each group member with one sheet of paper. Instruct them to write their problem at the top of the page. Then ask them to fold the paper in two and draw a line down the center.
3) In the first section ask them to *"draw what you are feeling, what is bothering you."*
4) In the next section, have them *"draw how you will take care of the problem."*
5) Discuss the completed projects and ask the following process questions: What is it that you want? What concerns do you have? Worries? What do you need in this situation?

In the final sections of this guidebook, *Communicating Expectations* works to expand on the client's assertiveness skills while identifying weaknesses and promoting awareness. *How I Feel* offers opportunities for self-disclosure while balancing reactions when faced with stressful circumstances. The last section, *Healthy, Wealthy and Wise* helps the group to develop a heightened awareness of both self and others through problem solving, cohesiveness, and healthy coping skills.

Skill 37: I Expect

1) Provide each group member with one sheet of paper. Instruct them to arrive at a topic, any topic, as a group, for this session's drawing.
2) Once this is completed, have them individually make a list of the items they would like to have included in the image. The list should be commensurate with the number of people in the group (i.e., five group members = a list of five items).
3) Ask them to *"pass your paper to the left. The first item on the list is what you are to draw. Draw that item now."*
4) When this is complete, ask them to once again pass the drawing to the left and *"find the second item on the list. Draw that item now."*

5) This continues until all items are drawn. Once the art is back to the original owner, have him/her title the drawing and discuss as a group using "I" statements. Ask members what expectations they had for their original drawing. Was the end result better? Worse? Was passing the drawing uncomfortable?

Skill 38: Pick a Word

1) Discuss with the group the definitions of passive, assertive, and aggressive. Have them define and provide examples of each type of communication style.
2) Provide each group member with one sheet of paper and a collage box of words. Have them choose up to seven words.
3) Once this is completed, have the members draw the feelings that accompany the words chosen.
4) Once this is complete, have the group members label the words as either passive, assertive, or aggressive.
5) Discuss the drawings. Explore the feelings they attached to the words chosen. How does someone look when they are passive? Assertive? Aggressive? Process how each client wants others in their life to view them.

Skill 39: What I Said

1) Provide each group member with one sheet of paper. Instruct them to choose one picture from the collage box of people and glue it to the paper.
2) On the top of the paper, have them write out a scenario describing what they think is going on.
3) Ask them to *"write what the person would say in an aggressive manner,"* under the image.
4) When this is complete, ask them to *"write what the person would say in a passive manner,"* under 3.
5) When this is complete, ask them to *"write what the person would say in an assertive manner,"* under 4.
6) Discuss the responses. Explore whether their voice would be weak and hesitant (passive), firm and modulated (assertive), or shrill and demanding (aggressive). Would their gestures be fidgety, relaxed, or abrupt? Their posture excessive head nodding, relaxed, or stiff and rigid? Which one of these choices seems the most effective in this scenario?

Skill 40: Where I Stand

1) Provide each group member with one sheet of paper.
2) Ask them to *"draw a self-portrait. Draw as best as you can. Make certain that it is of your entire body, not just a floating head."*
3) When this is complete, ask them to identify whether the picture has them looking assertive, aggressive, or passive.
4) Discuss as a group.

Skill 41: You Never _____

1) Provide each group member with one sheet of paper.
2) Provide them with the following sentence completions:

   You never ______.

   I'm always the one who ______.

   Everyone else is ________.
3) Ask them to *"choose one of the sentence completions and draw an image to accompany it."*
4) Have the client title the drawing and discuss the creations as a group using "I" statements. Question the members as to how they would label the statements: aggressive, assertive, or passive. Why? Explore how they would re-word the sentences using "I" statements.

Skill 42: From the Past

1) Ask the group members to recall a time, past or present, when they utilized anger or violence instead of communication.
2) Have them *"draw the other person and you in the conflict."*
3) Share the drawings and discuss with the group members. Was this a struggle for control? How did you feel during the conflict? How do you think the other person felt?
4) When this is complete, ask them to *"draw your feelings in the conflict."*
5) Have the client title the drawing and discuss as a group using "I" statements.

Skill 43: I Am Still Hurting

1) Ask the group members to recall a time when they felt hurt. Prompt them to look at their feelings of hurt rather than the physical or emotional sensation of pain.

2) Provide them with a piece of paper.
3) Ask them to *"draw a time when you were hurt."*
4) Have them title their drawing and discuss as a group using "I" statements.

Ask questions focusing on whether this incident still hurts them. What stops you from expressing your feelings? What would have happened if you expressed yourself? What would happen if you expressed your feelings today? What would be the worst-case scenario if you expressed yourself today?

Skill 44: Around and Around We Go

1) Provide each group member with one sheet of paper. Have them think of a scene or topic, in their mind, that they wish to draw.
2) Have them begin with markers. After three minutes, stop them and have them pass the drawing to their left.
3) Have them use the following media (in this order after passing their original drawing). The amount of time allotted is in parentheses. Continue passing until each member has his/her original drawing in front of them.

1	Markers	(3 minutes)
2	Graphite pencil	(3 minutes)
3	Pastel	(2 minutes)
4	Watercolor	(3 minutes)
5	Color Pencil	(2 minutes)

If there are more than five people in the group start at the top of the list and shorten the time from 3 to 2 minutes and 2 to 1.5 minutes.

4) Once the drawing is back to the original owner, have them title it.
5) Discuss as a group, making certain to emphasize "I" statements. Ask the clients what expectations they had for the drawing. Is the final drawing better? Worse? How does the picture make you feel? Was passing the drawing uncomfortable for you? What do you wish had been different about it? Is there something you particularly like in the drawing? What would you have done differently?

Skill 45: I Expect

1) Provide each group member with one sheet of paper. Have them draw a line down the center.
2) On the left side have them *"draw how you feel when your needs are ignored."*

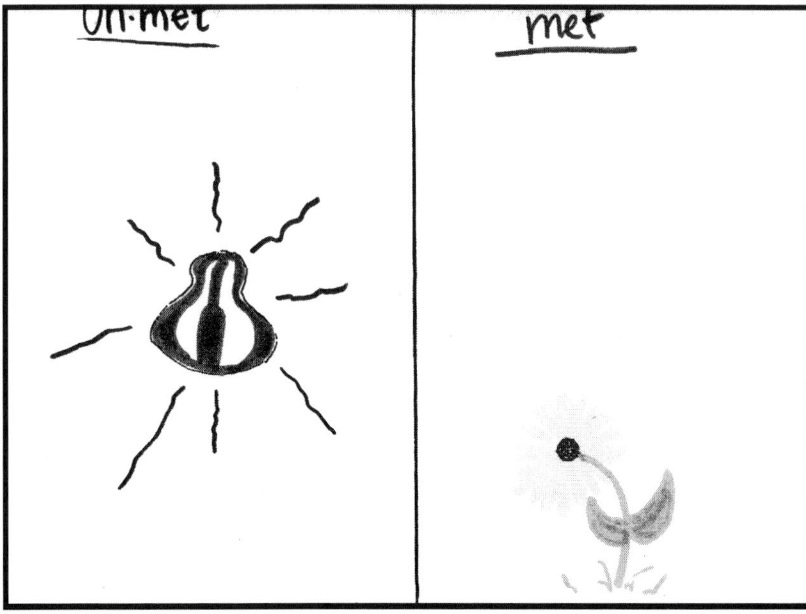

Figure 6.19 Acknowledgment

3) On the right side have them *"draw how you feel when your needs are acknowledged."*
4) Discuss as a group using "I" statements. Ask them what they could do to get their needs met. How do you create a scenario that leaves your needs unmet? What frightens you the most about asking for assistance?

The symbolic representation of Figure 6.19 does not require words. Utilizing shape, form, and color this male illustrated the anxiety that accompanies a world filled with doubt (left side) and the simple grace of a flower (right side), representing acknowledgment and connection.

Skill 46: I Can Handle It

1) Provide each group member with one sheet of paper. Instruct them to *"draw a picture of you upset"* or *"draw a picture of you in a tough situation."*
2) Once this is completed, provide them with a second piece of paper and attaching it to the first with tape, have them *"draw a plan to handle it."*

3) Have the client title the drawing and discuss as a group using "I" statements. What felt better: being "in charge" or feeling helpless? How is it better to take charge? Worse? What are some ways you can handle conflict without anger or violence? What could you say to defuse the situation or conflict?

The male who completed Figure 6.20 had an extensive history of assaultive and aggressive behavior toward others. In this drawing he depicts himself angrily kicking at a garage door because his car would not start. In the discussion phase he spoke of being so upset over this situation that he assaulted a family member after the incident. In the problem solving phase, he explored a multiplicity of ways to accept and resolve frustrating emotions without violence.

Skill 47: I Can Cope

1) Discuss as a group the following incomplete sentence *"violence won't get me ______."*
2) Have the group members complete the sentence. Once they all agree on a completed sentence, ask them to *"draw what that means to you."*

Figure 6.20 Just Kicking It

Variation:

Instead of having the group members agree on a common definition, have each member arrive at their own definition and *"draw what that means to you."*

3) Have the client title the drawing and discuss as a group using "I" statements.

Skill 48: Where I Stand

1) Present to the group members a brief review of the completed skills from this guidebook. Accomplish this by having them retrieve their folders and spontaneously discuss the past drawings.
2) Have the group members communicate with one another and arrive at an idea for a group "Violence Prevention Poster."
3) Monitor how the group delegates, decides, and navigates using assertive communication skills and "I" statements.
4) Create the poster.
5) When the poster is completed, display it in the group room and discuss the project with the group members.

As we move to the commencement of the second guidebook, *An Expression of Grief and Loss*, it is important to note that healthy resolutions and the promotion of connection assist clients with the development of a stronger sense of self. It is this final directive that coalesces each of the prior sections. In Skill 48, the solutions for the poster that they arrive at through first relating with one another and then creating an art production, provide a synchronicity that permits the group to experience and understand emotions on an interactional level.

Elisabeth Kubler-Ross (2016), stated, "People are like stained-glass windows. They sparkle and shine when the sun is out, but when the darkness sets in, their true beauty is revealed only if there is light from within." This quote is just as pertinent for those suffering loss, as those who grieve from excessive aggressive reactions.

References

Cirlot, J.E. (1983). *A dictionary of symbols* (2nd ed., J. Sage, Trans.). New York: Philosophical Library.

Grothe, M. (2008). *I never metaphor I didn't like: A comprehensive compilation of history's greatest analogies, metaphors, and similes*. New York: Harper Collins.

Kramer, E. (1971). *Art as therapy with children*. New York: Schocken Books.

Kubler-Ross, E. (2016, February 27). Retrieved from www.ekrfoundation.org/quotes/

Moschini, L.B. (2004). *Drawing the line: Art therapy with the difficult client.* Hoboken, New Jersey: John Wiley & Sons.

Patterson, S., Debate, J., Anju, S., Waller, D., & Crawford, M.J., (2011). Provision and practice of art therapy for people with schizophrenia: Results of a national survey. *Journal of Mental Health, 20* (4), 328–335.

Sadler, W.A., & Johnson, T.B. (1980). From loneliness to anomia. In J. Hartog, J.R. Audy and Y.A. Cohen (Eds.) *The anatomy of loneliness* (pp. 34–64). New York: International Universities Press.

Tillich, P. (1980). Loneliness and solitude. In J. Hartog, J.R. Audy and Y.A. Cohen (Eds.) *The anatomy of loneliness* (pp. 547–554). New York: International Universities Press.

Winnicott, D. (1968). The squiggle game. In *Voices: The art and science of psychotherapy, 4* (1).

7
An Expression of Grief and Loss

> Once upon a time there was a boy named John and he lost a ring. John loved the ring because it was special to him. John's ring was special because he got it from one of his friends. John got on his horse named Spirit and was riding on the farm looking for it. It turns out the dog stole the ring and then buried it in the dirt. And the boy didn't know he buried it in the dirt. John was on Spirit and he looked and looked and looked. After many days he never found the ring. It was gone.

The second guidebook, *An Expression of Grief and Loss*, is designed for mental health professionals who wish to blend the techniques of art therapy, working with clients who have experienced a grief response due to loss. As the grief experience is intensely personal and leaves the client emotionally vulnerable, the stages, as outlined in this guidebook, should be assessed on an individual level. Additionally, any loss can give rise to mourning; thus, the activities within this guidebook have been purposefully designed to incorporate not merely the permanent loss of a loved one, but also the myriad of losses that surround everyday living. Whether your client functions at a low or high level, this guidebook will assist with the understanding, expression, and management of deeply felt emotions and feelings. As such, the directives can be used singularly or as a complete treatment technique. Additionally, as outlined in *The Art of Anger Management* guidebook, each directive builds upon the preceding skill and therefore should be utilized in the order outlined within the guidebook. However, it is not necessary to complete each directive within each content area. Lastly, Table 7.1 outlines a section titled, "Distancing Directives." These tasks are offered for the mental health professional to incorporate when the feelings of loss swell to the point where fear and anxiety overwhelms the process. In this way, these directives can be used on any given day, in place of any of the skills, to aid the client's grieving process and to provide a break from its intensity.

Elisabeth Kubler-Ross (1969) postulated that the grieving process encompasses five stages: denial, anger, bargaining, depression, and acceptance. In addition, she outlined that people often cycle back and forth through a number of the stages before arriving at the stage of acceptance. She states, "Acceptance should not be mistaken for a happy stage. It is almost void of feelings. It is as if the pain had gone, the struggle is over." (p. 100).

For the purposes of this guidebook, instead of focusing on the end of life stages as Kubler-Ross proposes, I have modeled *An Expression of Grief and Loss* after Baker, Sedney, and Gross' (1992) three-staged model of grieving, from which the mental health professional can assimilate both the psychological and physical experiences that accompany loss. As such, the psychological tasks are broken into an early phase which promotes safety and security, the middle phase which focuses on acceptance and the emotional reality of the loss, and a late phase which endorses the formation of new relationships while preparing for the resurfacing of painful memories.

Table 7.1 outlines the Table of Contents for the guidebook, *An Expression of Grief and Loss*, and provides a choice of skills to accommodate both short- and long-term therapies.

The first section outlines the early stages of loss by laying a foundation of understanding and processing grief reactions through the client's personal stories. These skills begin by helping the group members compare life experiences and promote self-soothing where they can ultimately create feelings of comfort and safety. It should be noted that in this stage, the client can be exceedingly focused on protection of the self. As such, the ego gives rise to defense mechanisms in an effort to avoid the discomfort of emotional conflict.

Skill 1: My Story

1) Discuss with the group members the range of emotions and thoughts that accompany grief. Explore why people grieve (i.e., to regain control, to understand the loss, out of loneliness or fear, etc.). Explore the varied ways that people grieve (i.e., emotions expression, withdrawal, looking for answers, anger).
2) Provide each group member with a sheet of lined paper and have them *"tell your story of loss and grief. Make certain it has a beginning, middle, and end."*
3) Prior to having each group member read his/her story aloud, stress that we are not trying to make the group member "feel better"; instead we are listening and providing empathy and understanding.
4) If you wish, the mental health professional can begin an exploration around the group's collective loss experience: Was it sudden

Table 7.1 An Expression of Grief and Loss Table of Contents

Early Tasks	*Distancing Directives*
Skill 1: My Story	DD 1: Draw your problem
Skill 2: A Defining Moment	DD 2: Draw how you are feeling
Skill 3: What I Want	DD 3: What is it like _____?
Skill 4: My World	DD 4: Draw what you want
Skill 5: Four Expressions of Grief	DD 5: Draw your favorite activities
Skill 6: Pick One, Any One	DD 6: What do you do now?
Skill 7: Safe and Comfortable	DD 7: Draw using the colors of _____
	DD 8: Draw the most important thing
Middle Tasks	
Skill 8: A Place for My Grief	
Skill 9: My Tears	
Skill 10: Under Stress	
Skill 11: Grief Book	
Late Tasks	
Skill 12: In Control	
Skill 13: My World	
Skill 14: What I Like To Do . . .	
Skill 15: What Helped?	
Skill 16: Create a Linking Memory	
Skill 17: Fork in the Road	
Skill 18: What Now?	
Skill 19: What I Say to Myself	
Skill 20: A Relaxing Place	

or prolonged? Did the client, and others, have an opportunity for closure? If it was a death, did the client attend a funeral? What does the client remember the most about the funeral? Were people in the family, and the client, able to express fear, pain, guilt, and loss feelings or were these covered up? How has the client expressed feelings since the loss? How have things changed since the loss?

Skill 2: A Defining Moment

1) Recall the stories from Skill 1. Have each group member discuss the one thing they remember most about their story of grief and loss.
2) Discuss with the group how grief can be both contradictory and confusing. Allow the members to explore these issues as they relate to their personal stories.

3) Provide each group member with one sheet of paper.
4) Ask them to *"draw what grief is for you."*
5) When this is complete, have them add themselves to the drawing and write why this drawing represents grief.
6) Have each group member title the drawing.
7) Discuss the drawings as a group. Focus on and normalize problems related to behavioral issues (withdrawal, apathy, aggressive reactions), cognition (suicidal thoughts, hopelessness, self-reproach), physical manifestations (sleep problems, lethargy, headaches), and emotions (guilt, anxiety, nervousness, anger). Ask the group, *"What do you do with your feelings of grief?"*

Figure 7.1 illustrates two drawings completed in different groups. The left side was completed by an older female who incorporated layers of color and spoke of hiding behind her grief. In the writing task she asked, "How can I not be afraid of my grief? How can I accept it graciously and easily?" Conversely, the young adult male on the right side also integrated lines of varied colors that sweep over a faceless figure in the center. He correlated his grief to a "gray area" with each color representing a different stage of his sorrow.

The floating bodies and layered colors found in Figure 7.1 symbolize the anxious denial of two people seeking safety and security as an escape from the loneliness of loss.

Skill 3: What I Want

1) Verbally review the salient points as discussed by the group in Skill 2.
2) Provide each group member with one sheet of paper. Have them *"draw what you ____ (hope, wish, expect) to get from this group."* (Choose only one word for the group members to illustrate—not all three).

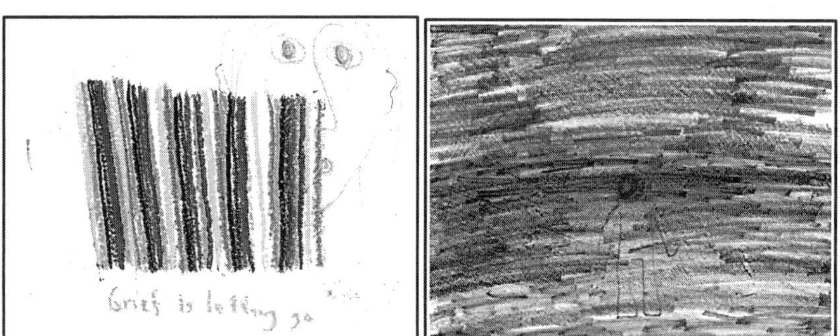

Figure 7.1 Grief Is Letting Go

3) While discussing the drawings, focus on issues related to "getting over" the loss as unreasonable. Create an atmosphere where adjustment, balance, and coping with the psychological pain are emphasized.
4) It is important that the clients understand that though grief can be mediated, it will not be eliminated.

In this stage, where safety and security take precedence, it is important to allow clients to both identify and discuss their personal expectations for the group; a member-to-member interaction which allows clients not merely to compare analogous solutions, but to interrelate. These early tasks, with their focus on here and now feelings, permit the therapist to play a supportive role which ultimately reduces anxiety so that new coping skills can be learned.

Both sides of Figure 7.2 represented an expression of hope through the gaining of insight. However, one struggled with motivation (left side), while the right side struggled with the acceptance of an encroaching mental illness.

Though both drawings offered much to be discussed in the post-drawing inquiry, it is the recurrence of eyes that grabs the attention of the viewer. These hypervigilant eyes symbolize the awareness that, in a clinical setting, we are both seeing and being seen. The left side of Figure 7.2 can no longer turn a blind eye to the motivation needed to confront her issues, while the right side of Figure 7.2 has acceptance right before his eyes if he can only assent to the loss that haunts him.

Skill 4: My World

1) Return to the last directive and have the clients explore things that interest them in their life. Follow this with a discussion surrounding things in the here and now that bring them pleasure and comfort.

   "What makes you laugh?"

   "What is your favorite color? Food? Flower? Smell?"

   "What activities do you do alone? With others?"

Figure 7.2 The Eyes Have It

2) Instruct the group members to draw the largest circle they can on the paper provided or have this prepared before the group session. Using art media, have the clients *"draw all the things that define your world."*
3) As a variation, when they are done "filling in their world," have them *"decorate the outside of your world."*
4) Discuss the drawings as a group. Ask them what they would have added if they had had time. Save this drawing as it will be referred to in the Late Phase directives.

Skill 5: Four Expressions of Grief

1) Discuss with the group members how problems related to grief and loss are multifaceted. Have the members verbally explore what they believe you mean by this statement.
2) On a chalkboard/grease board or a sheet of paper, write out these four categories:

Feelings	Behavior
Thoughts	Physical

3) Have the group members discuss the symptoms of their grief and where these symptoms or manifestations would fall within the four categories.
4) Provide them with a sheet of drawing paper and have them separate the paper into four.
5) Instruct them to write one of the four categories into each of the four squares and *"draw how each look using shape, color, and form."*
6) Discuss the drawings as a group.

Skill 6: Pick One, Any One

1) Provide each group member with one sheet of paper (used as a protective "covering" for the group room table) and baskets filled with multi-colored plasticine clay. Have them create their chosen expression of grief (see Skill 5) using the clay provided.
2) Discuss each member's clay representation from both a literal discussion and as a metaphorical interpretation. Keep in mind each group member's mode of interaction (demonstrative, denial of emotions related to the loss, aggressive reactions, dependency issues, etc.) when processing the completed clay creations.

If you return to Figure 1.23, you will recall that this adolescent female created a "robot" devoid of a heart. This clay representation served to protect her from further hurt and pain while expressing a wish for mechanical functioning, metaphorically preserving her safety and security through total mindlessness. Unfortunately, attempts to postpone the expression of loss is a common maneuver, but one that ultimately fails, as the wish to remove the self from the environment, cannot endure.

Skill 7: Safe and Comfortable

1) Discuss with the group members the importance of not only mourning the loss but also accepting the contradictory emotions that attend the experience. Normalize the desire to belong with the need to be separate, the overwhelming feelings, and the effort in rejecting those feelings.
2) Explore with the group the experiences of their own contradictory feelings.
3) Provide each member with a sheet of paper and have them *"draw a safe comfortable place; something meaningful and calming. This can be a real or imagined location."*
4) Discuss the completed drawings as a group. If any of the members drew an imagined place, explore how they could make that space into a reality. Explore why their drawn place is safe. Discuss here and now living spaces that are meaningful. Explore how each member self-soothes using the five senses:

Sight:	nature, paintings, watching a movie.
Hearing:	favorite music, sounds of nature, singing.
Smell:	scented candles, potpourri, walk in nature.
Taste:	favorite meal, flavors of ice cream, peppermint candy.
Touch:	warm shower, brushing your hair, cold compress on forehead, soothing clothing/cloth.

As we move into the middle stages, the *Expression of Grief and Loss* guidebook turns toward acknowledging and expressing the powerful emotions and feelings attendant to the sorrow and hurt of loss. Often emotional protection is established through detachment and isolation; in this way the client can manage the demands of the external world through the security of distancing themselves from overpowering feelings. In the end, the assessment of psychological pain coupled with the separation of behaviors and feelings is imperative if acceptance of the loss and its emotional reality is to be internalized. As such, the ensuing directives support not only the pain and hurt, but also tender recollections and remembrances.

Skill 8: A Place for My Grief

1) Discuss with the group members how grief is not only experienced in different ways but is managed in a multiplicity of ways.
2) Have the group members explore how they have managed and expressed their grief reactions in the past.
3) Retrieve the clay figures from Skill 6. Make available to the members a variety of arts and crafts supplies (tissue paper, construction paper, different shaped boxes, etc.).
4) Instruct them to look at the figures and *"make a place for your clay grief creation using any of the available supplies."*
5) Discuss the completed projects as a group. Explore with the members what they learned about grief. Process the different ways the clients acknowledged their feelings of grief and loss.

Skill 6 receives its denouement in Skill 8. As such, Figure 7.3 outwardly shows an inviting environment created out of brightly colored pink construction paper, blue wisps of feathers layered over a tableau of pink and orange felt pieces. Note the miniscule door on the left side of Figure 7.3 with an inaccessible window to glimpse the goings on, while the right side shows our "robot" figure sitting mechanically within—alone, safe, looking up at us with large, watchful, expectant eyes; an emotional reality of exclusion. Henry Laughlin (1970) states:

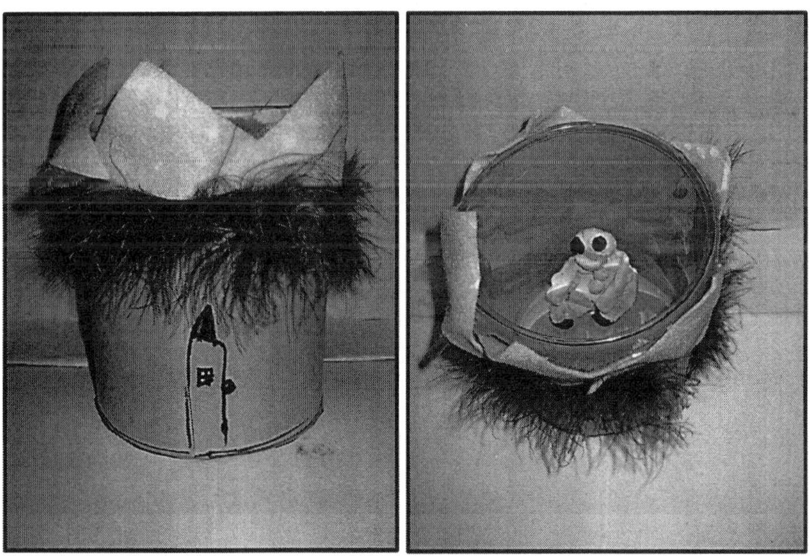

Figure 7.3 Safely Isolated

> Isolation is the intrapsychic defense sometimes evolved when the emotional charge has been too painful or too great. Divorcing its charge leaves the object emotionally isolated, or neutral. Through the dynamism of Isolation the ego secures the separation of otherwise intolerably painful affect from a given vent, striving need, idea, or event.
>
> (Laughlin, 1970, p. 477).

Skill 9: My Tears

1) This directive may take many weeks to complete. Have each group member choose a cardboard container. Ask them to cover the outside of the container using any of the paper provided and decorate the outside of his/her "crying jar." Have each member cut a slit in the top of their chosen container.
2) Provide each group member with white paper. Instruct them to draw as many tears as they wish, decorate them, and cut them out.

   Variation:

   Purchase balsa wood "teardrops," then provide markers to the group members. After the group members have chosen the amount of "tears" they want, have them decorate them in any way they desire.
3) After the tears are cut out (or chosen from balsa wood), for every ten tears (you can change the number as you see fit), have them write (on strips of lined paper) a memory of what they are grieving.
4) The provider may need to identify topics in ensuing weeks for the clients to write on their strips of paper. As each group is different, refer to the common issues that have arisen from the prior directives. Make certain to focus on the acceptance and reality of the loss.

Figure 7.4 shows two jars made by two adolescent females. The pile of balsa "tears" symbolizes the intensity of their losses. In this instance, both group members were shocked to see the amount of tears they had chosen. The group discussion focused upon the commonality of loss regardless of the content (some had lost parents; others were mourning the loss of friends, and freedom, while others focused upon themselves). In all, each client had experienced the collective element that bonded them while accentuating the building of relationships.

Skill 10: Under Stress

1) Discuss with the group members problems that arise when a loss is experienced. Question the members on whether they have experienced issues related to all the sensory preferences. Explore issues with behavior (lack of interest in activities, irritability, substance use or

Figure 7.4 The Crying Jar

other addictive behaviors), feelings (self-criticism, anger, loneliness, rapid mood changes), physical manifestations (fatigue, sleeplessness, skin problems, headaches, eating too much or too little), and thoughts (fantasizing, suicidal feelings).

2) Provide each group member with one sheet of paper and have them draw a line down the center.
3) Ask them to draw on the left side "*when I'm under stress I . . .*"
4) Ask them to write on the right side (have them be specific) "*when I see these symptoms I will . . .*"
5) Discuss as a group. Explore how our grief can be experienced and expressed through a myriad of behaviors and emotions.

Skill 11: Grief Book

This directive was adapted from a family intervention by Maxine Jung (1985).

1) Explain to the group that they are going to make multiple pages for a book about their experience with loss. This directive could take many weeks to complete.

2) Provide the members with a variety of art supplies and have them make a page for their "memory" book.
3) Should they need help, return to Skill 9 and have them begin by drawing one page for the memory book from one of the slips of paper they placed within the "Crying Jar."
4) In subsequent groups have them design pages around these ideas:

   Make a page/s about a positive memory.

   Make a page/s around what you wish you could have said.

   Make a page/s that shows at least one thing the deceased or yourself has missed.

   Make a page/s showing one emotion that you have covered up.

   Make a page/s of you and/or the deceased doing something.

   Make a page/s made up of your or the deceased's favorite things.

   Make a page/s based on something you would like ______ to know about you.
5) Some group members may have pictures that they can add to the Grief Book. Make copies of these and have them design pages. If they do not have photographs, incorporate collage images from magazines.
6) Some group members may have loved ones who wish to contribute to the pages. This should be encouraged.
7) After the pages are complete, have each group member add at least five blank pages to the completed book.
8) Have them choose a cover for the book and decorate this.

Again, the image that stands out, that begs to be seen, is that of the eye (Figure 7.5). This woman chose to create the last page of her Grief Book from the directive, *"make a page based on something you would like ______ to know about you."* In all, this page took two weeks to complete. The first week consisted of her collecting the four collage images, which from left to right (on Figure 7.5) shows a long tunnel situated on a desolate landscape, the peaceful gaze of a brown bear, the destructive forces of an ocean breaking over a safety wall, and a lunar module making its way through the mysteries of space. The artist explained that the collage represented the many stages of her grief especially that of anger. Situated in the center of the collage, a singular painted eye stares at the viewer. She stated her desire was to let her deceased brother see the "truth" about her.

The eye, with its prominent positioning, reminds one of the myth of the Cyclops and if we look to the folklore of Northern Spain, the Ojancanu, or

Figure 7.5 A Page in the Life . . .

Cyclops, "is, in sum, a symbol of the evil and destructive forces behind the primary or regressive side of Man" (Cirlot, 1983, p. 243). It is my contention that the "truth" which this woman wanted her brother to witness focused on her primary self which over time had degenerated to feelings of anger.

As we move into the final stage of the guidebook, *An Expression of Grief and Loss*, the late phase tasks focus upon the development of new relationships and the promotion of a personal identity without guilt. It is imperative that new relationships are endorsed as they prove fundamental if the client is to learn to both tolerate and integrate outside attachments. Consequently, it is through the member-to-member expression of pain, vulnerability, and remorse, coupled with the emotional reality of our losses, that leads group members toward acceptance; and acceptance offers group members the courage to generalize their learning into the larger community.

Skill 12: In Control

1) Discuss with the group members a time they felt in control.
2) Provide each group member with one sheet of paper.
3) Ask them to draw *"how it felt when someone heard what you had to say."*
4) Discuss the drawings as a group.

Skill 13: My World

1) Explore verbally with the clients issues related to interests, things in the environment, and/or people that bring them pleasure and comfort.
2) Instruct the group members to draw a large circle on the paper provided (or have this prepared before the group session). Using art media have the clients *"draw all the things that define your world."*
3) As a variation, when they are done "filling in their world," have them *"decorate the outside of your world."*
4) Discuss the drawings as a group. As a variation, review with the group their Skill 4 drawings and discuss any comparisons and/or additions to "their world."

At first glance, Figure 7.6 appears seemingly barren of emotion; however, in the post-drawing discussion an immense amount of information was provided about how this client copes with external stressors.

Prior to the directive, this client was discussing the intense amount of hate in the world given current events. In the drawing, she filled her world with

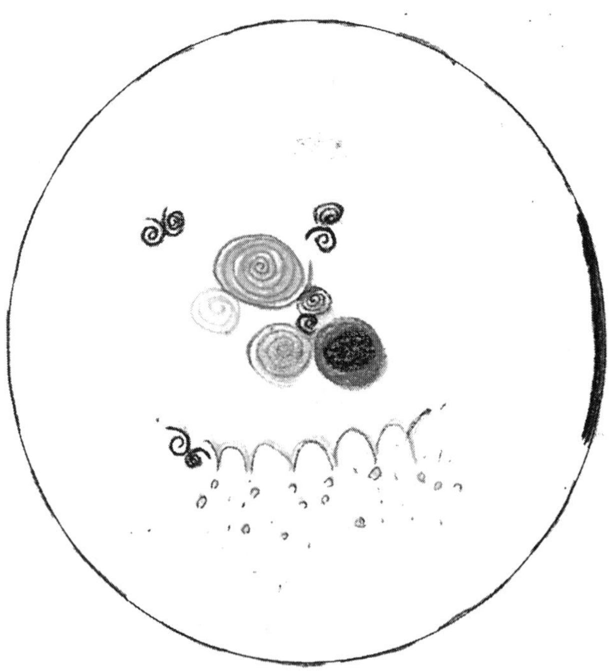

Figure 7.6 My World

two symbols, those of water and chaos. The water (bottom third of the circle) represented both a physical and emotional connection which sustains her in difficult times. The upper two-thirds, with its delicate spirals and pastel coloring, symbolized disarray, which is comforting in its familiarity. Importantly, when questioned as to why she decided not to decorate the outside of her drawing, she replied, "I try my best to avoid the outside world."

In this instance, the continued avoidance of the grief expression is problematic on a multiplicity of levels, but at its core, it impedes the formation of new relationships which are so integral to healthy resolutions. As this client receded into isolation, the therapeutic power of the group discussion offered her a connection that she would otherwise eschew; for it is in this portion of the group where hope can be nurtured and healthy adaptations practiced.

Skill 14: What I Like To Do . . .

1) Begin a discussion that focuses on the differences between isolation and interaction. Have the group members verbally explore these two words and how they relate to each of them.
2) Provide each group member with one sheet of paper. Ask the clients to draw a line down the center of the page.
3) Ask them to draw *"something that cheers you up."*
4) When this is complete, ask them to *"draw on the other side at least three things that you can do to cheer yourself up."*
5) Discuss as a group. Explore who is responsible for their choices. What do they do if problem-solving does not work? Explore what stress was underlying any feelings of depression or anger.

Skill 15: What Helped

1) Provide each group member with a 9" x 12" piece of paper.
2) Inform each member to be as specific and concrete as possible. Then ask them to *"draw all the things that helped you to survive your loss."*
3) Discuss the images as a group. Explore important people in the clients' lives. Ask the clients if they are willing to relate a specific memory that brings them comfort to this day. What are some things that they learned about themselves?

Figure 7.7, with its geometric shapes, heavy white space, and one dimensional lines presents ostensibly as simplistic. However, as discussed in Skill 13, the importance of the post-drawing inquiry cannot be underestimated. Specifically, this client described the forms on Figure 7.7 as "insurmountable objects; pain that could not be moved." She went on to describe the white space as the only place where she was able to "breathe" and "get things done."

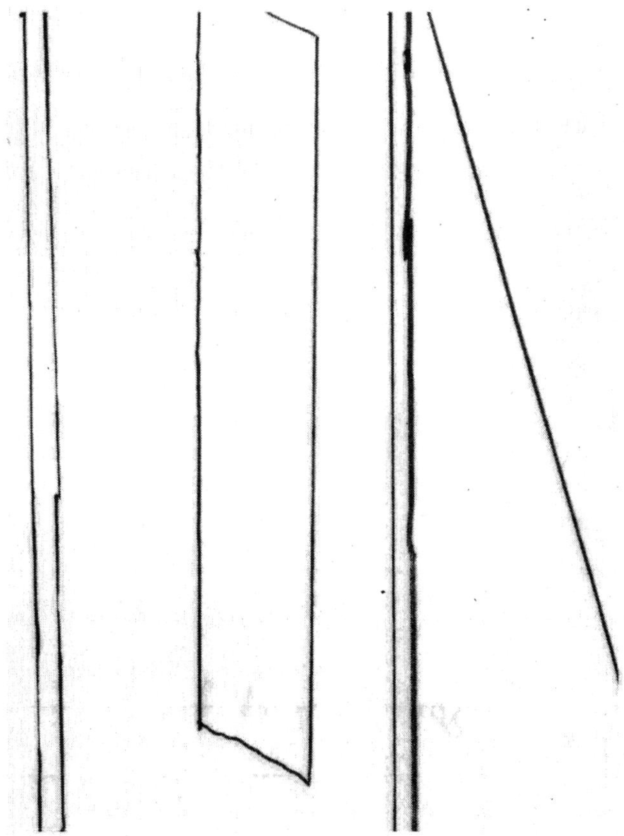

Figure 7.7 My Strengths

In this session, the group members were able to show their support and provide recognition that through pain and feelings of vulnerability, she ultimately found personal power; the power to move forward even though she wanted to remain insulated. And within this corrective experience the client began to appreciate her own strength. As Yalom (1985) delineated when he spoke about the 11 therapeutic factors, the fourth, altruism, outlines:

> Patients are enormously helpful to one another in the group therapeutic process. They offer support, reassurance, suggestions, and insight and share similar problems with one another. Not infrequently, a patient will listen and absorb observations from another member far more readily than from the group therapist.
>
> (Yalom, 1985, p. 14)

Skill 16: Create a Linking Memory

1) Discuss with the group members the meaning of a transitional or internal linking object. Explore with the members how the goal is not to forget, but to recall the memories and to continue the attachment in the here and now.
2) Ask them to think of what they have lost and, on the paper provided, to *"design something that will remind you. This will be a small keepsake and serve as a reminder of your memories."*
3) When this is complete, ask them to *"transfer your design onto the Shrinky-Dink® material."*
    - The completed Shrinky Dinks® keepsakes will be significantly smaller than the clients' original drawings. As a result, instruct the clients to draw their keepsake large. The provider may want to test a piece prior to completing this directive.
    - Shrinky Dinks® can be purchased online for a very reasonable cost.
4) Once this is completed, you will "make" the Shrinky-Dink® keepsakes and give them to the clients. Share the completed mementos as a group.

Skill 17: Fork in the Road

1) Provide each group member with one sheet of paper.
2) Ask them to *"draw a fork in the road."*
3) On one side of the fork, have them write out a list of both positive and negative events that have happened in the past.
4) On the other side of the fork, have them list what they are looking forward to in the future.
5) Discuss as a group: What are your present goals? What does it mean to live in the present? What are some things you should do but are afraid of? Why? What can you do about it? What will you do about it?

This skill focuses upon the client's need to develop a personal identity while continuing to have a connection to the loss which will ultimately support the inevitable resurfacing of painful memories. It is through acceptance that avoidance can be thwarted, through acceptance that satisfaction and understanding can be achieved, and hope proliferate. In time, the grief memories will re-emerge and it is integral that clients understand this occurrence. Additionally, it is important that clients recognize that the promotion of healthy adaptations will shape a personal identity without guilt or shame.

Skill 18: What Now?

1) Continue to expand upon Skill 17 and discuss with the group that painful thoughts and memories are inevitable, especially during times of stress, anniversary dates, and holidays. Explore with the group members their feelings and what they believe will be their most difficult times.
2) Give each group member a sheet of paper and ask them to *"draw a large heart on your paper. Decorate the heart any way you please."*
3) Once the drawing is completed, ask the members to list how they are going to deal with the feelings of re-emerging loss and grief in the area around the heart.
4) Discuss with the group: When you feel strong emotions, what are your thoughts? What activities or rituals will help you to process your feelings? Who is one person in your life that you can talk to? When has talking about your feelings helped?

Skill 19: What I Say to Myself

1) Provide each group member with one sheet of paper.
2) Ask them to *"list all the things you say to yourself when you are depressed or experience strong feeling states."*
3) Discuss as a group: What are some statements that will help you to feel better? What are some statements that make you feel worse? What do you say to yourself when you are angry? What is the feeling "beneath" your anger?

Skill 20: A Relaxing Place

1) Refer to the discussion from Skill 19. Have each group member discuss thoughts and images that they find pleasant and relaxing.
2) Provide each group member with one sheet of paper.
3) Ask them to *"imagine a secret world, deep within yourself, where you can go whenever you feel threatened, fearful, or alone. In your mind visualize a world that is calming, beautiful, and welcoming. Draw this place."*
4) Discuss as a group: What things do you feel, think, and experience when you are depressed? What do you do with your hurtful feelings? What is your "light at the end of the tunnel"? How do you feel when you imagine yourself achieving your goals?
5) After this skill, give each of the clients their Crying Jar from Skill 9.

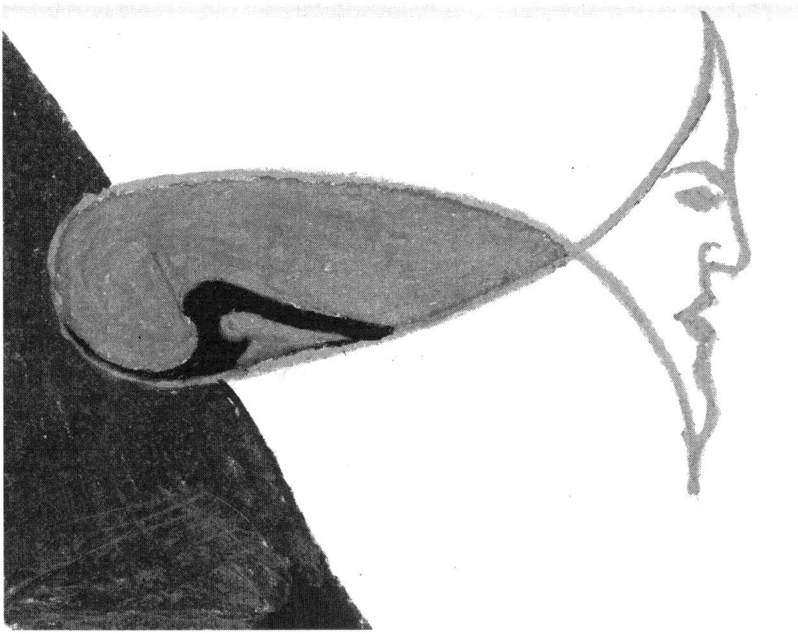

Figure 7.8 My Relaxing Place

In a prelude to the story, "Magic Mustard Seeds," William R. White (1986) stated, "The answer to sorrow, as well as loneliness, often lies in our willingness and ability to enter into the lives of others and share in their pain." (p. 42). His beautiful story tells of a grief stricken widow, who after being introduced to a holy man, implores him to bring back her son and ease her grief. The wizened man listens patiently to her pleas and eventually replies, "Bring me a mustard seed from a home that has never known sorrow. I will use that seed to remove the pain from your life" (p. 43). Without a second thought the woman set out upon her quest. She went from community to community; from magnificent manors to underprivileged neighborhoods and never once did she find a home untouched by loss or pain. Instead, what she found were stories, and within each story the widow listened patiently and consoled those who shared. After many months she forgot her search, for through her connectivity rather than distance, compassion rather than anger, the stories of others served to heal the pain that loss had produced.

In this, the final directive of the guidebook, connectivity takes the forefront through the comforting medium of pastels. Figure 7.8 typifies an integration of healthy adaptations, coupled with a growing personal identity. The artist of this drawing verbally expressed her gratitude to the group members for their unflagging support. She stated, "This is me . . . I have discovered that I have possibilities and that I can reach a point where I gain momentum and not the opposite."

In an environment of safety, each member is offered the opportunity to practice the building of new affiliations while undergoing a corrective experience to ease the fears of loss. The last section of Table 7.1 outlines a series of distancing directives which are provided to assist the mental health practitioner with issues related to the overwhelm that clients can experience throughout the course of this guidebook. As such, the group leader should trust their instincts and insert one of these distancing directives should they feel that the group is at a place where they require a respite from the concentrated work of loss. These directives provide concrete tasks which improve interaction and allow the expression of feelings in a safe setting.

Distancing Directives

1) "Draw your problem. Now wall it in or build a wall using construction paper."
2) "Draw how you are feeling and let the group know what you need."
3) "What is it like when you feel one way on the outside and another way on the inside?"
4) "Draw a picture showing what you want from ________."
5) "Draw all the activities that help you feel calm, relaxed, and joyful. Circle the single activity you like the most. Schedule a time to perform this activity."
6) "What do you do when you do something that is important to you?"
7) "Take some colors and put on the paper what you want to do today."
8) "Draw the most important thing that happened this week."

And So to Bed

> A metaphor is a kind of magical mental changing room—where one thing, for a moment, becomes another, and in that moment is seen in a whole new way. As soon as something old is seen in a new way, it stimulates a torrent of new thoughts and associations, almost as if a mental floodgate has been lifted.
> (Grothe, 2008, p. 10)

Whether the group leader is dealing with relational conflicts, affect-laden material, or personality issues, it is the exploration of a personal metaphor that offers the client emotional growth. The metaphor, with its inherent power to increase understanding, is deliberately designed to enhance awareness on an unconscious level.

In the preceding guidebooks, feelings of commonality brought on by the experience of loss and anguish ultimately stimulated the development of psychosocial proficiency. As such, the personal exchanges provided not only acceptance within a safe forum, but a place to practice and gain connectivity.

Throughout this book, the therapist's role has been active, directive, and involved. Art therapy is not a passive process, it is dynamic and reflective, it integrates and embraces differing perspectives, and it is the therapist who brings these collective interpretations into focus. As Yalom (1985) has stated:

> The therapist is an observer-participant in the group; the observer status affords the objectivity necessary to store information, to make observations about sequences or cyclical patterns of behavior, to connect events that have occurred over long periods of time.
>
> (Yalom, 1985, p. 146)

In each of the preceding chapters, metaphorical communication pointed toward the client's patterns of repetition; an understanding that we live the stories we tell. Much like a flowing river, pointed interpretation supports and aids differentiation which then affords the client the ability to move toward therapeutic change. As such, it is the mental health professional who establishes the goals of counseling and chooses the opportune moment for interpretation, but when exploring symbolic meaning, it is the client who should dictate the shift from a metaphorical discussion to that of the self.

It is important that when incorporating expressive arts into the therapeutic hour, it is done so in a manner that bespeaks of individual needs; a way in which the client can learn from the experience. As outlined in Chapter 3, an interdisciplinary approach allows for recovery of the whole individual for just as we live the stories we tell, we are the totality of our life experiences. To that end, harmonizing a counseling methodology with the practice of art therapy allows the therapist to focus on the primary themes while integrating interventions that are capable of touching upon a wide range of problems, disturbances, and diagnoses. It is my belief that in this manner, the mental health professional can assess motivation and readiness toward change while also highlighting the client's natural resources and resolutions.

Ultimately, personal metaphors have the power to increase understanding, promote the acceptance of feelings and thoughts, and will, in due course, guide the client as they strive to make sense of their environment and the larger world.

References

Baker, J.E., Sedney, M.A. & Gross, E. (1992). Psychological tasks for bereaved children. *American Journal of Orthopsychiatry*, *62* (1), 105–116.

Cirlot, J.E. (1983). *A dictionary of symbols* (2nd ed., J. Sage, Trans.). New York: Philosophical Library.

Grothe, M. (2008). *I never metaphor I didn't like: A comprehensive compilation of history's greatest analogies, metaphors, and similes.* New York: Harper Collins.

Jung, M. (1985). The book about daddy dying: A preventive art therapy technique to help families deal with the death of a family member. *Art Therapy 2* (1), 4–10.

Kubler-Ross, E (1969). *On death and dying.* New York: Macmillan Publishing Company.

Laughlin, H.P. (1970). *The ego and its defenses.* New York: Appleton-Century-Crofts.

White, W.R. (1986). *Stories for telling: A treasury for christian storytellers.* Minneapolis: Augsburg Publishing House.

Yalom, I. (1985). *The theory and practice of group psychotherapy* (3rd ed.). New York: Basic Books.

Index